East Prawle through the Ages

A story of the coastal village
at the southernmost tip of Devon

Kate Jennings

EVE – Eden Valley Editions

Book Layout by Fred Deakin and Kate Jennings

Cover Design by Fred Deakin

Cover photographs from the East Prawle History Society

Website: www.katejenningsprawle.co.uk
Email: katejennings02@gmail.com
Telephone: +44 1548 511382

All profits from the sale of the book will go towards the repair of St Sylvester's Church, Chivelstone.

ISBN 978-0-9929723-6-3

To Mark for his patience

Drawings by Elli Caddick, Gilli Harris, Jane Shadbolt and my niece Ellen Deakin – without their help this would be a duller book. A very big thank you to Roger Barrett for creating the maps.

Photographs from the East Prawle History Society database, the Cookworthy Museum in Kingsbridge, Roger Barrett and others.

The help given by all those who gave photographs is gratefully acknowledged. Every effort has been made to trace copyright holders and the author apologies if any have been inadvertently omitted.

Extracts from the Woodleigh Deanery Magazines from 1900 are with permission from the Cookworthy Museum, Kingsbridge, and copies of the magazines can be viewed at the Museum's Local Heritage Resource Centre.

Inspirational

Winnie Easterbrook, Derek Wotton, Richard and Jane Partridge (for their attention to detail), Roger and Vicky Tucker, John Tucker, Brenda Jeffery, Pat Farleigh, Ashley Ford, Margaret Mitchelmore, and Bill Login, all played a large part in helping and inspiring me to put this book together.

Other people to thank include Alice Stone, Diana Shelvoke (née Thorpe), Jane Shadbolt, Marilyn Rose (née Robson), Sarah Trinick, Tim Blyth (who found lots of snippets for me), Ann Lidstone of the Kingsbridge History Society, Reg Hannaford (evacuated in the war from Torcross to Chivelstone).

Roger Barrett's book *Prawle Point and the Coast between Start Point and Salcombe Bar* has been instructive and I draw on it many times. Similarly *A Century of Memories* by Stephen Pedrick.

Chris Martin, former Librarian at South West Water, has been a source of fascinating information about how and when mains water came to East Prawle and Peter Lamb, of the South Western Electricity Historical Society, about the electricity. I am also indebted to the many various reports and articles for the early part of the history. Where possible I have given reference to the original documentation. Much of the earlier history is taken from the 'Chivelstone Parish Heritage Appraisal'. Other sources are credited in the text and in the Bibliography.

I have to thank my nephew, Fred Deakin for guidance in the layout of the book and the design of the cover, my sister Rose for all her support and constructive criticism and Jenny Brown for proof reading the manuscript.

List of Subscribers

Because the inspiration for this book has been talking to local people about East Prawle and its past, much of the book is based on oral history.

For this reason I have had immense support from local people, many of whose names are listed below, who are prepared to spend money buying the book. The other names listed are those, although not local, who are also prepared to support me in buying the book.

Audrey and Alan Ayton
Helen and Richard Barcan
Richard Barker
Roger Barrett
Elaine Bishop
Anne and Tim Blyth
Sarah and Mark Bolton
Jennie Bond and Jim Keltz
Lou and Bill Bonham
Nicola and Tudor Brown
Ruth and Kenny Browne
Sarah and Rob Bunn
Bunny Campione and Iain Grahame
Did Caudery
Rosie and Cliff
Margaret Coke
Louise and Nick Coombes
Kath and Richard Cordy
Gill and Mike Corly
Ann Cripps
Katie and David Hampden-Smith
Anne and Steve Dooley
Ashley and James Douglas
Andy Elliott
John Farman
Lynn and Mark Ford
John Gaisford
Nicki and Bob Grainger
Cindy and Neville Higgins
Kate and Charles Hobson
Rosie Horseman
Rowena and Alan House
Judith Howard
Sarah Howden
Vickie and Douglas Howie
Judith and John Ingram
Brenda and Brian Jeffery
Tim and Helen Johnson
Ren Hill and Andy Johnston
Celia and Dai Jones
Chrissie and Mark Konig
Viv and Chris Lally
Jeni and Roger Lawson
Ali and Peter Lennon
Ann Lidstone
Jane Lutyens
Christine Martin
Hilary Matthews
Lizzie and Nick Millard
Heather and David Morgan
Tessa Mack and Richard Pain
Sarah and Mike Pain
Jane and Richard Partridge
Michael Partridge
Jane and Bob Payne
Stephen Pedrick
Ann and Willy Potts
Pauline Rainsbury
Caroline and Adam Raphael
Jan Reading
Hazel and Jim Roberts
Janet and Len Starling
Alice Stone
Tim Stone
Linda and John Storey
Jane and Michael Sturdee
Gillian and Nigel Timmins
Elaine and Mike Trant
John Tucker
Lin and Kim Tucker
Marilyn and Richard Tucker
Vicky and Roger Tucker
Val and Alan Walford
Jo and Patrick Walsh
Robert Waterhouse
Lesley and Peter Webber
Graham White
Tim White
Gill and Nigel Whitmore
Paula Wolstenhome
Linda and Peter Wotton
Kelly Wotton

Contents

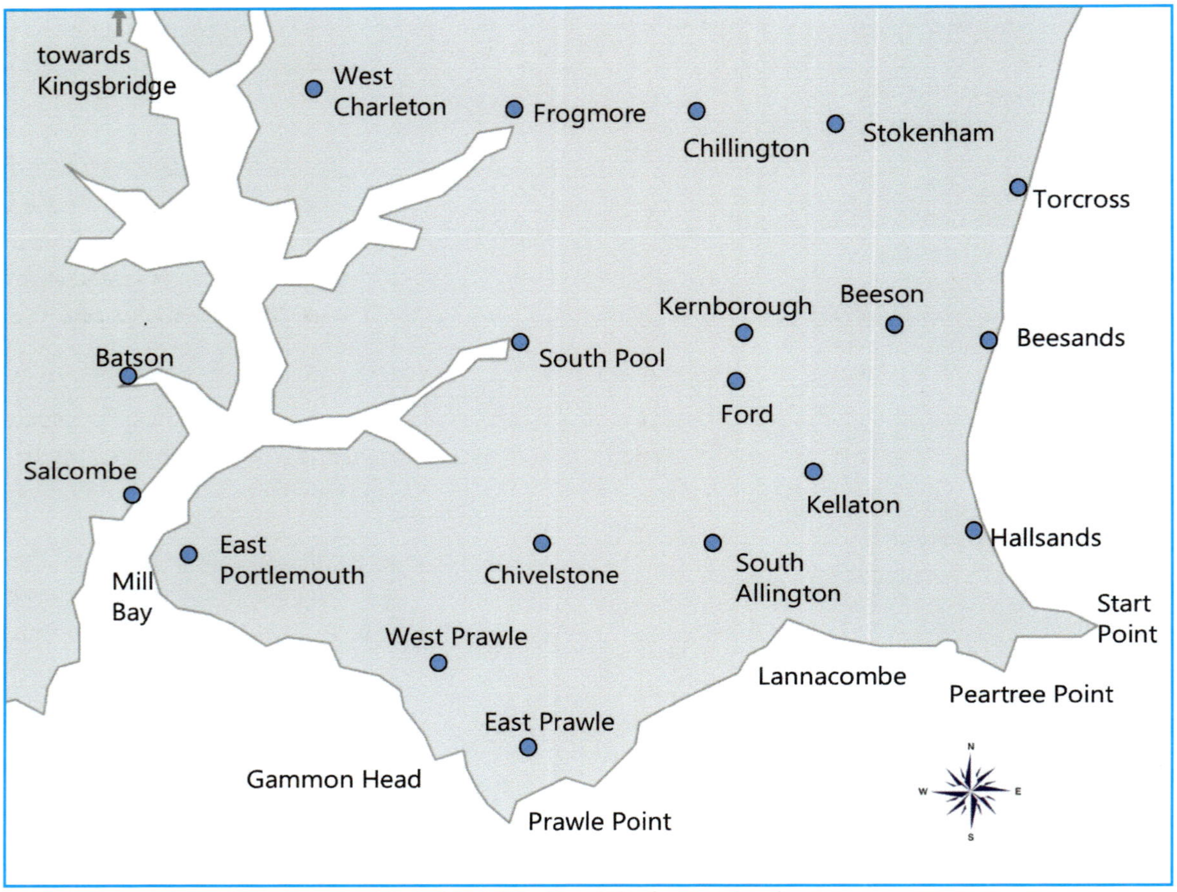

Map of East Prawle and the Surrounding Area

Why This Book?

This book came about because many of the residents of East Prawle had memories and information about the village and the South Hams area of Devon, which have not been written down. Their contribution to history could so easily be lost.

The book started off as an exercise in oral history. However, I became so absorbed and fascinated by the subject matter, the stories and references to things obscure to me, that I turned to written records to help fill out the picture and gain a deeper understanding of rural traditions and local events. While the result is heavily based on verbal accounts and the reminiscences of various villagers, I frequently dart off to expand on the traditions, local methods and the ancient history of the area.

Inevitably the majority of the material is more about the last 150 years than earlier. So much has altered beyond recognition in that time, from horse drawn transport, water from wells, candles and oil lamps after dark.

Many stories are anecdotal and have come down through the generations. I hope none of the material will cause upset. I have tried to record as accurately as possible the information I have been given, although there may be occasional differing accounts. History is not black and white.

Our links to East Prawle

In the 1930s two doctors, Anni Noll and Hesketh Pearse, came to Gara Rock to write a book about the Peckham Pioneer Health Centre, which was a famous venture into community health in the 1930s, and which they (and my father) helped to found. Exploring the coast they discovered and fell in love with East Prawle. For many years Anni and her husband, Haschi Wassermann, came and rented the Station Officer's house down New Houses, from William Richard Ernest (W R E) Tucker, Winnie Easterbrook's father. In 1958 they bought Foss Cottage. Haschi died in a plane crash in 1971 but without Haschi we might never have come to East Prawle. I go into more detail when writing about Foss Cottage on page 26.

My sister, Rose Deakin, inherited Foss Cottage in 1971 and Mark and I spent our honeymoon there in 1973. We returned to Foss three or four times each year until we bought 1 Sea View, one of the old coastguard cottages from Phyllis and Derek Wotton in 1993. More and more of our time has been spent in East Prawle and in 2005 we sold our London house to buy Sea Rocket Barn, where we now live. This was the Threshing Barn for Lower House Farm.

Phyllis Putt at home

This project began to take place in my mind as a result of spending many hours talking to Phyllis Putt, our near neighbour down 'New Houses', who died in 2003. Phyllis had lived at no 4 Sea View for over 50 years and remembered times without electricity or running water. Sadly, because we were working in London, although coming down as often as we could, I never managed to do more than listen. Later I started to record conversations, with this book in mind.

Over many years in Prawle we used to buy fresh vegetables from Derek Wotton and Winnie Easterbrook. Winnie stopped growing vegetables when her husband, Wilf died in 1997. However, Derek continued to grow vegetables (including shallots, strings of which were very popular Christmas presents for many of my friends) and we would see him frequently. We also used to buy the most wonderful pies from his wife, Phyllis before she died. In particular, great favourites were her treacle tarts – I used to take some back to London and freeze them. Scrumptious!

Therefore, when I started to write this book, the two most obvious people to talk to were Winnie and Derek. Over the years I have spent many happy hours with them. Winnie was born in 1912 and Derek in 1931; so there is quite an age gap between them.

Winnie Easterbrook at 90

The next phase of my research started when I met Richard Partridge – Phyllis Wotton's brother. Both he and his wife Jane have been tremendously supportive.

I have spent many hours with Roger and Vicky Tucker. Roger has a houseful of photographs, maps and documents. In 2011 the East Prawle History Society was formed. We have created a database of photographs and many of these are included in the book – with many thanks to all those people who have allowed me to use them.

This book is not specifically about the families in East Prawle. However, failure to mention them would leave out an important element of a social history.

In 2013 Stephen Pedrick gave the East Prawle History Society a talk with recordings and photographs of people born and bred in East Prawle in the early 1900s. What became apparent from the recordings was how closely inter-related the families were: Putts, Stones, Tuckers, Partridges. In the *Elizabethan Court Roles of Stokenham Manor 1560-1602'* translated by W A Roberts, Partridges, Tuckers and Collyns are mentioned throughout. The Tithe map of 1842-47 records land lots with some of the same names still existing today. Many of the local families are related in one way or another.

Derek Wotton

Tithes: Today the rector is paid directly from the Church's diocesan centre, but until the 1840s a rector was expected to live off tithes. Originally tithes were paid 'in kind' (wool, milk, honey, fish, barley). By 1836 tithes were still payable in most parishes in England and Wales, but the Government decided on the commutation of tithes – the substitution of money payments for payment 'in kind' all over the country. The term Tithe map is usually applied to a map of an English or Welsh parish or township, prepared following the Tithe Commutation Act 1836. The map and its schedule gave the names of all owners and occupiers of land in the parish. The Tithe was an annual payment of an agreed proportion (originally one tenth) of the yearly produce of the land, which was payable by parishioners to the parish church, to support it and its clergyman.

Life in East Prawle was very self-contained – everybody knew everyone else. People could, and often did, live all their lives without even going as far as Kingsbridge.

This book has taken me seven enjoyable years of research.

Jane and Richard Partridge

Roger and Vicky Tucker

A Bit of History

Roger Barrett wrote in *Prawle Point and the Coast between Start Point and Salcombe Bar* of evidence of an occupation in the Bronze and Iron Ages (4,500 to 2,000 years ago) and perhaps the first settled farming during the Neolithic period (6,500 to 4,500 years ago). Robert Waterhouse in the 'East Portlemouth Heritage Appraisal' considered the Hamstone Valley, east of Moor Sand, where scatters of flint working debris was found. Anne Born in *The History of Kingsbridge and Salcombe* commented 'the most spectacular Bronze Age finds are the bronze artefacts from an underwater site off Moor Sand near Gammon Head, protected since 1978.' She also noted the Bronze Age people were followed by the Celts of the Iron Age, who left much more evidence of their presence.

Prawle Point lies at the southernmost tip of Devon; 'Prawle' is old English for 'lookout' or 'look-out hill'

The Early Tourist Guides

In *Murray's Handbook for Travellers in Devon and Cornwall,* first published in 1850, it recommended the coastal path from Torcross to East Portlemouth and suggested that Prawle Point was 'perhaps the finest headland on the S coast of Devon'.

However, Ellen Luscombe in *Myrtles and Aloes* (1861) described the area rather differently: 'In spite of his (Mr Pengelly, Chief Boatman at Prawle) hearty welcome and reiterated invitations to repeat our visit, we never had the courage to return to Prawle, though after a long absence from wild scenery even that dreary place would have charms in our eyes.'

Sarah Prideaux Fox (S P Fox as she liked to be known), in *Kingsbridge and its Surroundings* (1874), commented from the *Londoner's Walk to the Land's End*, the following reference to the scenery between Start Point and Prawle Point:

Those who have been disappointed with foreign travel would do well to bend their steps to this little-known part of our own country. One may journey far before he finds so much to satisfy the eye and charm the imagination, as came before me in this day's wandering. A coastguard, whom the 'Londoner' met with, remarked to him, 'Tis as rough a bit of country as any part of Devonshire, but 'tis well worth looking at. An Englishman don't know what England is till he has been along here.'

The Geology

The geology of the Prawle area is unique in England. Stretching from Bolt Tail to Start Point is a plateau of 400-450 feet above sea level, bound to the southwest and southeast by 'fossil' cliffs.

An article from Devon County Council explained why:

Start Point to Prawle Point is a truly beautiful stretch of south Devon coastline. It is underlain by rocks that are very different to those of the rest of Devon. These are known as mica schist, found at Start Point (SX 828372), and hornblende schist, which has a green tint and is found at Prawle Point (SX 772352).

These rocks are the result of intense pressure and heat acting on the original rocks during a collision of tectonic plates. The mica schists were originally shales, siltstones and sandstones, whilst the hornblende schists were once lavas and ashes, all probably of Devonian age (nearly 400 million years ago).

The area displays good examples of beach platforms including the present wave-cut platform in the intertidal zone. An older beach platform occurs just above the present beach and extends back to an old cliff line. Deposited on this older platform are raised beach deposits which consist of beach sand and cobbles mixed with rock debris, known locally as 'head', deposited as a result of rock movement during the Ice Age.

The two lines of fossil cliffs by Prawle Point are clearly shown on this postcard (reproduced in a thesis written in 1964-65 by Philippa Louden (née Tucker)

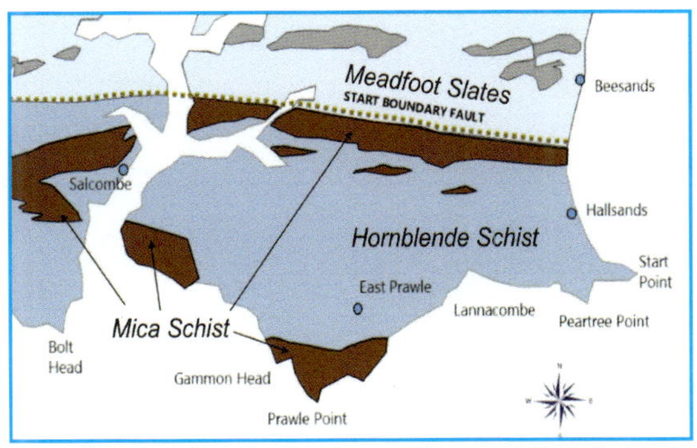

Map showing the distribution of Mica and Hornbelende Schist rocks based on the British Geological Survey

Walking from Prawle Point towards Gammon Head you can see very large standing stones which were the ancient field boundaries. Flint tools found along the coast suggest it was occupied about 12,000 years ago. Bronze Age burial mounds (known as barrows) were in the fields on the outskirts of East Prawle, near Vinivers, although the majority have been ploughed up and no longer exist. They were made by digging a circular ditch and piling up the earth inside in a rounded heap over a pottery vessel which contained the burnt ashes of the dead.

The Queen's Golden Jubilee Project for Chivelstone Parish in 2002 produced a memorial on the village green, with a map and brief historical descriptions through the ages of East Prawle. It includes a description of a collection of very rare ceremonial stones from 3800-4500 years ago, typical of the Bronze Age.

Queen's Golden Jubilee Project 2002

Two examples of standing stones

On the western slope of Deckler's Cliff, towards Gara Rock, are the remains of a Bronze Age Field System.

Sir Harry Jephcott gave the land to the National Trust in 1963 on a 465-year lease which ends in 2428. Subsequently, Roger Tucker took over the lease – from Moor Sand to Sunny Cove – from the National Trust at £1 a year for 500 years.

The scrub was completely overgrown, but Roger cleared the area and the Bronze Age field system can now be clearly seen, which has enabled maritime grassland to grow and allowed

Bronze Age Field System

the cirl bunting, a rare bird local to East Prawle, to feed on insects which live in the short grazed grassland.

The Cirl Bunting

Chivelstone Parish

S P Fox described Chivelstone as 'a small village, but the parish extends southwards to the romantic sea cliffs between Start and Prawle Points; it includes the fishing village of Prawle, and the hamlets of Ford and South Allington.'

Today the parish of Chivelstone is in the district of the South Hams, an ancient name which comes from the old English word 'hamme' or 'hamm', meaning a low-lying meadow or enclosed pasture. The South Hams is within an Area of Outstanding Natural Beauty with stunning coastline, rivers and estuaries, golden beaches and wonderful countryside.

According to W G Hoskins 'much of the parish consists of a plateau of pre-Cambrian rocks, dissected by deep and beautiful combes of which Lannacombe is the best. Field-walls of grey slate on the plateau are an unusual sight for Devon.'

It is quite possible most of the farms date back to Saxon times. The name of the parish, first recorded in the Domesday Survey of 1086, derives from Coefel's farm, while Prawle may derive from Præwhyll, meaning a look-out hill. The survey recorded three manors in what was to become Chivelstone Parish, all owned by Iudhael of Totnes.

For population information in Chivelstone Parish throughout the ages, see Appendix I.

According to *The National Gazetteer of Great Britain and Ireland (1868)*:

Chivelstone, a parish in the hundred of Coleridge, in the county of Devon, 7 miles S. of Kingsbridge, its post town. It is pleasantly situated in a valley and contains the hamlets of Ford, South Allington, and Prawle … The living is a curacy annexed to the vicarage of Stokenham, in the diocese of Exeter, and in the patronage of the crown. The church, dedicated to St Sylvester, is an old stone edifice, with a beautiful screen and curious pulpit. Thomas Newman, Esq, is lord of the manor.

Apparently introduced by the Saxons between 613 and 1017, a hundred was the division of a shire for administrative, military and judicial purposes each with enough land to sustain one hundred households.

Mining

Quoting Robert Waterhouse:

An iron mine, operated by the East Portlemouth Consolidated Mining Company Limited, was opened on Deckler's Cliff in 1857 by a group of Cornish entrepreneur miners, known as 'adventurers'. Reports in the Kingsbridge Gazette for 1857 describe the excavation of adits and shafts, while the local historian Sarah Prideaux-Fox stated that the mine was abandoned by 1859-60 after a ship loading iron ore was wrecked on the cliffs below the mine.

The site survives today as a complex of pits, adits and dumps, laid out along two veins or 'lodes', on an east-west axis 30m apart. The western adit on the southern lode entered the hillside directly off the coast path, where it now appears as a collapsed gulley. A tramway zig-zagged down the coastal slope onto Deckler's Island, where iron ore was tipped from the trucks down a stone chute onto a quay below. Ore was stored on platforms on the south side of the island before being shipped, and an inclined railway constructed of timber, which climbed the west side of the island, brought materials up to the mine.

Going down from Gara Rock towards Seacombe Sands, just after the footbridge over the stream, are the remains of the blacksmith's hut where the ponies used for the iron mine

The chute at Deckler's Cliff

The mine at Deckler's Cliff

were shod. Derek believed the blacksmith was in operation up to the early 1900s, and remembered once digging up a collection of pony shoes.

Remains of the Blacksmith Hut

Barbary Pirates

Fishermen and people dwelling near the coast in 17th century Britain lived in dread of being kidnapped and sold into slavery. The Barbary pirates (from the Barbary Coast of North Africa) raided all round the English coast including South Devon.

The height of this activity was around the 1630s when England's navy was weak. While anything of value was fair game, their main quarry was slaves. In the beginning they targeted the crews of West Country fishing boats, but as the pirates grew bolder they came ashore to find victims.

In 1995 the South West Maritime Archaeological Group of divers discovered a treasure trove of gold coins at the Salcombe Cannon Site. The find consisted of around 400 coins ranging in date between 1578 and 1635, with Marrakech as the dominant mint. Islamic jewellery, probably of Moroccan origin, and gold finger ingots were also recovered. Most of the ingots and jewellery had been deliberately cut suggesting trade in weight rather than the objects themselves. During the 17th Century there were many ships visiting the Devon coast – was the mystery ship with Moroccan gold a trader or Barbary pirate ship trafficking white slaves?

Coins ranging in date between 1578 and 1635 (South West Maritime Archaeological Group)

5000 Years Ago

Roger Tucker in his talk '120 years farming in and around East Prawle' told about removing a hedge on the farm. It was an earth hedge and the soil conditions were very dry. While cultivating the soil to level the ground and picking up the trash and stones, Richard, his youngest son, spotted some unusually shaped stones and brought them home. 'We kept them for many years not knowing what they were, until Robert Waterhouse (now the Archaeological Officer for the Channel Islands), came to visit. Robert was speechless at first as these stones are very rare. We agreed for Robert to take the stones to the Natural History Museum in London who reported that the stones were the property of an important person/tribal leader 4-5000 years ago and the hedge we removed was part of a burial mound. Many hedges are six or seven hundred years old, dating from the time when the medieval landscape was created. There is good evidence to suggest that some may be prehistoric.

Stones from more than 5000 years ago (from Roger Tucker and Richard Partridge)

The Romans

In *A History of Devon* Robin Stanes wrote:

> Cornwall and Devon, and that part of Somerset west of the river Parrett, made up what was known to the Romans as Dumnonia. It cannot have been entirely unfamiliar to them before their invasion of Britain in AD 43. Its deposits of tin had been known about in the Mediterranean since the fourth century BC, and there were trading links through Brittany with the Mediterranean. Cornish tin was certainly being exported to Marseilles in the second century BC.

There is no evidence that the Romans came to Prawle, but they did reach Exeter. However, Roger described hand picking potatoes in the field which is the highest on their land and the whole of the Prawle/Portlemouth plateau. Roger was driving the tractor with the Ransomes elevator chain digger and stopped to assist Hathor Hamilton, a local friend helping, when he spotted a small disk on the ground. On one side he could just make out a head.

The coin was taken to Reading Museum, examined and although very corroded, from the type and the style of the head they believed it to date from the Roman period, First Century or possibly early Second Century (Hadrian). Clearly, the coin had lain undisturbed for centuries, suggesting to Roger the Romans did come to Prawle.

Roman coin, 1st or 2nd Century AD

Burial in the Cliffs at Prawle Point

On 14 June 1996, it was reported in the Kingsbridge Gazette that an off-duty police officer from Wales discovered human bones on the cliffs near East Prawle, dating more than 100 years.

An excavation and recording of a burial were commissioned by Devon County Archaeological Service and undertaken between 29-31 July 2002:

The excavation revealed the grave of a single individual in the cliff face. The skeletal remains probably represented a male with a stature of around 1.579m (5ft 2ins). He was aged over 29 years and suffered from a degree of osteoarthritis. The teeth had evidence of dental disease, suggesting a relatively modern diet high in carbohydrates. There is no evidence of trauma on the surviving skeletal remains and, given the nature of the burial and its location, drowning is the assumed cause of death.

The radiocarbon dating of the bone fragments has indicated a wide date range for the burial, between the late 17th and the early 20th century. However, the remains are most likely those of a shipwrecked seaman washed ashore in the late 18th or early 19th century.

According to Parson Hawker (author of The Remembrances of a Cornish Vicar), prior to the 1808 Seaman's Burial 13 Act 'it was the common usage of the coast to dig, just above high-water mark, a pit on the shore, and therein to cast, without inquest or religious rite the carcasses of shipwrecked men' (W.S. Horner pers. comm.).

It is not possible to determine whether this burial pre-dates the 1808 Act, and the unfortunate individual was buried where he was washed ashore, or post-dates it and represents the burial of a shipwrecked mariner washed up on a remote Devon shoreline too far from consecrated ground to be easily transported for burial. The nearest churches in the post-medieval period were at East Portlemouth, 4 km (2.48 miles) to the northwest, and Chivelstone, 3.6 km (2.24 miles) to the north.

The report continued: 'Given the relative remoteness of the location, and the number of wrecks recorded in the vicinity of Prawle Point, it is probable that there are other burials of shipwrecked mariners in the area.'

The Burial of Drowned Persons Acts 1808 provided that unclaimed bodies of dead persons cast ashore from the sea should be removed by the churchwardens and overseers of the parish, and decently interred in consecrated ground. ... Prior to this act it was customary to bury drowned seamen unceremoniously, without shroud or coffin, in unconsecrated ground.

More about Sand Burials

James Fairweather in *Salcombe and Neighbourhood* quoted from Hamilton's '*Quarter Sessions under James I*' that pirates: '...often foraged and stripped the country adjoining of sheep and other

The cliffs between Landing Cove and Western Cove where the bones were found

commodities, and took from poor fishermen their boats and barks. Moreover, the report goes on, they murdered each other, and buried them in the sands by night, and committed daily sundry other outrages.'

The wrecking of the *Chantiloupe*, from the West Indies, in 1772 at Thurlestone Sands, has been told several times. One from Frank Coope, vicar of Thurlestone Church from 1897 to 1923, who wrote about a wealthy passenger, Mrs Burke (said to have been related to Edmund Burke), dressed in all her jewellery and fine clothes, no doubt with a view to saving them. She came ashore alive, but half drowned, only to be caught by wreckers who tore off her earrings and cut off her fingers to get the rings, and thus did her to death. Later they buried her mutilated body in the sand, but soon after it was dug up by a dog. Mrs Ilberts, of Horsewell House, South Milton, arranged a Christian burial. The vicar continued with the warning: 'It is well known, however, in the neighbourhood who did it, and their surnames are remembered to this day ... all came, it is said, to a bad end within the year.'

S P Fox told the same story in more detail in *Kingsbridge Estuary with Rambles in the Neighbourhood* but went on to write:

Is it not sickening to think that such scenes ever were enacted in this professedly Christian country? – but the days of these savage deeds are long past away, and now instead of the greedy wrecker, we may picture the life-boat launched and manned by a brave and honest crew, eager to risk their own lives in the endeavour to save those of their fellow men. ...

Many years ago, some young relatives of ours were amusing themselves by digging in the sand just under Bantham Ham, and to their astonishment they came upon a human skull. It was apparently that of a negro – certainly not that of an Englishman. Afterwards, several other skulls were disinterred near the same spot, and it seems probable that they were relics of those who perished either in the wreck of the Ramillies, or of the Chantiloupe.

Stokenham

Stokenham played such an important role in several hundred years of history. Stokenham was called Stoke in Hamme in the 13th century to distinguish it from other Stokes.

Robert Waterhouse wrote in the 'Stokenham Heritage Appraisal':

Stokenham Parish, an unusually large one by South Hams standards, owes it size and importance to its status as part of an Anglo-Saxon royal estate. This was originally of considerable size and included the current parishes of Chivelstone to the southwest, Sherford to the northwest and Blackawton to the north.

In his 'Stokenham Occasional Papers 1 (Queen Katherine's rental 1547)' W A Roberts wrote that Henry VIII gave Stokenham Manor to Katherine, his sixth and final bride, as part of her marriage dowry.

In 1580 Henry, the third earl of Huntingdon, and Richard Pooley, his gentleman servant, began to break up Stokenham Manor. They obtained licences of alienation from the King's court … and disposed of substantial parts of the manor to the sitting tenants with 3000-year leases. He then sold the remaining bulk of the estate, still considerable, to Edward Ameredith in 1585.

There are still traces of the Earl of Huntingdon in the area, reaching as far as East Prawle. Richard Partridge has a copy of a deed of enlargement where his grandmother, Emily Partridge of Rosario, in 1956 had a 3000-year lease changed to freehold.

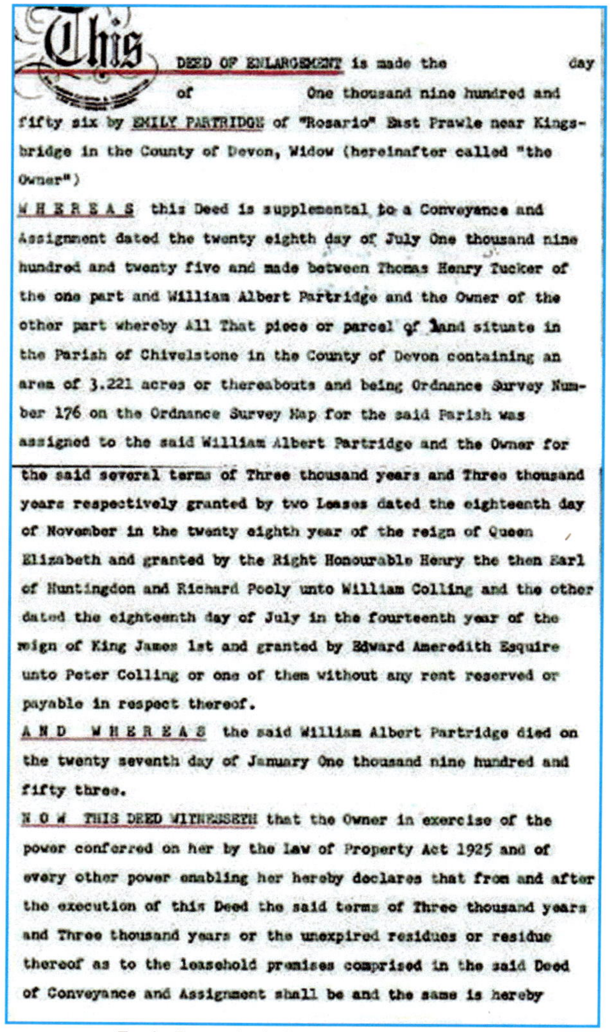
This DEED OF ENLARGEMENT is made the day of One thousand nine hundred and fifty six by EMILY PARTRIDGE of "Rosario" East Prawle near Kingsbridge in the County of Devon, Widow (hereinafter called "the Owner")

W H E R E A S this Deed is supplemental to a Conveyance and Assignment dated the twenty eighth day of July One thousand nine hundred and twenty five and made between Thomas Henry Tucker of the one part and William Albert Partridge and the Owner of the other part whereby All That piece or parcel of land situate in the Parish of Chivelstone in the County of Devon containing an area of 3.221 acres or thereabouts and being Ordnance Survey Number 176 on the Ordnance Survey Map for the said Parish was assigned to the said William Albert Partridge and the Owner for the said several terms of Three thousand years and Three thousand years respectively granted by two Leases dated the eighteenth day of November in the twenty eighth year of the reign of Queen Elizabeth and granted by the Right Honourable Henry the then Earl of Huntingdon and Richard Pooly unto William Colling and the other dated the eighteenth day of July in the fourteenth year of the reign of King James 1st and granted by Edward Ameredith Esquire unto Peter Colling or one of them without any rent reserved or payable in respect thereof.

A N D W H E R E A S the said William Albert Partridge died on the twenty seventh day of January One thousand nine hundred and fifty three.

N O W THIS DEED WITNESSETH that the Owner in exercise of the power conferred on her by the Law of Property Act 1925 and of every other power enabling her hereby declares that from and after the execution of this Deed the said terms of Three thousand years and Three thousand years or the unexpired residues or residue thereof as to the leasehold premises comprised in the said Deed of Conveyance and Assignment shall be and the same is hereby

Emily Partridge's Deed of Enlargement

The Village

Little in East Prawle has changed over the years - the landscape is still the same. The exception is several of the farm buildings are converted into housing (including the threshing barn where we now live).

1920s East Prawle Village Green

For the last two or three centuries East Prawle has been predominantly a farming village. Being so close to the sea has also given it a connection with the fishing industry.

2015 East Prawle Village Green

The shape and life of the village has always been, and to a lesser extent still is, strongly influenced by the existence and position of farmhouses and out buildings, with the many cottages and smaller houses surrounding them. Despite this there are some larger houses, which are part of the village but just outside it.

Its pubs have a special importance and have made East Prawle widely known and visited. Apart from a brief period in the 1980s, there were two pubs for several centuries, although the Providence Inn is now shut, there is still the Pigs Nose. The shop and café are open for eight months of the year.

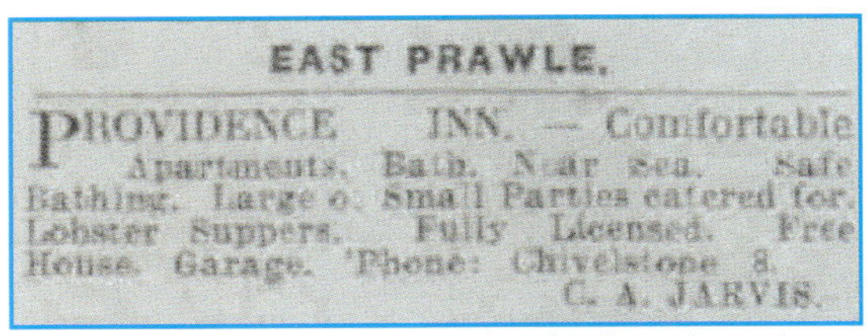

EAST PRAWLE.

PROVIDENCE INN. — Comfortable Apartments. Bath. Near Sea. Safe Bathing. Large or Small Parties catered for. Lobster Suppers. Fully Licensed. Free House. Garage. 'Phone: Chivelstone 8.
C. A. JARVIS.

7 June 1933: an advertisement for the Providence Inn in the Western Morning News

With the changes in agriculture that have reduced the number of agricultural workers this focus has inevitably shifted. The sale of Lower House Farm, located at the heart of the village and its conversion into residential accommodation had a big impact in the late 1980s. Although there are several families who have lived in the village for many years, the numbers are dwindling.

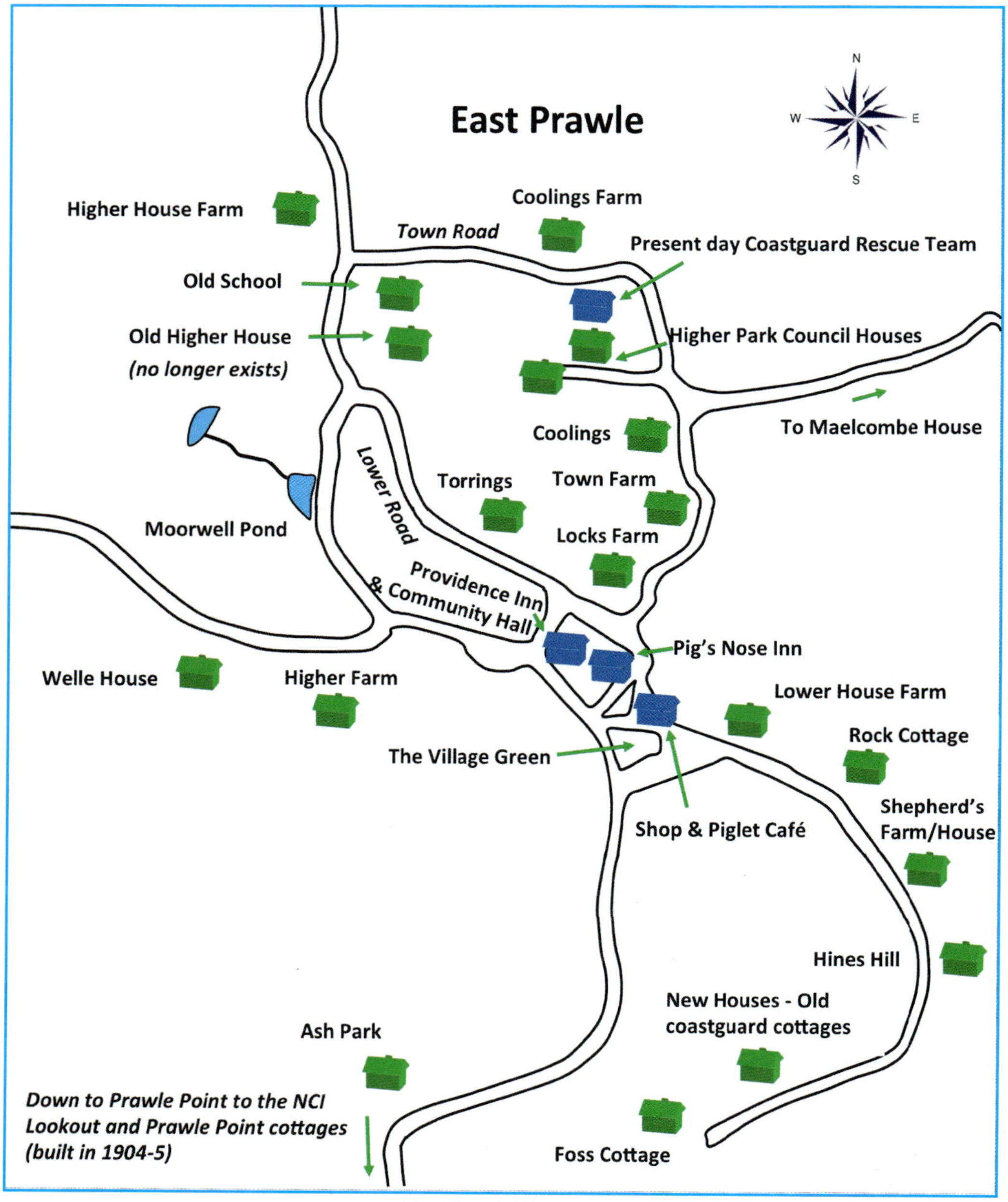

East Prawle Village

East Prawle has become a popular holiday village and many of its cottages are owned by second home owners, although recently there has also been quite a substantial number of new permanent residents. The release of coastguard cottages, unneeded farm workers' accommodation (the building of council houses for the farm workers, in the 1940s-1950s), and the conversion of barns has made this possible.

Tourism is a principal source of wealth today in the South Hams. Planning authorities – and the National Trust – recognise this and made sure the whole coastline is not built over in a rash of bungalows. Before holiday cottages, bed and breakfast was an industry, certainly as far back as 1916. We know that Granny Partridge took in bed and breakfast – Richard Partridge has a copy of a postcard dated 1916 on which is written 'stayed at Rosario, very nice stay and rates reasonable'.

Particulars of Farmhouses and Country Lodgings, Hotels, Boarding-houses, Hydros, Restaurants, Cafes, Estate Agents, etc.

Mrs Partridge, Bowhay House, East Prawle – Apartments, boarding, 2 sitting rooms, 5 bedrooms. 15 minutes from sea. Good cooking. Homely. Indoor sanitation.

Mrs Tucker, Locks Farm, East Prawle – Apartments, 2 sitting rooms, 4 bedrooms. Near sea. Safe bathing.

Mrs A Quick, Sunnyside, East Prawle – Apartments, 2 sitting rooms, 2 bedrooms. Near sea. Safe bathing. Indoor sanitation.

Mrs Webster, Bona Ventura, East Prawle – 6-roomed furnished bungalow. Indoor sanitation. Every convenience. Own grounds. Magnificent sea view. Safe bathing.

Mrs B O Old, Shepherd's Farm House, East Prawle – Board residence. Beautiful scenery. Overlooking sea, beach. Safe bathing. Recommended.

Providence Inn, East Prawle – Comfortable apartments. Bath. Near sea, safe bathing. Large or small parties catered for. Fully licensed. Free house. Garage. Proprietor: C A Jarvis.

Extract from Great Western Railway Holiday Haunts, dated 1934 [from the Cookworthy Museum]

In *Devon* W G Hoskins wrote:

The watering-places became transformed into holiday resorts with the increasing penetration of railways into rural Devon, and with the institution of the Bank Holiday and Sunday School 'treats'. ... And the seaside towns of Devon flourished increasingly throughout the second half of the 19th century.

In September 2005, according to the 'Chivelstone Parish Heritage Appraisal', there were 220 households (104 were second or holiday homes) the majority in the hamlet of East Prawle.

We ourselves used to spend our holidays here, but we now live permanently in East Prawle.

For population information in Chivelstone Parish throughout the ages, see Appendix I.

Some of the Buildings in East Prawle

There are many interesting buildings in East Prawle and I have selected just a few.

Farm Houses

In the past, farmhouses and yards were built first and foremost where there was a good spring of water or a never failing well. Apart from a human need, water was vital for animals.

Farmhouses were often built from the rock or earth on which they stood: the most common materials are stone and cob which is made from subsoil, water, some kind of fibrous organic material (typically straw), and sometimes lime.

The farmhouse, known as a longhouse, became the most common type in Devon. It consisted of two rooms divided by a cross passage. To one side of the passage ('above') was the hall where there was a fire and where people lived. On the other side of the passage ('below') were the cattle with their heads to the outside walls and a dung channel between them with a drain hole at the lower end.

The earliest of these are thought to have been built in the 13th century, and they continued to be constructed throughout the mediaeval period and into the Early Modern. However, Robert Waterhouse suggested: 'The first longhouses' probably appeared during the later Anglo-Saxon period. These were somewhat longer rectangular buildings, aligned up and down the slope with a byre for the cattle at the lower end, residential accommodation at the higher end and a shared entrance passage.

Higher Farm

Higher Farm was called 'Adams, Dearings, Knowle Hill, Partridges and part of Hawkins' on the Tithe Map of 1842-47.

1919 Higher Farm

The Rev Marcus Dimond Dimond-Churchward, MA, vicar of Northam was one of the principal landowners in East Prawle, owning Higher Farm and Lower House Farm. He died in 1917 and his niece, Miss Ellie Augusta Sarah Braine-Hartnell, inherited and continued to rent out the 314 acres of Higher Farm. From 1905 the Sawtells rented it until 1923 – see the poster of the goods for sale on the next page (it should be Higher Farm, not Higher House Farm).

The Woodleigh Deanery Magazine of October 1909 carried the report of a fire at Higher Farm:

We are thankful that Mr Sawtell and family were not burned out of house and home, in the late fire at Prawle. The wind mercifully carried the flames and sparks away from the village. We suppose the fire originated in the barn at the back of the farmhouse - as it was, the outbuildings were destroyed and their contents, including farm machinery - a serious loss, as well as inconvenience. The darkness and inadequate supply of water made matters worse. The Coastguards were most helpful, as they always are, and when the fire engine arrived from Kingsbridge the worst was over.

1921 Country transport: at Higher Farm

HIGHER HOUSE FARM
EAST PRAWLE.
4 MILES FROM STOKENHAM AND 8 FROM KINGSBRIDGE.
Important Sale of 143 Sheep besides Lambs, 25 Pedigree and 17 other South Devon Bullocks, 7 Horses, Implements, Furniture, &c.
RENDELL & SAWDYE
Have been instructed by Mrs. Sawtell, who is giving up this Farm at Lady-day, to Sell by Auction there, on
Friday. March 23rd. 1923
the following LIVE and DEAD
FARM STOCK

SHEEP.
20 DOUBLE COUPLES.
70 SINGLE Do
7 BARREN EWES.
24 EWE HOGS
20 WETHER HOGS Mostly Fat.
1 Two-year-old RAM, bred by Mr. W. Savery, Staverton
1 Four-year-old Ditto, bred by Mr. J. Hoare, Staverton
The above are a well bred lot of South Devon Sheep, and the Lambs are strong and healthy.

BULLOCKS (Pedigree).
8 COWS in Milk and Calf
7 Fine HEIFERS, forward in Calf.
2 Two-and-half year old HEIFERS.
2 Two-year-old Ditto.
6 Yearling Ditto.
OTHER SOUTH DEVON BULLOCKS.
2 COWS, forward in Calf.
6 18-months to 2-year-old STEERS.
9 YEARLING and YOUNGER STEERS.

1923 The top of the bill of sale

The Tolchards took over until 1939-40 and Jack Partridge was there up to 1943. In 1944 Geoffrey Hill Tripp, married to Dorothy May Partridge, rented the farm and finally bought it in 1964, employing six men. Today the farm is owned and managed by his son, Geoffrey Tripp, with his wife Sally, who run the farm together, with occasional help from family.

In the 'Chivelstone Parish Millennium Book', Geoffrey described it as a 'two story L shaped building with about 15 rooms, built of local stone in the early 18th century and originally thatched. There is also a range of traditional farm buildings surrounding the courtyard.'

For many years several social occasions were held at Higher Farm, including barn dances in the summer.

Lower House Farm

Lower House Farm was burnt down in the 1800s, date unknown, and was rebuilt. Miss Braine-Hartnell also inherited Lower House Farm from her uncle, the Rev Marcus Dimond Dimond-Churchward.

From the Tithe map and apportionments (1842-47), we know that the Fosses farmed Lower House Farm from the 1840s, and they were still there in the 1930s. Harry Foss and his two sisters were the last of the Fosses to run the farm, when Douglas Trinick took it over.

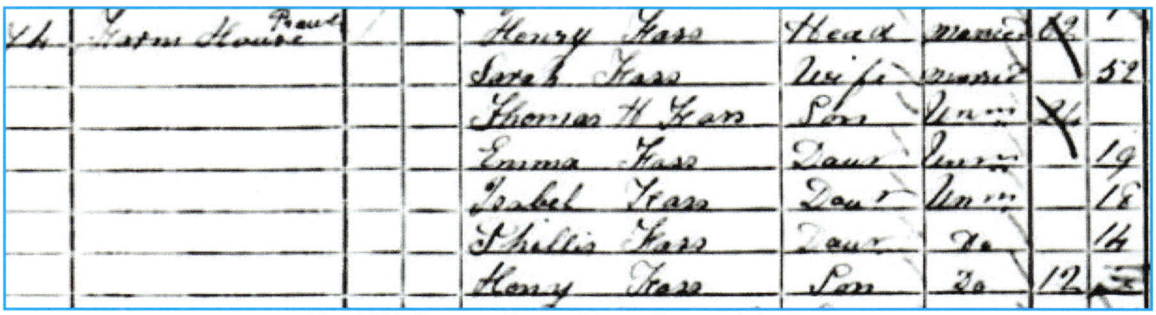

44	Farm House Prawl	Henry Foss	Head	Married	62	
		Sarah Foss	Wife	Married		52
		Thomas H Foss	Son	Unm	24	
		Emma Foss	Daur	Unm		19
		Isabel Foss	Daur	Unm		18
		Phillis Foss	Daur	Do		14
		Henry Foss	Son	Do	12	

The 1881 Census of Lower House Farm and the Fosses

In 1938 W R E and Frances Ann Tucker (Winnie's parents and Roger's grandparents) rented it when John Francis, their son and twin brother of Winnie, married Molly Wood. The farm was rent free to begin with, but the Tuckers rented and then bought it in the 1960s.

Lower House Farm was sold in the 1980s once it became impractical for large lorries to get through the small roads and round the difficult corners to the farmyard. The barns have been converted to residential accommodation (we live in the old threshing barn). As a result, the agriculture atmosphere of the village changed quite considerably.

Aerial View circa 1960s of Lower House Farm and surrounding area, including what is now the shop (on the left) and Pigs Nose, with Locks Farm at the top right

The field below Lower House Farm used to be an orchard and by the side of the hedge (not visible in the photograph above) was a sheep dip which was used by Geoffrey Tripp, Jack Tucker and Derek Wotton, all three of them used to dip the sheep there, helping one another.

Locks Farm

Richard and Jane Partridge compiled the history of Locks Farm from 1560 to 1964:

On the 1842-47 Tithe map the owners of Locks Farm are listed as the Canons of Windsor, part of Queen Anne's Bounty. Tenant: William Pearse RN. Queen Anne's Bounty was a charity for the augmentation of the maintenance of the poor clergy. The Canons of Windsor purchased Locks Farm from Thomas Hoopel and Peter Colliver in 1823. Thomas Henry Tucker rented Locks Farm from about 1895 and bought the farm in 1922. Dorothy

Locks Farm early 1920s

Tucker married John Henry Partridge and they bought Locks Farm in 1944, from Thomas Tucker's executors and lived there until 1955, when they built the Retreat and moved there.

Town Farm

Town Farm, once Collings Farm, was renamed Town because it was too similar in name to Coolings Farm, which was directly behind Town Farm.

There have been Tuckers and Partridges in the Parish for several hundred years. In 1720 a John Tucker from Chivelstone was married in Stokenham Parish Church. Roger's description of some of the family and Town Farm is below:

'Uncle' Richard Tucker was born in 1786 and died in 1857 without children. He left Town Farm to his brother John Tucker's son, William Eales Tucker [1831-1909], my great grandfather. William Eales left Town Farm to William Richard Ernest [1873-1950], my grandfather.

Town Farm, Frances Ann Tucker, Miss Jane Way and Blanche Tucker, circa 1912

Town Farm passed to Uncle Bill, William George Tucker [1903-1955] after my grandfather (W R E), and it then passed to my father's children. Mother holiday let Town Farm until Vicky and I got married in 1964 when we moved into Town Farm.

Town Farm was originally three cottages (made into two at some stage) and the lavatories were at the bottom of the garden overhanging the stream. In the yard in front was a feed store, a large swill boiler for cooking all the waste food from the RAF Camp, pigs houses, a hay and straw barn with a chaff cutter driven by a Blackstone Oil Engine.

The chaff was hay and straw cut into short pieces to feed the horses, eight in total. The last two I remember were called Victor and Damsel. Across the road was Town Linhay where the lorries were garaged and produce was stored. On the south side of the Linhay was a very large greenhouse in which peaches, grapes, tomatoes, lettuces and chrysanthemums were grown all the year round. Below the Linhay was a barn, now a garage, which was the cider house, and next to the two Poor House cottages.

The Poor Houses

On the incline of Town Hill there were once two cottages for the poor, called Collings Cottages. Tim Blyth has photographed the Chivelstone Poor Book from 1763. Members of the village contributed towards the upkeep, and in the Woodleigh Deanery Magazine of January 1923 Miss Braine-Hartnell was thanked for the £2.2s.0d she gave for distribution of coal to the poor of Chivelstone Parish.

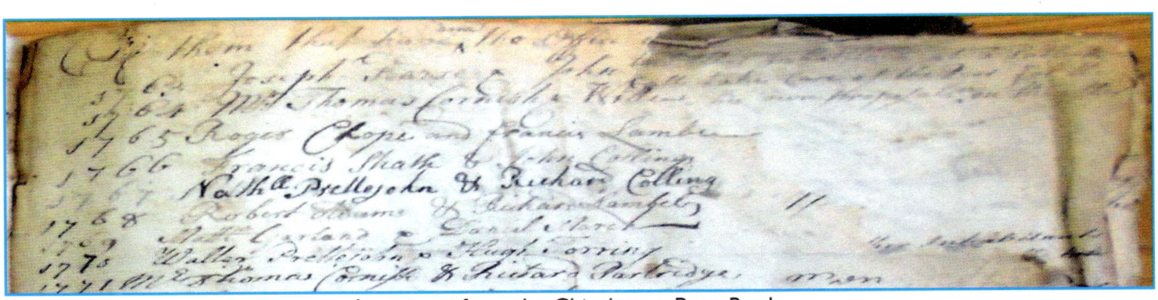

An extract from the Chivelstone Poor Book

Coolings Farm

From the Tithe map apportionments of 1842-47 Coolings Farm was owned by Walter Prettyjohn and rented by Richard Foss. Coolings and the Thatches were originally a single 17th century house. Read more about the Thatches later in this chapter.

From Richard:

One of the Prettyjohn's family married one of the Pitts in the late 1800', and Coolings farm passed to the Pitts family. W R E Tucker rented it from the Pitts in the 1900s. Richard Albert Partridge, My grandfather, bought it in 1922 and William Albert Partridge, my father, and family went to live in Coolings in about 1925 and farmed it until his death in 1953. Phyllis and Derek Wotton moved into the farm in about 1955 and bought it from W R Partridge (my brother, known as Bob) in the early 1960s.

Pubs

Union Hotel/Pigs Nose Inn

The Union Hotel was renamed the Pigs Nose Inn in 1949.

1920s John Francis Tucker on the horse

2011 The Pigs Nose

The table below lists the owners from Kelly's Directories:

1842 - c.1850	William Cole
1866	James Stone
1878	Ambrose Patey Jn (and shoe maker)*
1889	Peter Adams
1906, 1906, 1914, 1919	Mrs Emma Sture
1926, 1930, 1939	Mrs E A Rendle
1960s	Larry Wootton
Late 1960s early 1970s	Graham Fisher

* Also Innkeeper in 1872 at the time of the Maria Teresa wreck and ensuing drama of the Italians

After Graham Fisher, John Ireland took over the Pigs Nose; from 1974 for 13 years Joan and Jim Bailey ran it for John. Then Ben and Ann Newport and finally Lesley and Peter Webber, who still run the Pigs Nose today.

Didi Caudery recalled being sent out by Larry to see if Snowdrop, the local bobby, was around! After closing time, the practice was to go upstairs with your drinks, and the lights turned off in the bar... Elaine Trant also recalled in the late 60s the publican Larry used to have a small shop in what is now the snooker room (see the chapter on Shops on page 69).

Diana Shelvoke was told that periodically fishermen from Hallsands used to come across the cliffs to the pub and drink themselves silly. When this happened, all the villagers would shut themselves indoors and say 'Out of the Union and trust in Providence'. There used to be one man (Diana thought he was called Frenchie Billy), when he walked back he used to shout and when asked what did he shout for, he replied to frighten the ghosts.

In *Sisters at Sea,* by Ruth and Frank Milton, a mission room at Hallsands is mentioned, where people from Prawle went for gatherings.

The Providence Inn

The Providence Inn served the public since 1840 and is thought to date back much earlier.

From the 'Chivelstone Parish Heritage Appraisal': 'the Providence Inn, East Prawle, has a brewhouse with floor of stone slabs laid on solid rock. Shown on 1880s OS 25" map as corner group of adjoining buildings.'

Brenda Jeffery remembered next to the stairs there was what they called the trap door and 'if we wanted to go in – we used to nip over if we wanted a packet of crisps or something. Mum would give us some money 'oh go over and ask your Auntie May for one'. Brenda's aunt and uncle ran the pub for many years.

Sadly the Providence Inn closed on 1 November 2008, and as Tim Johnson, the last publican, put it: 'Running a village pub was becoming just an expensive hobby.' So another piece of rural history disappeared. The Providence had been quenching thirsts for centuries.

In 2010 Arnold Mann, the owner, sold the Providence and it has been refurbished and modernised as a private residence. Arnie told me apparently the pub was affectionately known as 'Putts Providence', because the Putts built it.

Pre 1920s Providence Inn before the Assembly Room

1964 Providence Inn with Assembly Room

1850	Mary Putt
1866	Miss Kerziah Putt
1875	Mrs Putt
1883	John Putt
1889	Philip Hutchings
1897	Sampson Putt
1906	Mrs Ann Thornton
1914	John Thornton
1919	No mention
1926-1930	George Henry Jarvis
1939	Arthur and May Jarvis took over from George
1969	Richard and Janet Smallman
1960s	Sean Featherstonehaugh (son)
1978	Penny and Richard Twigg
1990s renamed Freebooter	John and Delphine Swaddle
2002 renamed Providence	Arnie Mann
2007	Tim Johnson

Owners of The Providence Inn taken from Kelly's Directories of Devon or White's Directories & others

The list of publicans for the last 50 years of the Providence Inn may not be completely accurate.

The Assembly Room

I had been in East Prawle for 37 years before hearing about the Assembly Room in a conversation with Brenda about euchre.

The Assembly Room is attached to the Providence Inn and belonged to it, but was sold separately and converted into a flat when Arnold Mann bought the Providence in 2002.

Peter Kingston told me John Henry Putt – Pat Farleigh's father – helped build the Assembly Room for George Jarvis, which puts the date around 1926-30. (He was always called John Henry because there were several Johns and Jacks in the village at that time.)

However, an extract from the Woodleigh Deanery Magazine of September 1922 reported: 'An "American Tea", followed by a Whist Drive and Dance took place in the Assembly Room at Prawle on Tuesday, August 1st.' This suggests it was built earlier.

Winnie, born in 1912, certainly remembered going to dances as a teenager. Winnie had great affection for the Assembly Room. They would dress up in their long party frocks and go to the Assembly Room for dances.

… a lovely room where we used to go dancing, and my sister played the piano. It was a lovely place. You go up the steps like you do now and opposite there was a little cloakroom where you could go in, there's a mirror, take off your coat, get yourself ready to walk out into the room, sit down ready to be asked to dance.

The Assembly Room with the windows open next to the Providence Inn and with the remains of the RAF camp in the distance

Richard's mother (Blanche, Winnie's sister) used to play the piano and people (including Harry Foss) also played the violin as well at the dances. Richard mentioned that Arthur Jarvis had the garage below the Assembly Room where he repaired local cars.

Euchre and whist matches also took place in the Assembly Room. Once a fortnight in the winter months there were tables for euchre on one side of the room and tables for whist on the other. The Pigs Nose would play the Providence and teams from East Portlemouth and South Pool would come up there to join in.

Brenda told me how her mother, Mrs Nellie Blank, Mrs Rendle, and Mrs Webster would take a sponge cake, loads of sandwiches and refreshments. They always had three prizes, one for each side and a booby prize. The money went towards the Youth Club. This went on for years, once a fortnight.

In talking to Derek:

Well, the Assembly Room was a great going thing, more than the Pigs Nose. I mean the Pigs Nose used to have dances in the hall, but euchre and whist drives and Christmas parties were always at the Provi.

Euchre is a trick-taking card game most commonly played with four people in two partnerships with a deck of 24 standard playing cards, plus a joker called the 'benny'. Euchre was very popular in Europe during the eighteenth and nineteenth centuries. Apparently the most important pub and club card game in Devon and Cornwall is euchre, but how it turned up in the West country is unknown. Whatever its history, euchre has been played in East Prawle for years. Euchre is still played in the winter in the Pigs Nose.

Sarah Trinick had tap dance lessons in the Assembly Room, and Cindy Higgins embroidery classes and sewing. The children's Christmas parties started by Mrs Webster, Christopher Trinick's granny, were in the Assembly Room. They still continue but in the Community Hall.

Cottages

In the early 1900s, all the cottages were lived in by people born in East Prawle. Children were able to run around freely – no danger of being kidnapped in those days!

As Pat Farleigh put it:

I've lived here in the village all me life and when I was a girl all the cottages were lived in by people who were born and bred here, they went down the generations – but Prawle isn't like it was. Us was allowed out in the winter for hour after tea; we'd play hare and hounds, go over where the ricks were and down around the willow grove – we didn't have no watches then, we used to guess the time ... but if us was late getting back in us would get jawed!

The Original Coastguard Cottages

The land on which the cottages were built was leased from Richard Tucker on a 60-year term from 1 January 1823. Five cottages and the station officer's house (a communal wash house was later built on the land of No 1 for the use of all the cottages) formed the East Prawle Coast Guard Station. On the 1825 map it is written as 'Preventative Station'.

The lease below expired in 1882 but the Admiralty took on a fresh lease for a further 21 years from 1 January 1883. This expired in 1904, by which time the coastguard cottages at Prawle Point had been built.

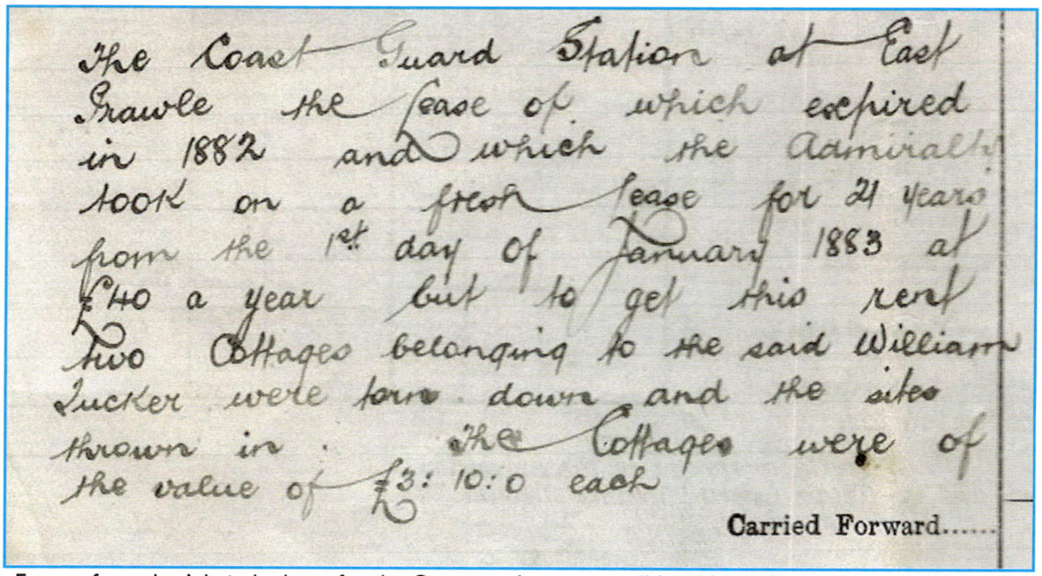
The Coast Guard Station at East
Prawle the lease of which expired
in 1882 and which the Admiralty
took on a fresh lease for 21 years
from the 1st day of January 1883 at
£40 a year but to get this rent
Two Cottages belonging to the said William
Tucker were torn down and the sites
thrown in. The Cottages were of
the value of £3: 10:0 each

Carried Forward......

Extract from the Admiralty lease for the Coastguard cottages at 'New Houses', given to me by Roger Tucker

The land with the cottages and station officer's house passed back to William Tucker, the nephew of the original owner, Winnie's grandfather, and Roger and Richard's great grandfather (Granfer Tucker). He left the five cottages to his son Thomas Henry Tucker and the station officer's house to William Richard Ernest Tucker, Winnie's father.

When the cottages reverted back to the Tucker family, they were deemed to be worth very little and lay empty for a while. At the time of the Hallsands disaster in 1917 some of the families from Hallsands came to live in these cottages.

Thomas Henry Tucker retired to No 5 Sea View in 1935 and below is an extract from his will:

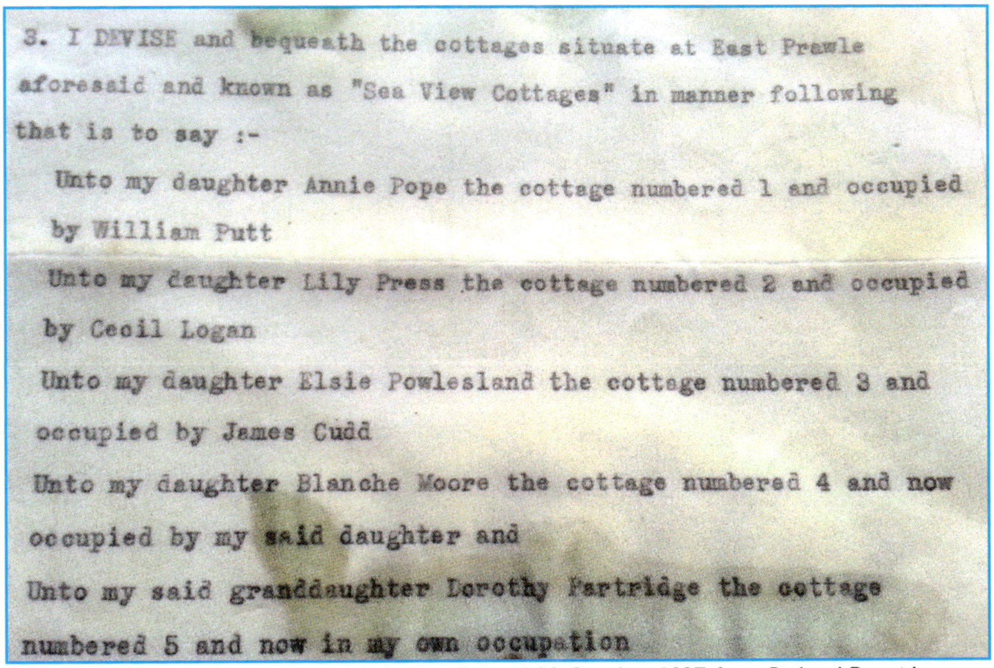

3. I DEVISE and bequeath the cottages situate at East Prawle aforesaid and known as "Sea View Cottages" in manner following that is to say :-

Unto my daughter Annie Pope the cottage numbered 1 and occupied by William Putt

Unto my daughter Lily Press the cottage numbered 2 and occupied by Cecil Logan

Unto my daughter Elsie Powlesland the cottage numbered 3 and occupied by James Cudd

Unto my daughter Blanche Moore the cottage numbered 4 and now occupied by my said daughter and

Unto my said granddaughter Dorothy Partridge the cottage numbered 5 and now in my own occupation

Extract from Thomas Henry Tucker's will dated 29 October 1937, from Richard Partridge

1 Sea View

In 1993 Mark and I bought No 1 Sea View, one of the original coastguard cottages (mentioned above and renamed Sea View), from Phyllis and Derek Wotton. Phyllis Wotton (née Partridge) inherited No 1 Sea View from Osmond Moore, whose second marriage was to Mary Blanche Partridge, sister to Winnie, and Richard and Phyllis's mother. Richard and Mike lived there for five years with the family before getting married themselves.

Early 1900s Coastguard Station ('New Houses')

2004 Sea View cottages ('New Houses')

Gladys Login, Margaret Mitchelmore's mother, lived at No 1 Sea View from the age of two (1906) but moved to Lannacombe when she married. .Margaret and Bill walked with their mother every Sunday to stay in No 1 Sea View with their grandparents to go to school.

Coastguard Cottages at Prawle Point

Roger Barrett wrote:

In 1903, the Admiralty changed its policy of renting coastguard stations and financial provision was made to either buy outright existing stations or build new ones. Accordingly, with the lease of the old station at East Prawle due to expire in 1904, the Admiralty decided in 1903 to establish a new station for the CG detachment at Prawle Point when the necessary accommodation had been provided.

Richard recounted how the bricks came on the train to Kingsbridge, then by steam traction engine and wagons to Prawle Green. From there they were unloaded and taken down to Prawle Point by horse and cart. It was pretty rough going down to the Point in those days.

1904-5 Prawle Point coastguard cottages – the chief officer's house on the left

2015 Prawle Point cottages, now privately owned

The Rev B N Adams wrote that 'in summer time the approach to these houses is fearsome enough, but in the winter it becomes a literal wade through a sea of mud. But it is well worth the toil at any time, for Prawle Point is a spot, once visited, never to be forgotten.'

Foss Cottage

Mention has to be made of Foss Cottage, which now belongs to my sister Rose and her family. It is the very last cottage down New Houses at the end of the row with the old coastguard cottages.

The Chivelstone Parish Council minutes of 14 November 1913 recorded that there were '2 cottages at the extreme end of Prawle connected with Mr Foss'. However, the Miss Foss sisters, and their brother Harry, moved down from Lower House Farm to Foss Cottage – known as 3 West End Cottages in those days – certainly by 1935.

1970s Drawing of Foss Cottage

The Miss Foss sisters

The Miss Fosses had a busy life, weaving, keeping bees, and making wheat wine. Diana Shelvoke recalled they used to say the bees came to tell them when anyone had died – they said the bees brought the news.

One of the Miss Fosses used to go around collecting money for the church and the chapel, as well as collecting for a hospital. Derek remembered his wife, Phyllis, telling him that as a child she and her mother used to help count the money – Phyllis had it all worked out before Miss Foss did, who crossly said 'sit back brain box!'

There are many stories about Harry Foss, but one was that he used to give Alice Stone's family a Christmas pudding every year, because Jim Stone, her father, would empty the privy buckets down at Foss Cottage early every Saturday morning.

Emma Foss was the last of the family to die in 1957. At the time Miss Leonard and her aunt Mrs Leonard were renting Nos 1 and 2 West End Cottages (next to Foss Cottage). The three cottages came up for sale as a single lot and Haschi Wassermann bought all three (Rose thinks the price was £1500), on the understanding that he would sell Nos 1 and 2 to the Leonards.

Before purchasing Foss Cottage, Haschi and his wife, Anni, rented the Station Officer's house from Winnie's father. They were familiar figures in the village and walked for miles around the coast with their Dalmatian dog.

Dr Anni Noll, or Dr Wassermann as she was known in the village, was a top baby specialist at the Heidelberg Clinic before the war. Anni was very helpful in diagnosing Winnie's daughter's ailment of Pyloric Stenosis at two or three weeks old.

Derek used to deliver cream, butter and eggs to the Wassermanns, and Maurice Putt and his father used to look after Foss Cottage and the garden.

Haschi Wasserman

Dr Anni Noll

Maelcombe House

Maelcombe House was a large Edwardian property built in about 1905, on a wonderful site sheltered in the lee of Prawle Point and enjoying fabulous views along this unspoilt stretch of coastline, most of which is now owned by the National Trust. Recently it has been rebuilt. It was pulled down in 2014 and Nicola and Tudor Brown moved into the new building in 2016.

Aerial view of Maelcombe House (undated)

2016 Maelcombe House rebuilt

There are many theories about the building of Maelcombe House, but Winnie said:

A coastguard at Prawle Point had the place built but when it was finished he couldn't pay for it and the Helbys bought it from him. Captain Helby was the father, Hugh Helby the son, and another brother, a brigadier. Miss Rosemary, the daughter, was presented at Court. They were a lovely family. My mother was invited to Mr Hugh's wedding in the Tower of London.

Winnie also thought the bricks he used were of insufficient quality for the Admiralty to use for the cottages at Prawle Point. The story is the clerk of works had so many bricks rejected – many were damaged in transit – he was able to build Maelcombe House with all the rejects.

Roger Barrett's account of the building of the Prawle Point cottages is similar:

The builder of the new coastguard cottages, J. Wilson, apparently had enough bricks rejected by the Admiralty's clerk of works, or otherwise left over at the end of the contract to build a new house for himself along the coast at what is now known as Maelcombe House. (Running out of money, Wilson subsequently sold the house to Captain Harold Helby, who between 1908 and 1909, as Lieut. Helby, was Inspecting Officer of Coastguards for the Salcombe division.) Wilson also got the contract to insert a telescope window up at the Prawle Point signal station at a cost of £108 and in 1908 William Tucker installed, at a cost of £12.10s., two galvanised iron, 200 gallon, water tanks 'to remedy the inadequacy of the existing supply to the Lookout House.

Ash Park

In 1915 Richard Foss bought the ground from the Rev Marcus Dimond Dimond-Churchward and built the house which he called Ash Park.

Ash Park before it was burnt down in the 1980s

Present day Ash Park

Richard acted as guarantor for Emma Wood, Pat Farleigh's mother, in 1915 so that she could become the post mistress at East Prawle. Richard is buried in St Sylvester's, Chivelstone. See the inscription on his gravestone below:

Richard Henry Watson Foss died January 27th 1937 aged 88 of Ash Park Prawle. Hermione wife of R H W Foss who fell asleep July 26th 1919 aged 67. Resting.

The Relles bought Ash Park in the late 1930s. Diana Shelvoke (née Thorpe) remembered that before the war her family had bought a piece of land next to Ash Park with a view to building. However, soon after the Relles decided to sell Ash Park to the Thorpes. Mrs Relle bought No 9 the Coastguards cottages but she continued living in Ash Park until after the war when Wing Commander Thorpe retired.

The Thorpes sold Ash Park in about 1981, and shortly after it burnt down. Although there was a well in the field behind the house, this does not seem to have been used to help put the fire out. Water had to be piped from the well at New Houses, across the fields. It was rebuilt in 1982 and has recently been sold to Cathryn and Chris Vanderspar.

The Thatches

The Thatches and Coolings Farmhouse, now a pair of houses, was originally a single 17-century house, extended in the 18th century and altered in the early 20th century.

Ashley Ford lived in the Thatches as a child:

Grandf'er, Philip Putt, initially rented the cottage at £4 per annum and subsequently bought it for £160 from the Rev. Prebendary M D Dimond-Churchward of Northam Vicarage, who owned a good deal of land and property around Prawle. They were wealthy land owners in the South Hams.

Thick cob walls, under a thatched roof, was in today's jargon very eco friendly and on a winter's night with a cooking range alight at one end of the house, an open fire at the other and a couple of oil lamps alight in the two downstairs living rooms made for a cosy existence. Minus the fires the interior was cool in the summer. The

The Thatches

bedroom floorboards were the ceilings of the room below, you could see the upstairs light through the cracks between the floor boards. A serious downside was the lavatory (bucket) at least a hundred yards away in the vegetable garden adjacent to Town Farm house, freezing in winter, vile in summer. There were, of course, chamber pots under the beds. No H&C water on tap.

My grandfather died aged 82, leaving the cottage to mum who over the years acquired H&C water, mains electricity, a comfortable bathroom and a Rayburn stove (the poor man's Aga!) which for much of the year was continuously burning and kept the old place warm and dry. The thatch had to be renewed every 30 years or so.

Mum left the cottage to Barney and me and we sold it for £70k in 1997 to fund her care for the last five years of her life. She lived 95 years in the old place and it was a wrench parting with it.

The Council Houses

The first council houses in East Prawle were originally built shortly after the war for farm workers. The houses were built in three stages: 1 to 6 Higher Park in 1948; the Kingsbridge Rural District Council laid a water main across Torrings Meadow which belonged to W R E Tucker; 7 to 16 Higher Park were built on land compulsorily purchased from Roger's father in 1953; and 17 to 26 were built in 1993 when Roger had taken over the farm. Roger stipulated that the houses built on his land would always be for rent, never sold by the Council. As long as local people put their name on the housing list they get first priority.

Pre 1972-73: Higher Park Council Houses

Brenda has her father's Agreement of Tenancy from the Kingsbridge Rural District Council dated 17th November 1953, at a weekly rent of fifteen shillings (see the next page). She said:

My parents moved from Town Cottage, then owned by Mr Tripp of Higher Farm, into No 8 Higher Park in December 1953. The rent was fifteen shillings a week but if you had lodgers, my grandmother who lived with us, you had to pay 5/- a week extra. When I left school and went out to work they had to pay 2/6 a week extra; the same again when my sister finished school. Mum and Dad and Pat Farleigh were the only people to remain in those two houses until they died, aged 57 and 61 years respectively.

Fore Street

Fore Street is the main road into East Prawle when approaching from Moorwell Pond, and was not tarmacked in 1916. The first house on the left is Bowhay House and Jane and Kenneth Shadbolt wrote in the Millennium Book:

In 1835 a Mary Gunn of Charleton had made a will leaving the house and 11 fields to her son William and a granddaughter. She was the sister of W Watts of Watts' Tenement, Prawle and died in 1857. William Gunn rebuilt

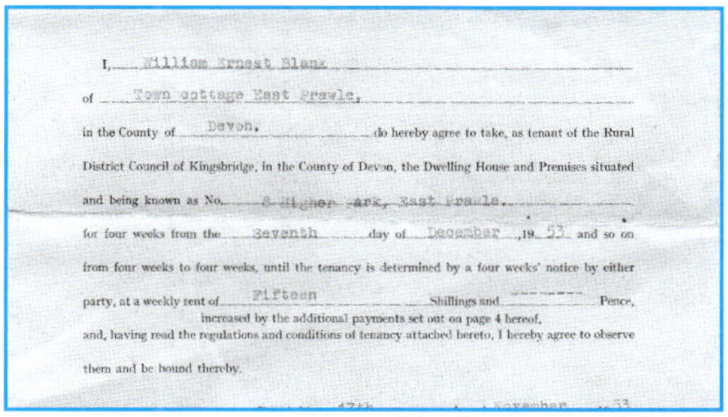

I, William Ernest Blank

of Town cottage East Prawle,

in the County of Devon. do hereby agree to take, as tenant of the Rural District Council of Kingsbridge, in the County of Devon, the Dwelling House and Premises situated and being known as No. 8 Higher Park, East Prawle.

for four weeks from the Seventh day of December, 19 53 and so on from four weeks to four weeks, until the tenancy is determined by a four weeks' notice by either party, at a weekly rent of Fifteen Shillings and -------- Pence, increased by the additional payments set out on page 4 hereof, and, having read the regulations and conditions of tenancy attached hereto, I hereby agree to observe them and be bound thereby.

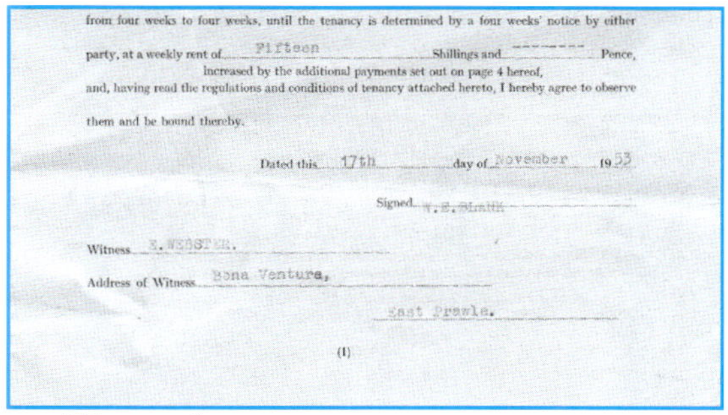

from four weeks to four weeks, until the tenancy is determined by a four weeks' notice by either party, at a weekly rent of Fifteen Shillings and -------- Pence, increased by the additional payments set out on page 4 hereof, and, having read the regulations and conditions of tenancy attached hereto, I hereby agree to observe them and be bound thereby.

Dated this 17th day of November 19 53

Signed W. E. Blank

Witness E. WEBSTER.

Address of Witness Bona Ventura,

East Prawle.

(1)

The front page of the Blank's Council Tenancy Agreement

the house in 1858. Between 1835 and 1839 tenants had been Thomas Bennet and Peter Giles. After William, Edward Gunn lived there until 2 June 1870 when the house was sold at Putt's Providence Inn to Stephen Lewis-Adams Bowhay for £80. He was the village carrier and died in 1894; his yard was alongside the house. His son, James Harley Bowhay and family lived here until his death in 1916. W A Partridge and family lived here as tenants 1921-28 when Mr J H Partridge bought the house and garages opposite for £325 from James Lewis Bowhay, a South Pool rabbit trapper. The extension (which does not form a 180° line with the house - more like 170°!) was built between 1928 and 1931 on land containing a cottage garden between the house and Rosario, bought from C T Tucker in 1922 for £8. Building stones came from Rockfield. A small stable fronting the road was still surviving after a fashion when we came to Prawle - sold later to Rosario to become their garage. Mr J H Partridge and wife lived here from 1931-40. Subsequent tenants of theirs between 1940 and 1958 were a Mr and Mrs Hopkirk and Mrs Hopkirk's brother, Mr Dick Putt - and in 1958 we purchased the property. From 1965-72 it was let to the Pigs Nose while we were in New Zealand but from '72 when we returned it became properly the family home to my wife Jane and me, and to our four children.

Rosario was built by Richard Albert Partridge (Richard's grandfather) in 1903. It was named after a port in Argentina, which he visited when in the Royal Navy, and was built by a Mr Brooking for £241 in the garden of what is now known as Rosario Cottage.

Rosario Cottage is probably several hundred years old, being only one room with open hearth and walls 3-4 feet thick. In Victorian times two further rooms were added and the roof lifted to provide a room above the living room.

The two Corner cottages (at the other end of Fore Street) were built by 1865, and described as bounded on the north by Eastern Green Common (the village green). In Kelly's Directory 1902 William Beer was the sub-postmaster for East Prawle at No 1. No 3 Corner Cottages, Little Eldner, derived from the reverse spelling of Rendle: Jack Rendle, who used to live there, was well known in the area for his transport business. The Post Office was on the opposite side of the road from 1915 to 1983, with the first telephone in the village.

(before 1928) Fore Street

2011 Fore Street

About the House

Life at home was always busy without modern equipment. No hoovers, washing machines, dishwashers, microwaves etc, far fewer luxuries. Children's nappies – endless washing, no plastic pants or disposable nappies in those days. As well as no plastic bags!

The Weekly Wash

Before washing machines, the weekly wash was an awesome task taking the whole day. Monday morning was always washing day and certainly it was for Winnie Easterbrook. In the outhouse, they had a copper boiler which they filled and a fire grate underneath for the fire to heat the water. Once it was boiling hot, all whites, sheets and pillow cases were put in the copper boiler. (Winnie said she never used the popular peg dolly used to plunge and agitate the clothes, it was always by hand.)

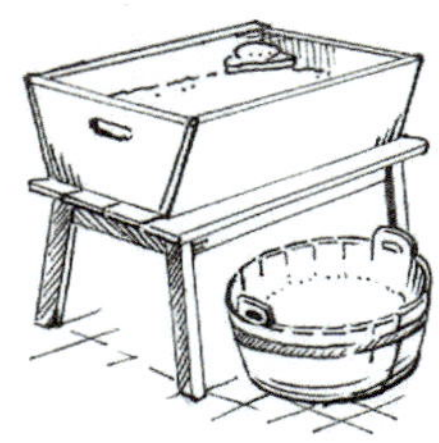

Winnie had one tub soaking the clothes with soap, one with clear water and the blue bag. She dipped the blue bag in and out of the rinsing water ('streaming' – Winnie's word for rinsing – possibly originating from rinsing clothes in streams). This whitened the clothes and couldn't be left too long or the laundry would turn blue. The clothes then went through a mangle before hanging on the line in the meadow – nothing better than to see washing whiter than white flapping in the breeze.

Until the mid-20th century Reckitt's blue-bags were well-known in many countries, sold as penny cubes to be wrapped in flannel or muslin, or sold ready bagged.

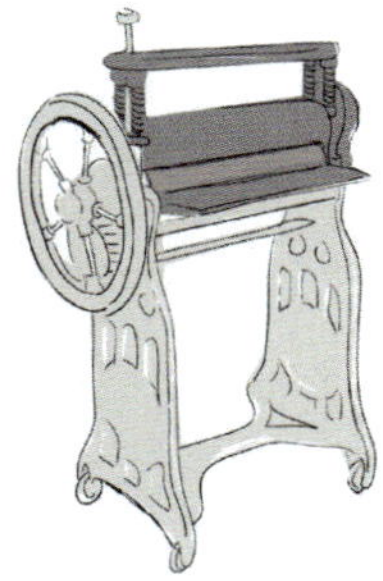

Winnie also remembered when they had finished with the copper boiler it was put out in the garden up the other end, and it slid down into the field, where it probably still is to this day.

The copper was not only used for washing clothes, but also for cooking potatoes for the pigs as well. As Winnie said: 'Just the little potatoes, big ones they would bag up to take to market. They were only little, scruffy potatoes. Of course then after you had cooked the potatoes, they were a bit muddy, so you had to clean the copper before you could use it again to do the washing.'

The five Sea View cottages, the original coastguard cottages down New Houses, had a communal washhouse. Richard Partridge lived at No 1 Sea View for a time with his mother and stepfather and I asked him how they coped with so many cottages using the washhouse on the same day. He thought perhaps it rolled over to Tuesdays. Margaret Mitchelmore, whose grandparents lived in No 1 before Richard and his family, said each cottage had a day allocated.

Maurice Putt told Richard that they hired a fisherman's donkey on a weekend to collect 'furze' (gorse) and wood which had washed up on the shore, for his mother's washing on a Monday. The tops of the gorse were burnt off in the winter time so just the sticks were left, which they brought in for putting in the copper's grate.

A superstition: Blankets were never washed in May. Winnie never washed blankets in May, she didn't know why not, but it was the superstition:

Wash blankets in May
Wash a dear one away

Another superstition is 'Marry in May, Rue The Day'. It was believed that May was an unlucky month, especially if you were to be married within the month. Further to this, children born in May were thought to be sickly children. The unluckiness apparently applied to cats as well. Any cat born in May was thought to be useless for catching rodents.

Winnie used to buy unbleached sheets from Rudd Prinn of Dartmouth, who came round once a fortnight. After two or three washes the sheets would be completely bleached white.

Hanging out the Washing

The pegs known as 'gypsy clothes pegs' because gypsies from Chillington made them and came round knocking at doors selling them. They cut sticks from the hedges to make the clothes pegs. They also made linen buttons – metal buttons covered with fabric. They carried their heavy baskets for miles with a wide variety of goods to sell to the villagers.

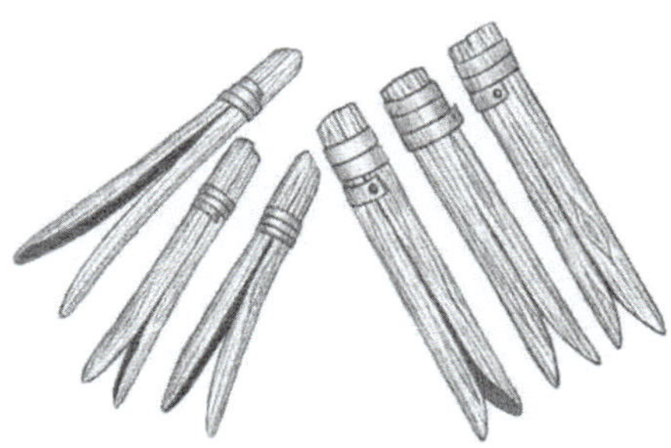

Clothes pegs made by the gypsies

Ironing

If washing was done on a Monday, it followed that ironing was done on a Tuesday.

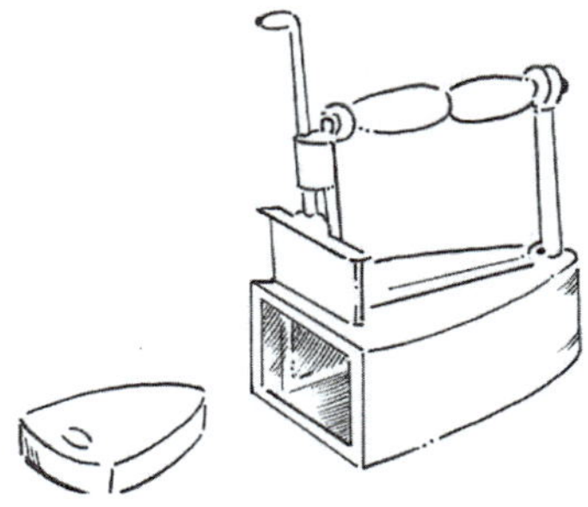

Box iron with a slug

According to Winnie:

You stood a flat iron on the stove to get hot, but I had a box iron as well. We had two iron slugs to go inside this box. You'd put them right in the fire and take them out one at a time. We had an open fire then and we had a poker to take the iron out of the fire. Take it out with a poker, a crook, pull up the lid [of the box] put the iron in, put the lid down and it was ready to iron and while one was in the box the other was in the fire. Over the years putting them in the fire they would get smaller, and the blacksmith, Charlie Yalland, used to re–make them bigger.

Managing the House

Winnie remembered cleaning always as hard work – on your hands and knees on flagstone floors, with mats on them. The bedrooms had lino flooring with small mats either side of the beds and polish would be in a tin (like shoe polish), put it on and rub off with a cloth.

Stone and tile floors were mopped frequently using long handled string or rag mops. Mopping was quite a skill – the floor had to be left clean... Sprinkle salt or tea leaves on the carpet before brushing it with a hard brush. The tea leaves would clean up the dirt of the carpets...

Lidstone fireplaces and grates all had to be black leaded, a laborious task but kept them looking bright and clean. Even now fire grates are often black leaded.

Washing the Dishes

Elaine, Winnie's daughter, remembered as a child they would wash the dishes in a bowl of water on the table and a tray to put the dishes on, but they didn't have Fairy Liquid. 'Mum had a wire mesh box that would open to put a bar of soap in and shut down. You'd shake it out in the water to get your soapy water.' All the pieces of soap were saved and pushed together.

It was similar for Brenda but the water was thrown away outside into the road, or on the garden.

Personal Hygiene....

The concepts of cleanliness are a lot different today from a hundred years ago. There certainly wasn't much washing. As Ashley Ford said, 'If you were out in the fields there wasn't much you could do about washing your hands before eating a sandwich.'

Ashley told me his grandfather, Philip Putt, never bathed – they didn't have a bath. Ashley himself remembered Saturday night was bath night in a tin bath that hung behind the kitchen door: Elwin first as the youngest, Ashley second, their mother third and their father fourth – same routine every Saturday. Hot water was so precious, not one drop could be wasted.

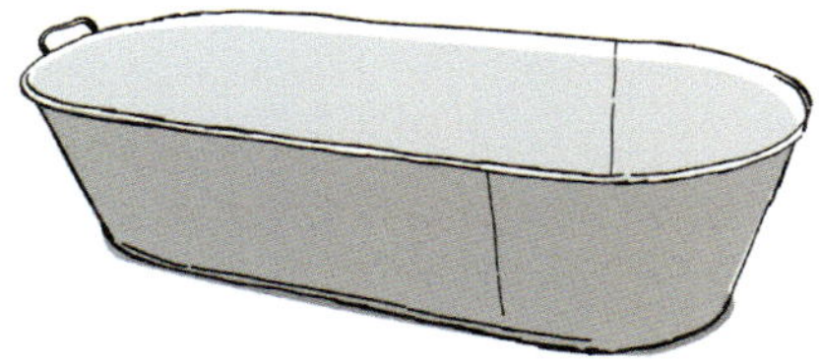

For Winnie, it was standing up and bathing. Elaine, her daughter, said they never had a bath at Sea View – they just washed using a bowl. Brenda also remembered, when living in Town Cottages, they had a tin bath and as with the washing up, the water was literally thrown out into the road. 'It wasn't until my sister had scarlet fever in 1949/50 and the health inspector came and demanded that there was proper drainage.'

Whether washing people, clothes or dishes, it must have been a relief to have mains water, baths and sinks. (See page 50 for the chapter on water.)

Sanitation

Until mains water came to East Prawle (in 1942 and 1953), there were few indoor lavatories; for example in 1934 Bowhay House and Sunnyside advertised indoor sanitation.

Winnie told me there were four privies down at the end of Town Farm, one for her family, two for the Town cottages and one for Mrs Ford. 'The toilet was right down through the court at the end of the garden where the stream is.'

Brenda lived in one of the Town cottages and remembered very well having to walk all the way down to one of the privies at the end of Town Farm. Waste was frequently buried in the garden or thrown into a nearby stream. Brenda's father used to light a cigarette before setting off for a digging session.

Iris Brialey (née Hannaford) staying with her Aunt Carrie Beer, the postmistress at 1 Corner Cottage, told me she had to go out of the cottage, down past the blacksmith, past Sunnyside and turn left into a garden to get to the privies – the horses at the blacksmith used to terrify her. The people in the next door cottages had to walk right across the green to the field the other side. But Alice Stone was all right in Hanley Cottage because they had a garden at the back.

When Phyllis Putt's daughter Elizabeth was a child at No. 4 Sea View, Phyllis used to take her down the passage way, up some steps, along a path at the top and then round a corner to their outside lavatory. It was behind the communal washhouse shared between the five cottages, and very scary with spiders....

Well into the second half of the twentieth century newspaper was the norm in 'end paper' (surely the forerunner of recycling). With no television, a daily newspaper was considered a must, and the chore of cutting up the squares invariably was delegated to the children.

Winnie said they had squares of newspaper with a piece of cord threaded through a hole at the top and hung on a nail on the wall. They always had a chamber pot as well, one was plain white, and another had pretty flowers on it.

Lighting and Electricity

Until the advent of electricity, life was very different. People's lives were dependent on daylight. Oil lamps date from the first quarter of the 19th century and kerosene (paraffin) lamps from the 20th century.

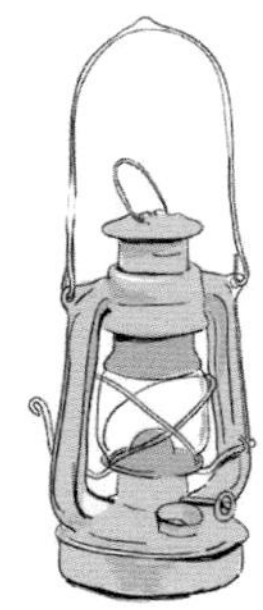

When we first came to East Prawle in 1973 it was commonplace to have power cuts. One New Year's Eve was spent roasting our meat in the fireplace. However, nowadays even if there is a power cut it is not likely to last long.

To discover precisely when electricity was brought to East Prawle, I got in touch with Peter Lamb, the Chief Archivist and Secretary of the South Western Electricity Historical Society, who hazarded a guess that it was somewhere around 1952/53. Rural Development started in 1950 and Peter was personally part of the process in 1957 of extending the Totnes to Harbertonford line out towards Kingsbridge, but he is uncertain about Prawle. Certainly, Brenda remembered there was electricity when the council houses were built in 1953. Roger remembered electricity being installed. They used a lot of dynamite to make holes for the poles and it was very messy.

Winnie moved from Town Farm to down New Houses in 1946 and there was no electricity then. Winnie remembered candles and lamps, and when the electricity came she remembered going upstairs to switch on the lights in two bedrooms, just to see what the light would be like.

And another priceless story from Richard: A lovely old lady living in the village (not to mention names), when the meter man came to read her meter he said 'you have hardly used any electricity, do you turn it on, or is something wrong?' 'Oh no,' she said, 'I turn it on to see to light my candles and oil lamp.'

Didi Caudery used to stay down at the Prawle Point cottages and they were still using gas lamps until the late 1950s.

Roger, aged about 10, remembered very clearly the noise and mess as they put dynamite down to make holes for the poles.

A story told by both Winnie and Richard about Ash Park. I understand there was some sort of lighting generator before electricity came to the village, and someone said: 'Oh I hear you've got a lighting plant down there.' The reply was 'Oh no we've got a lighting *tree*!' Apparently a plant wasn't big enough. Diana Shelvoke said there was an unused generator there when her family lived at Ash Park. Uncle Jack Partridge maintained their lighting plant (tree) through the 1920s and early 1930s.

Sarah Trinick talked of Bert Stone the shoemaker, who lived in Rock Cottage before her. He didn't want to have electricity, but one day he had to go to hospital and it was installed while he was away for the day. Electricity was installed but only in a very basic way. When Sarah moved in, some of the rooms had no plugs. There was one light switch and just a central ceiling light.

My earliest memories when we farmed in Gloucestershire are of no electricity. To this day I hate the dark probably because I had to go to bed in the pitch dark, leaving everyone downstairs in the light and warmth.

Brenda told me that before electricity, Moyseys of Kingsbridge used to come round once a fortnight with accumulators to charge batteries up for the radios – or 'wirelesses'. They picked up the accumulator, took it to Kingsbridge to charge, then brought it back the next time they came. People had two accumulators, so while one was being charged there was always a second.

The Queen's Coronation, on 2 June 1953 in Westminster Abbey, ushered in the television age. Permission had never been given before for television cameras in the Abbey. Some felt it wrong for people to watch such a solemn occasion while drinking tea in their front rooms. However, about 20 million TV viewers saw the young Queen crowned. Diana Shelvoke remembered they had a tiny television especially to be able to watch the coronation.

Refrigeration

As a child, Elaine Trant didn't have any refrigeration, and she used to go to the shop for the ice cream which had to be eaten the same day. (See more on food and drink and preserving food on page 49.)

I remember we had an enormous fridge in our kitchen – it was very noisy, similar to the one on the right here.

Keeping Warm

Before central heating, almost every room in a house had a fireplace.
Firewood and peat were the only local sources of warmth before the 18th century. Furze or gorse was also used as fuel. It was burnt or singed before cutting to remove the prickles, and then made into faggots of 'black sticks' for firing the household boiling coppers. Driftwood was also collected from the beach. On many occasions my children were made to carry driftwood up for the fire.

Of course, the main room also had either an open fireplace or later a Lidstone stove, which probably kept the whole place warm.

From Richard's grandfather, Richard Albert Partridge's diary, it is clear that he was collecting coal with a horse and wagon and a van from Goodshelter in the 1920s. He then delivered the coal around the village. The coal was delivered to Goodshelter by barge or boat.

Medicine

In the early 1920s, and probably earlier, the doctors used to come across on the ferry from Salcombe, then hire a pony and trap to make calls on the sick in the village. It's thought to have been on Mondays, Wednesdays and Fridays. Winnie remembered the medicine was always in flattish shaped bottles never in tablet form.

Wilf Login told Stephen Pedrick that his mother had to have her leg amputated in 1929 and was provided with a peg leg. However, all the villagers of Prawle got together and raised enough money to buy her a prosthetic/aluminium leg - a great story of charity starting at home.

Childbirth

We don't have a lot of information about babies being born in East Prawle even though, until the 20th century, most children were born at home.

From Winnie:

They had big families then. I remember there was always six or seven. They had no sort of preventatives, they were often living in just 'one up, one down', but they managed, it wasn't like it is today. Hygiene standards were much lower than today, you wouldn't wash your hands very often in hot water! You just couldn't do it! Sometimes when there were complications; they just had to deal with it as best they could.

Doris Wotton's grandmother, Alice Bowhay, was the parish midwife and brought most of the Chivelstone parish children into the world. She lived in one of the cottages just over the bridge at South Pool, and Richard Wotton, Doris's husband, told me that people often used to go and pick her up with a horse or a trap to get her back quickly. Derek Wotton remembered she was tall with glasses, very friendly and helpful. (Richard also told me that Doris's mother was a Bowhay and her father (Louis Bowhay) was the first carrier in East Prawle with a horse and van.)

Many people knew Nurse Rundle, the District Nurse, who later also became the midwife. She lived at No 2 Lower New Houses (South Allington) before she married Albert Rundle when they lived at Fairfield, Knowle Corner. She is listed in the 1939 Kelly's Directory as Rundle A. (Mrs.), nurse, Fairfield, East Prawle, Chivelstone 214.

Vicky told the story of Roger's mother having a baby. It was a Sunday and Nurse Rundle said: 'Unless it is Mrs Tucker, tell them I am out. If it is Mrs Tucker, say I'll be right there.' When the telephone went, her husband said she was out. Nurse Rundle came rushing in and asked who was on the telephone. Her husband replied: 'Mrs Tucker. I said you were out.' With that, she galloped in the road to Roger's mother at Lower House Farm. The arrival of Roger.

Doreen Shepherd in her book on *South Pool Portrait of a South Devon Village in the mid-twentieth century* wrote: 'Babies were born at home usually attended by Nurse Rundle from Prawle. Grandmothers and neighbours also assisted by boiling large amounts of water and helped to look after other children in the family.'

Stephen Taylor, who now lives at Fairfield, told me that Nurse Rundle built the chalet at the back of Fairfield, for RAF wives to stay if their husbands were here for any length of time.

However, during and after the Second World War, several of the *Prawle* children were born at Flete House, near Modbury. Plymouth was badly bombed during the war and the maternity ward at the City Hospital (Freedom Fields) was destroyed. Flete House, therefore, became a maternity hospital. Winnie's children, Derek's son, Gregory and Pat Farleigh's son David were all born at Flete.

The first baby to be born at Flete arrived on Monday 14 July 1941, and by the end of 1941 there had been a further 124 births. The hospital closed on 8 May 1958, less than a month after the last baby was born there.

Natural Remedies

Savoy Cabbage

For mothers suffering from mastitis, a leaf of Savoy cabbage is recommended. Put in the fridge or a cool place and, once cold, it is very soothing to press a leaf against the sore part. I can say that I have actually had experience of this, albeit for a slightly different reason.

Savoy Cabbage Leaf

Elder

Winnie said: 'Mother used to make Elder ointment. They picked the green elder leaves and I can see them drying outside …. Wire netting outside up home, and I don't know how she did it but she used to make elder ointment. For sores or anything.'

Elder tree: Legend says elders are in fact witches turned into trees by the saints but still able to cast a curse if you upset them. From early times the flowers, fruits, leaves, bark and roots have been used in herbal medicine. Elder leaf ointment is good for chilblains; elderflower and peppermint teas promote perspiration, reduces temperature and is also a mild stimulant. For those who considered alcohol unladylike, elderflower cordial was acceptable. Always say please and thank you to an elder tree and, if no-one is looking, curtsy.

Garlic

Garlic is very effective for relieving earaches. Garlic oil (which is simply garlic infused into olive oil) can be warmed and used as ear drops. Garlic contains powerful aromatic compounds

that have an antiseptic and anti-inflammatory action. It is often thought that garlic is quicker and more powerful at fighting ear infections than pharmaceutical antibiotics.

Another way to use garlic is to take a fresh clove and cut a piece to the size that will fit comfortably in the outer ear. **Do not put the garlic clove into the ear canal;** you only want to rest it on the outer ear like an old-fashioned hearing aid.

Onions

Onions have been used medicinally for thousands of years by ancient societies throughout the known world. They are another way of relieving earache pain quickly. Steam or bake an onion with the skin on until it is soft, (keeping the skin on helps to hold the onion juices inside). Place some of the warm juice in the ear. Usually, this relieves the pain in minutes.

Phyllis Hutchings talking to Stephen Pedrick:

Mum used to put an onion in the fire 'til the juice was coming out – you'd let it cool off a bit to put in your ear for earache. Then she used to make this ointment ... we used to go and pick penny-pancakes and primroses ... lots of things... done with 'sweet oil'. Houseleek ... and ground ivy, to make Mummy's ointment, boil it and strain it.

In *Sisters from the Sea*: 'an onion was boiled and placed on the ear for earache, and also eaten boiled and piping hot with a lump of butter for colds.'

A most popular remedy for chilblains was to rub them with a cut edge of an onion. Winnie remembered her mother doing this for her.

Bread Poultice

Bread poultice makes a great remedy for boils and eczema. It can also be used for treating bruises, wounds and cuts, inflammation, arthritis, sprains and removing splinters. Pour milk or water on a slice of bread and lay it on the affected part.

Goose Fat

When they killed a goose they'd save the fat as it was the ointment for all ills. During the 1930s and 1940s goose fat was highly prized and saved for medicinal purposes. To remedy 'colds on the chest' goose fat was smeared onto brown paper and applied to the chest or back as a poultice. Sore throats could also be cured with a spoonful of 'goose grease'.

Michael Partridge told the story of when he was a small boy going with Uncle Billy up to the field of bullocks where the RAF camp was based later on. He fell into a bed of stinging nettles, and hollered all the way home. His mother put goose fat all over the stings to soothe.

Michael remembered that goose fat was used for all ointments, as Vaseline is today.

In the Kitchen

Cooking

Prehistoric man cooked with sticks and an open flame. From *The National Trust Book of Forgotten Household Crafts*:

In an Anglo-Saxon farmhouse, a wood or peat fire was built in the middle of the floor. Sometimes a small hole was cut in the thatch to allow the smoke out, but more usually the smoke had to find its own way out.

The widespread introduction of the chimney in the fourteenth century made cooking a much more pleasurable business, for it was then possible to keep an eye on the cooking without being choked by the smoke. The hearth was gradually moved from the centre of the room to the side, where the fire was built on the ground or on a stone slab.

When the wood fire was in the centre, any baking was done under a pot (or outside the house). When the fire was moved to the side wall the 'oven' became built in.

From Winnie Easterbrook:

Years ago, they used to cook in the chimney corner. They didn't have stoves. They'd bring in a great faggot of wood and cook from the heat of the wood. All the fire places had an open chimney corner, and you'd light the fire right on the floor.

Manor Farm kitchen – cooking on an open fire (permission from Edward Baker)

The kitchen was the most important room in the house, where everyone would sit for their meals. The farmer's wife, the housewife, or in Winnie's case the 'missus at home' – the wife was expected to run the house, feed everyone including large numbers at harvest dinners, all from the earnings from vegetables, milk, butter, cream, eggs etc. Winnie never had wages, but it was never a problem. That's simply the way it was. She never lacked for anything.

Running the household was hard work for women and much planning was needed to prepare for a day of cooking. The cook had to rise early to light the fire.

Large pots or cauldrons stood in the fire or were suspended over it first by means of a wooden stick or rope, or later by an iron chain or rod fixed to a wooden or iron crossbar.

Wilf Login told Stephen Pedrick how in 1939:

Mrs Elliott who lived down at Walland (in the valley from West Prawle) had a fireplace eight foot – ten foot wide, and two could sit in it, one chair on each side. There was a big hook coming down the middle of the chimney with notches on and you could put your cooking pots on whichever height you wanted. She had a big oval iron pot, I reckon he'd hold about three gallon of soup... she'd sit there and if she wanted some soup she'd just scoop it out with a gert big iron ladle... and there'd be plenty of meat in there, rabbits... and potatoes, vegetables... keep putting it in, so it became full of flavour.

In the eighteenth and nineteenth century kitchen ranges came about as a result of the coal and iron age, with coal being cheap and plentiful and gradually taking over from wood.

The Lidstone Kitchen Range

In *Lidstone of the South Hams of Devon* by Hugh R G Lidstone, a note about John Lidstone:

Who founded the Kingsbridge blacksmith's business, died in 1803 and his only son took control and expanded it, particularly in the manufacture of edged tools and the famous Lidstone kitchen ranges, which were installed in very many farmhouses, inns and cottages throughout the South Hams for over a century. In these days of electricity and gas stoves, the Lidstone range has become obsolete but is sought after eagerly by antique collectors.

In *Sisters against the Sea* by Ruth and Frank Milton, the cast-iron range in the kitchen was central to people's lives.

It had a small oven at the side and an open grate with an iron bar across the top, from which the big black kettle would hang and permanently steam away. ...Often there was a saucepan bubbling away for supper containing a boiled suet apple dumpling, wrapped in a pudding cloth, knitted at the top.

A Lidstone stove (from Ann Lidstone). The Lidstone factory was near the former Post Office in Duke Street. The foundry was taken over by the Admiralty in 1939 and destroyed by German bombs in 1942.

Winnie's family had a Lidstone stove.

That was the rage, the cooker that everybody had. They didn't have electricity. You had to light it with wood and coal every day – if kept in it would burn too much wood. You had to black lead it. Lovely little things.

Roger Tucker's mother, Molly, saved up enough money from her laying hens to buy her four oven Aga and Agamatic boiler which was fuelled by furnacite (black eggs) and kept going 24 hours a day. Roger described it as heaven!

A Triplex drawn by Jane Shadbolt and Alice Stone

Alice Stone remembered when her father bought Hanley Cottage, in East Prawle, it had a Lidstone, but they took it out and her mother cooked with a Valor Perfection and paraffin oil. In the 1930s they had a Triplex with two little doors on the top, a fireplace, open grate and an oven by the side, and it was tiled. On the left is a drawing by Jane Shadbolt helped by Alice's memory.

Food

Food was available only in season – everything was local as far as basic food was concerned: local butter, milk and eggs, local vegetables, local meat: beef, pork, chickens and rabbits. There were regular deliveries to the village.

Rabbits

Until 1953 when myxamatosis arrived, rabbits were in abundance and an enormous source of protein, as well as a profitable business, particularly during the winter months. (See Rabbit Trapping on page 122.)

Winnie remembered roast rabbit, rabbit pie, rabbit stew, every sort of rabbit. Harold Widger talking to Stephen Pedrick '...harvest time we used to catch the rabbits, and Mother would do us a rabbit each, roast rabbit, or in a pie, it was beautiful!'

A paragraph on meals from *Sisters Against the Sea:* 'The most frequent meal at Eliza Anne's table was rabbit, either as a stew made with potatoes, turnip, onions and "dough boys" (suet dumplings), or served in a pie with a crusted top. '

Dorothy Hartley has many recipes for rabbits, but I like the Elderly Rabbit (in pie) best:

An elderly rabbit is best in a pie. Joint it, putting head and ribs to boil down for gravy. Rub the meat joints with lard, then pepper and dust with fine oatmeal. Put a slice of bacon over a bay leaf at the bottom of a deep pie-dish; lightly fry the joints and pack down onto it, scattering chopped parsley and onion on top, small chopped carrots, parsnip thinnings, mushrooms if you have any, and some elderly peas – a few capers are good; lacking mushrooms, a spot of mushroom ketchup will not come amiss, or if you can, pack the old rabbit with a little finely chopped ham or bacon, a blade of mace, nipped up fine. A spoonful of cider, or a chopped apple, should be added, and season well, making it good and spicy. Whatever the filling, let the top layer be thickly sliced potato, capped with chopped parsley and butter.

Other Meals

Most houses kept a pig. At the time of killing the pig, there was plenty of pork, although much would be salted for preserving (see food preserving on page 47 and pig rearing on page 121).

There was always some sort of stew on the go. It would be left simmering away. The Sunday joint was a treat and anything left over would be added to a stew. Fish, of course, was also part of the staple diet. A whole chapter is devoted to local fishing from page 140.

Richard remembered fisherman would bring around mackerel, which they ate frequently and spider crabs, as there was no commercial sale for them. They also ate dried fish, which needed to be soaked overnight to remove the salt. They got winkles from the rocks, mostly at Shallowpool. All the villagers had a vegetable plot with plenty of vegetables. They also ate rabbits, chickens and ducks. Mostly they had roast beef on Sunday, cold beef on Monday, which was washing day, then cottage pie on Tuesdays, if there was any meat left. Rice pudding, Bird's Nest Pudding, which was made with apple and sago, or Nelson's squares were often eaten for desserts - very filling.

From Wilf Login, born at 'New Houses' East Prawle:

I used to go bird-baiting because there was a Depression on, and there was no work: we couldn't catch any fish because nobody had any money to buy anything. It started, I think, in 1929/30 and it went on for six years. We never got no meat, the butcher didn't come round because nobody had money to buy meat. I used to catch starlings..... I'd pick 'em and clean 'em for me mother, and then she'd make a pie out of them, it was nice.

From Robin Stanes:

West Country folk also ate seabirds and their eggs in some quantities. Young herring gulls, black headed gulls and kittiwakes were eaten, and some were caught alive and fattened on liver or corn. Puffins were thought to be too rank, 'fit only for servants', but the young of the cormorant were used to take the place of pigeons in squab pie.

Milk

Milk for many centuries has played an important part of man's diet. It has been used by mammals to feed their young forever.

In the early 1900s, there were several farms in East Prawle and there were around 6-10 cows at each farm for milking, to provide milk for the family and then the village. This only changed when transport became readily available for the collection of milk churns. Most of the farms produced butter, cream and clotted cream. Cream and butter making were at the heart of the Devon farm. The cows at Town Farm where Winnie lived were South Devons.

Winnie's memories:

When they brought the milk over, they would put so many pints in big enamel pans for people to come and buy straight from the cow, the rest they'd put in the separator. … We'd keep the milk in the dairy, where it was cool, and people would bring their jugs and cans. We'd dole it out either a pint or a quart. And we always made sure we saved enough before we put it in the separator to supply the village, in case they wanted some more.

The cows were kept over Torrings Farm and the milkman would milk the cows and walk the milk, carrying it in buckets from Torrings over home to separate. Coming Around Castle with two buckets of milk, he had quite a way to bring the milk every time.

Derek Wotton was married in 1951 when he worked for Jack Partridge at Locks Farm, and also Coolings. A few years later Derek recalled: 'I knew everybody because I did the milk round. We used to sell all our milk going round the village, going round with a churn, a ten gallon churn, and we'd have a pint measure.'

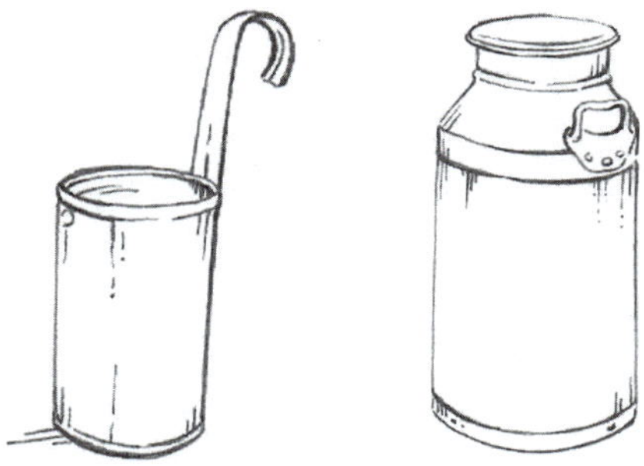

Clotted Cream

I had many conversations with both Winnie and Derek about the joys of dealing with milk and cream. I understood they used to have two types of cream: clotted and separated (the separated cream was thickened).

Clotted cream was made from fresh cow's milk. You'd leave it to cool in a pan in a cold dairy and the next day you would scald it by putting the milk pan in a second pan with hot water, bring it almost to the boil – but making sure it doesn't boil – then let it stand again. Slowly the cream would rise to the top of the inner pan for you to scoop it off. It would form a lovely yellow crust on the top and become clotted cream.

As a child, I wasn't allowed to have full fat milk and so the milk was left in a white enamel basin and when the cream had risen we would skim it off. This was thin cream, but delicious. I understand the separated cream Winnie made is more like double cream, as we know it today.

Antique cream skimmer

Again from Winnie:

We had a separator that separated the milk from the cream. It had two spouts: milk came out of one and cream out of the other. We gave the milk to the cattle or to the pigs, and the cream we would scald, in the same way as clotted cream.

When it spins, the milk, which is heaviest, is pulled outward against the walls and the cream, which is lighter, is collected in the middle. The cream and milk then flow out of separate spouts.

Derek remembered there were 25 to 30 cups [bowls] – stainless steel cups which the milk had to drain through to separate the cream from the milk. Very fiddly to wash every time.

Thunder and Lightning from Roger: if Mother had not sold the clotted cream, she made thunder and lightning, which is bread, clotted cream and treacle drizzled over the top. At one of Roger's talks his brother John brought some bread, clotted cream and treacle – we all tried it – Roger is right, absolutely wonderful!

Cream Separator Advert from 'The Lister Standard' (June 1929)

Butter

In most English counties butter was made in a butter churn, but in Devon the tradition was an open wooden tub, turning the butter by hand.

When making butter they would also separate the cream from the milk, but they wouldn't scald it. Winnie would make butter most days, particularly in the summer, unless the weather was cool enough for the milk to be saved. Sometimes there was only a little cream to turn into butter.

Both Winnie and Derek remember the sheer enjoyment of making butter.

Again from Winnie:

I used to love making butter. You had a wooden butter bucket. In the winter when it was cold, it would take no time at all to turn, but in the summer when the cream was soft, it took longer .... You can hear it gradually, not slushing, but gradually getting the milk out of it. The butter milk. Then you'd weigh it – ½ lb or a pound and finish it by shaping it with butter hands or pats.

The wooden tub had to be kept scrupulously clean and was washed first with boiling water and then very cold water.

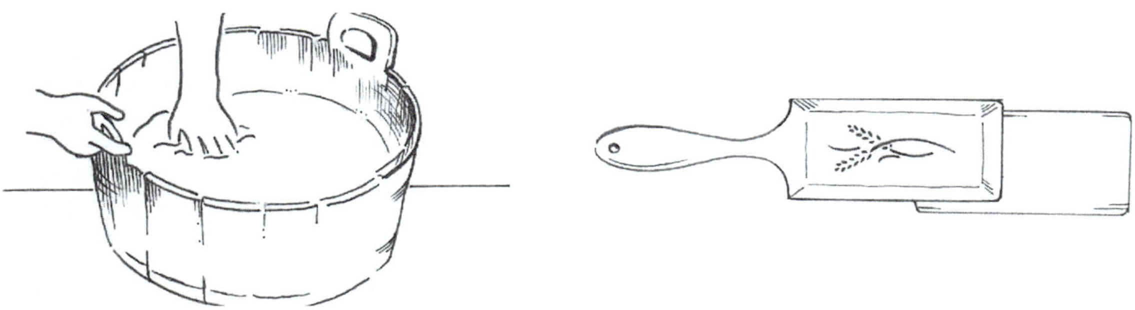
The wooden butter bowl and butter pats

Bread

Bread has been one of the principal forms of food for man from earliest times. Although many homes made their own bread, Winnie's family didn't. Winnie only recalled deliveries from Thorntons at East Portlemouth and Lapthorns of Frogmore.

Roger remembered their bread was made and delivered by Allan and Florrie Thornton from East Portlemouth. They usually arrived between 6 and 9 pm in the evening and always had plenty to talk about. Later the bread came from Frogmore Bakery, delivered by Ned Arundel. When Frogmore Bakery stopped delivering, Eddie Bowles started delivering for Mother's Pride Bakery. Roger always said Eddie could sell sand to the Arabs.

Food Preserving

Pickling, potting and drying food goes back way before the Middle Ages. All kinds of preserves were made: jams, chutneys and pickles.

Salting is the preservation of food with dry edible salt. It is related to pickling (preparing food with brine, ie salty water). It is one of the oldest methods of preserving food, and two historically significant salt-cured foods are dried and salted cod (usually referred to as salt fish) and salt-cured meat.

From Robin Stanes in *A History of Devon*:

From the late 16th century for at least three centuries the Grand Banks and the Newfoundland fisheries must have been familiar territory to Devonshire fishermen. Every year from the 1570s up to the end of the 19th century, the cod fishermen set out for the North American coast to fish for and salt the abundant shoals that formed part of the diet for the poor in Devon and the Mediterranean lands. Dried salt cod, crudely known as 'Toerag', was cheap and nutritious. The parson of Newton Ferrers described the diet of his parishioners in the mid-18th century as consisting of 'mutton, beans and Newfoundland cod'. Every sizeable fishing village and town sent ships and men to the Banks and some ships, having loaded salt, cordage and provisions for the Atlantic crossing, then took salt fish to Catholic Spain and Portugal, and returned with fruit, salt and port wine.' This was a famous triangular trade.

By Elizabethan times there was emphasis on pilchards, herrings and sardines which were preserved and packed into hogsheads. Oil pressed from these fish was used in dressing leather and earlier had been used as a soap base.

Brenda recalled that Lapthorns also sold salt fish. 'It would keep for months once salted. It used to be very dry and Mum used to soak it and then fry it, or steam it, or make a batter and fry it.' Richard also remembered 'Father used to have fish as well, buying it in Dartmouth years ago. Dried fish, soaked overnight and cooked the next day.' Derek remembered the salted meat at High House Farm hanging from hooks.

To preserve pork, Winnie said the pig would be hung up in the chimney corner to make a lovely ham – smoked ham: 'Mother would also cut it up and keep it in standards – big earthenware jars which were kept in the dairy. The meat was soaked in salt brine and those hams would stay in there until the liquid had sunk right through.'

Robin Stanes in *Old Farming Days* described the salting of pigs:

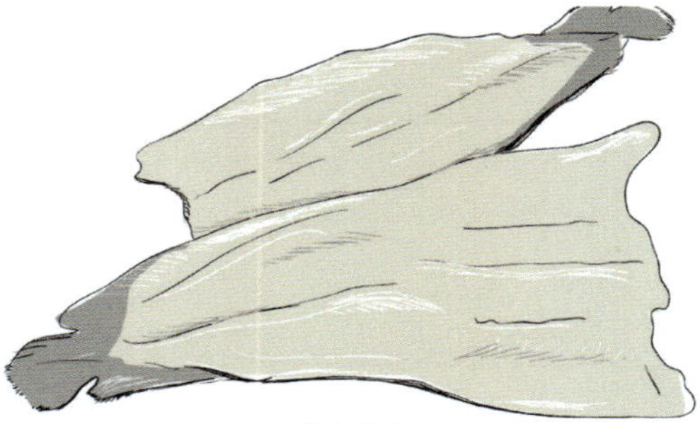

Salt fish

The gammons and hams were then salted in salting 'tryes' or 'keeves', great earthenware troughs, glazed inside. There were many recipes for salting; some used bay salt (from the Biscay coast) or 'salt prunella' or just coarse salt to which saltpetre was almost invariably added. Sometimes beer, treacle, brown sugar or juniper berries were added to the cure. The meat lay in salt for three or four weeks, turned every day in the cure, and the nooks and crannies of the meat rubbed hard with salt. Once cured it was often hung up the open chimney to smoke. This would preserve it better and give it a distinct flavour.... The joints were then wrapped in cloth and hung from the roof where they would keep for a year or more if properly cured.

He went on to write 'the pig's insides also provided some delicacies'. For more read his book!

Drink

Water was not the most popular form of drink. Apart from water, the choice was cider or beer. Not much is known about the types of beer which were brewed but there was one famous Devonshire beer, 'white ale', made at Kingsbridge, Slapton and elsewhere in the South Hams. This was still being drunk there in 1864.

W A Roberts stated in the *Elizabethan Court Rolls of Stokenham Manor 1560-1602*:

Brewing – Ale was the only beverage available to most households for all the meals and purposes of the day, as well as for social occasions. The variable water supply was certainly not a competitor, as the many court accounts of its pollution or diversion will indicate.

Cider was certainly made in Devon by the thirteenth century. Most farms had an orchard and every cottage had some apple trees.

Jim Hananford with his cider cask (Richard Partridge)

In 1878 Philip Putt's first job at Lower House Farm was leading the donkey to and fro to the cellars where their rough brew cider was stored. All the men had kegs (small barrels) and he kept them supplied from the donkey all day long.

Bill Blank told Richard that as a boy when they were harvesting out Prawle Point way, he'd be all day carrying cider out for the men. He'd carry it in a little cask – and all day long Bill would go back and forth carrying the cider.

The photograph on the previous page is of Jim Hannaford, the pig killer, with a cask of Lower House Farm cider under his arm. Both his father and grandfather worked there almost all their lives. There was an orchard below the house but they removed the trees for Mollie Tucker to be able to see the sea.

The Cider House to Lower House Farm (now modernised) had the cider press because it was a cool building. The top part of the building was the granary where they used to keep the corn.

However, nowadays in Prawle, orchards have largely disappeared. Although Winnie's family did not make cider, she remembered a barrel was always stored in the Town Farm Cider House down towards Around Castle where the men were allowed to fill their kegs when working.

Tea, that most quintessential of English drinks, is a relative latecomer to British shores. Although the custom of drinking tea dates back to the third millennium BC in China, it was not until the mid 17th century that it first appeared in England. It was too expensive for ordinary people until the late eighteenth century. When King Charles II married the Portuguese princess, Catherine of Braganza, she brought tea chests to England as part of her wedding dowry and soon popularised the custom of taking tea at court. 50 years later tea became still more popular when Queen Anne started drinking tea with her breakfast rather than the customary beer.

Sloes: Another story from Richard:

Bob and his mates, when they were 12 and 14 years old, used to go down Horsley way to pick sloe berries, and Granny Tucker would take them into Dartmouth to sell. They would be down picking sloe berries as quick as they could. Anyway … must have been harvest time and they had bought some cigarettes.

They went down and picked these sloe berries and they smoked their cigarettes and then they accidentally, or on purpose, set fire to the brake down there, and smoke was flying. When they come home Bob, partly because he was smoking, went early to bed. A week or ten days afterwards Uncle Billie had a rabbit that was all scorched. His fur had been burnt and Uncle Billy held this rabbit up and said to Bobbie 'I think you might know something about this rabbit.'

Sloe Gin

From Dorothy Hartley: 'Sloes are best preserved in gin ... Sloe gin is a recent adoption into modern cocktails. Previously blended with penny royal and valerian, it had long been used by old-fashioned country wives in connubial emergencies – hence the nickname "Mother's Ruin".'

My Mother's Constance Spry Recipe:

1 ½ pints sloes	a few bitter almonds pounded, or a few drops of almond essence
¾ lb sugar-candy or loaf sugar	1 quart gin

Prick the sloes and put into jars. Add other ingredients. Cover tightly. Shake from time to time and after 3 or 4 months strain, bottle and keep. It improves with keeping.

'Many sloes – many cold toes.' Sloes are best preserved in gin. **After the first frost** gather the sloes direct into the sloe-jar, and fill the interstices with gin. Cork securely, and set away in a warm, dark cupboard. By Christmas-time it may be poured off and used, but may stand longer with advantage.

Water

Water and Wells

I have only once experienced a total shortage of water in East Prawle, as described by Richard Partridge on page 59.

Water is an essential part of our lives. Farmhouses were usually built near a spring, a stream or a well. In East Prawle the water came from the many springs and wells; latterly most of the wells had pumps.

Before mains water came to the village, one of the main sources of water was the well at Around Castle (going towards Town Hill). Nobody knows why it is called that, but that is how it's known. The water was carried back to the houses in buckets – see the map of the wells in the village on the next page. If the village became short of water in the wells and pumps, they would have to fetch water from the well at the back of Moorwell Pond.

Winnie Easterbrook told me that when she came to live at Sea View in 1946, they had no electricity and no mains water. Water was from the well. There was a tap to the well by the letter box down at New Houses.

Marilyn Rose, Vera Hannaford's daughter, who lived at Channel View (now known as Crab Cottages), said they also had to walk right to the end of the path to the tap by the post box.

Sadly in 2013 this post box was removed. Instead there is a sign indicating the public footpath.

As Winnie said:

There have always been wells – that was the only source of water. …. And they said when they brought the mains that the well water wasn't worth drinking, course they're bound to say that but it didn't kill people.

Warwick Harwood remembered that the man who came into the house to tell him the mains water was now installed, commented that it should be OK even though there was a drought at the time. Warwick replied he could always use the water from the well to which the man replied 'but it hasn't been tested.' Warwick's response was 'well it was OK yesterday!'

Diana Shelvoke remembered, when they lived at Ash Park, they obtained their water from a large well, about 150 yards away, in the field above belonging to Higher Farm. They paid a shilling a year for the use, until they bought the rights to the well. Diana also remembered that George Rundle and Dick Putt expanded the well and at that time were paid four pence halfpenny an hour.

 = approximate position of each well

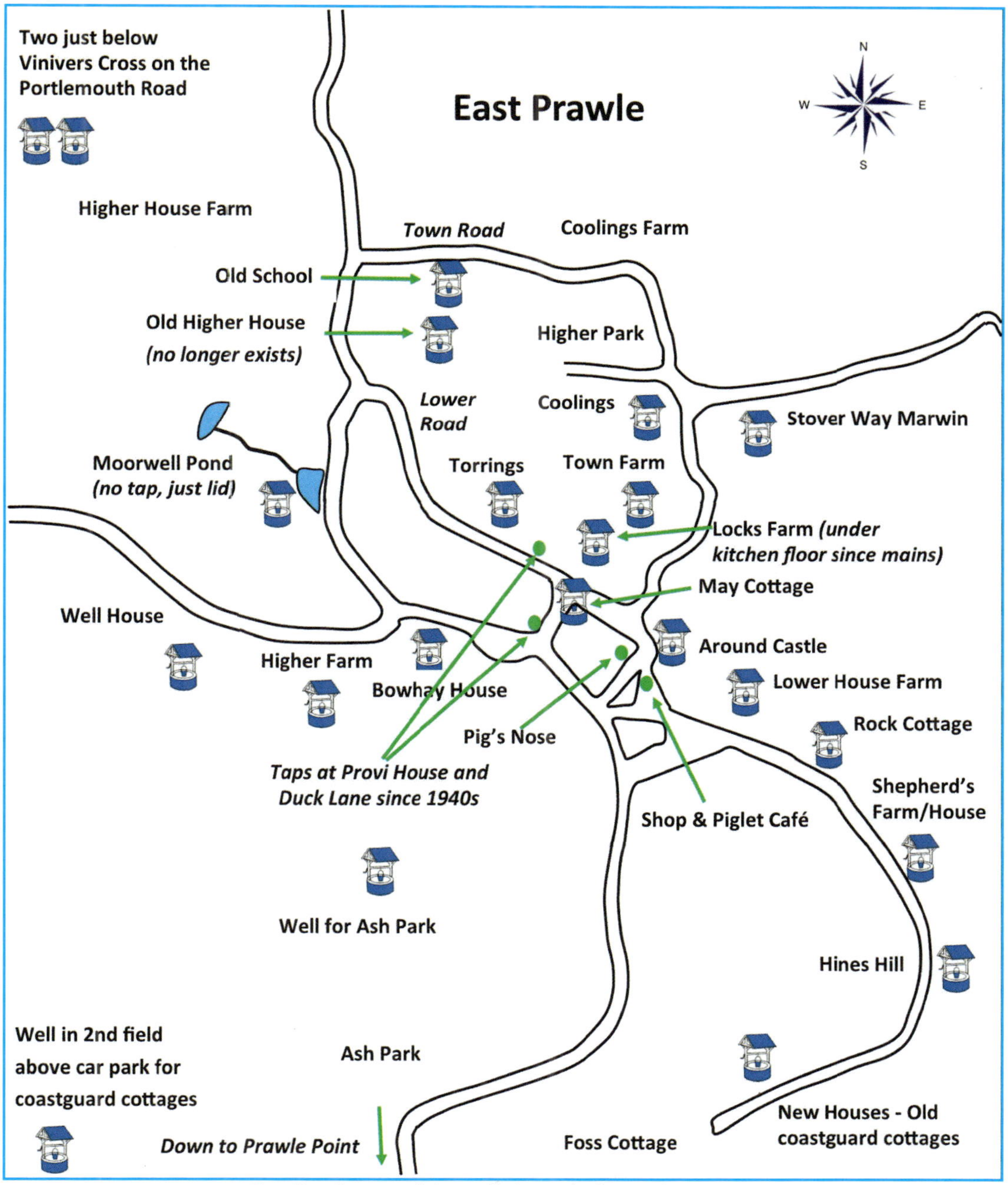

East Prawle map of the wells in use before mains water

The arrival of mains water was very popular.

Mains Water

It has been quite a challenge to find out exactly when and how mains water came to East Prawle. It is clear that there were two phases of mains pipe laying during the Second World War as a result of both the RAF at West Prawle and the RAF domestic site at East Prawle. These phases still did not cover the whole village: the third phase was in 1953.

I have been coming to East Prawle for over 40 years, but until I started researching this book I had never heard the RAF had been stationed here. Although there are still some RAF buildings at West Prawle, there is very little evidence of the domestic site here in East Prawle. (See more about the RAF on page 164.)

Derek said that, before mains water, the RAF brought their own lorries and collected water, for both East and West Prawle, in large tanks from various wells, but mainly from Vinivers. Before that: 'Well there weren't many tractors. Horses and carts, and anybody with a van used to do little trips. A 200 gallon tank, slide it in the back and take it over to West Prawle to the camps.'

Richard Partridge said the RAF paid £1 a week, for five to six weeks, to Thomas Henry Tucker, whose well was by Vinivers, to fill their water bowser for building the RAF camp.

I know from several people, including Derek and Richard, there was a water tower (which held 5000 gallons) near the RAF camp on the bend of the road almost opposite the new coastguard station on Town Road/School Lane. This was in case of fire. There was also a large pond nearby (like a swimming pool), providing plenty of water to put fires out if they were bombed.

Photograph of the Pigs Nose Inn with the RAF water tower in the background

In July 2010 I telephoned South West Water to ask the date when mains water was first brought to East Prawle. I was told they were first installed in January 1953 and relined on 1 June 1992.

Somewhat puzzled, in September 2010 I contacted Chris Martin, the Librarian at South West Water who was extremely helpful, and after much searching around the Devon Record Office, found the East Prawle water and sewerage plan. This contained the layout of roads and buildings, eg Higher and Lower House Farm, the layout of water and sewerage infrastructure: unfortunately this plan is undated (see the map on the next page).

However, almost 18 months later in April 2012, Chris Martin told me that one of the works managers had alerted her to some old documents and amongst them was a bundle of correspondence on the East Prawle water supply, the RAF and the water tower.

Part of East Prawle Water and Sewage map (undated)

I spent a couple of days in Exeter at South West Water with Chris going through fascinating documents. The water supply of East Prawle had been the subject of investigation for many years by the Council. There was talk about supplying water to the south eastern parishes of Kingsbridge Rural District Council and also the AMES (Air Ministry Experimental Station) at West Prawle as far back as March 1939.

Below are extracts from some of the documents (with permission from South West Water). On 25 July 1940 the civil engineering contractors wrote to the Air Ministry Directorate: (Figure 1 on the next page):

On Monday last, the 22nd instant, we were informed by your Clerk of Works and by the Contractors, ... that instructions had been received to proceed with the construction of a 3" main from the reservoir at Sherford Cross, the property of the Kingsbridge & Salcombe Water Board, to the A.M.E.S at West Prawle and the living quarters at East Prawle, a total length of about 9.500 yds. and including the necessary booster.

And later in the same letter (Figure 2 on the next page):

When we originally estimated £5,000 as the approximate cost of the 3" supply main to West Prawle we had no knowledge of the extension to the living quarters for W.A.A.F. and R.A.F. personnel at East Prawle, involving an additional 1,500 yds. of 3" pipe line at an extra cost of approximately £1000: the total cost of the works for a supply for the Air Ministry only would be therefore about £6000.

There were many delays along the way and in March 1941 it was agreed there should be an electrical booster water pumping station at Cousins Cross and finally, a letter from the contractors on 29 November 1941 confirmed the water supply was first made available to the RAF at East and West Prawle on 1 June 1941 (Figure 3 on the next page):

Dear Sir, We confirm our telephone message of this morning that the water supply was first made available to the R.A.F. at East and West Prawle on 1st June 1941.

After the mains water came to the RAF camp, two standpipes were erected, one at Ducks Lane (beside Locks Farm) and the other at the top of Provi Hill. This made carrying water buckets much easier. Derek helped Betty Partridge with her water – he used to carry buckets from Ducks Lane when she lived near Locks Farm and, when she moved above Provi Hill, he carried buckets from the standpipe there. She certainly had no mains water. Although mains water came for the RAF with two standpipes, the rest of the village still used the wells.

> On Monday last, the 22nd instant, we were informed by your Clerk of Works and by the Contractors, that instructions had been received to proceed with the construction of a 3" main from the reservoir at Sherford Cross, the property of the Kingsbridge & Salcombe Water Board, to the A.M.E.S. at West Prawle and the living quarters at East Prawle, a total length of about 9,500 yds. and including the necessary booster. We were favoured

Figure 1

> When we originally estimated £5,000 as the approximate cost of the 3" supply main to West Prawle we had no knowledge of the extension to the living quarters for W.A.A.F. and R.A.F. personnel at East Prawle, involving an additional 1,500 yds. of 3" pipe line at an extra cost of approximately £1000; the total cost of the works for a supply for the Air Ministry only would be therefore about £6000. If the sizes of the mains are

Figure 2

> Dear Sir,
>
> We confirm our telephone message of this morning that the water supply was first made available to the R.A.F. at East and West Prawle on 1st June 1941.
>
> Yours faithfully,

Figure 3

Copies of the original letters regarding the mains water supply in the 1940s

The water was to be piped from Sherford, down through to Frogmore, Kernborough, up to Cousins Cross, down to Pucka Pitts and onwards to West Prawle, with additional piping to East Prawle. Derek recalled there were workmen from Loddiswell and also the prisoners of war at Pucka Pitts were put to work. (See more on Pucka Pitts on page 173.)

When talking to Margaret Mitchelmore in early 2012, I was much puzzled because Margaret was clear there was running water when she got married in 1949 and moved to Sunnyside on the green. Although she had to heat the water to take it upstairs for the children's baths, she definitely did not have to fill buckets (Richard, her son, was born in 1952).

However, a decision to extend the water mains to the village is first found in a letter of 19 March 1942 asking when the work will commence (Figure 4 on the next page):

East Prawle Water Supply. I have been directed to inquire when it is expected that the work of extending the water main to the village of East Prawle will commence.

Also, a further memo from the Public Health Committee dated 7 July 1942 (Figure 5 on the next page):

East Prawle Water Supply: Public Health Committee: 7/7/42 (Minute No. 369(a)(i). Recommend Council to authorise carrying out of extension of main to The Green, East Prawle, as suggested by the Sanitary Surveyor...

East Prawle Water Supply.

I have been directed to inquire when it is expected that the work of extending the water main to the village of East Prawle will commence.

Yours faithfully,

Figure 4

EAST PRAWLE WATER SUPPLY.

Public Health Committee: 7/7/42 (Minute No.369(a)(i)).

Recommend Council to authorise carrying out of extension of main to The Green, East Prawle, as suggested by the Sanitary Surveyor, and to suspend Standing Orders relating to Contract for the purpose.

Figure 5

(1)..The work to be carried out consists of connecting up 3" Cast Iron Pipes to the existing 4" main at the top of Ducks Lane, and carrying the pipe line to The Green. at East Prawle, via Providence Inn, thence turning left past the Post Office, and thence left again on to The Green, terminating outside the Union Inn Garage.

Figure 6

Further letters regarding the water supply to East Prawle

In July 1942 (Figure 6):

(1)..The work to be carried out consists of connecting up 3" Cast Iron Pipes to the existing 4" main at the top of Ducks Lane, and carrying the pipe line to The Green, at East Prawle, via Providence Inn, thence turning left past the Post Office, and thence left again on to The Green, terminating outside the Union Inn Garage.

At this stage I must point out that Sunnyside, where Margaret Mitchelmore lived, is the cottage on the green just before the Union Inn – now the Pigs Nose – a mystery solved.

A further note is that Bill Elliott, in Stephen Pedrick's *A Century of Memories*, was born in 1911. From the age of 13 he worked on a farm for 27 years. There followed a job building the sea wall at Torcross and a bit later, some rabbit trapping and gardening. Bill then joined the gang laying the water mains. This, therefore, must have been around 1952-53, which fits in with what South West Water told me in 2010, that the final mains were installed in January 1953 and relined from 1 June 1992. So from 1953 the entire village was on mains water.

Copies of the maps planning the construction from Sherford are in Appendix IV.

The Water Tower at Vinivers

There was concern that the original water mains were not sufficient, particularly if the booster at Cousins Cross failed. On 23 November 1945 a letter from the construction engineers (Figure 7 on the next page):

The laying of a 3" ring main far from completes the scheme required for this village (East Prawle). At the present time East Prawle relies on about three-quarters of a mile of 4" pipe for its 'reservoir', and should the booster fail at Cousins Cross within about two hours the village is without water.

In a letter of 11 December 1945 (Figure 8):

We note and agree with your Council's desire that a high level tank near the school should be eliminated, and we shall propose a reservoir on the high ground near Vinivers. The construction of this reservoir, however, is to some extent affected by the future occupation or otherwise of the R.A.F. site at East Prawle.

2015 the Water Tower (see Appendix IV for the map)

Although I don't have a precise date for the water tower being built, there is a letter accepting a tender for the construction of the water tower at East Prawle, dated 13 May 1961, and also a letter from the South Devon Water Board dated 30 January 1962 stating: 'I understand that the Water Tower being constructed ... is likely to be completed in four to six weeks.'

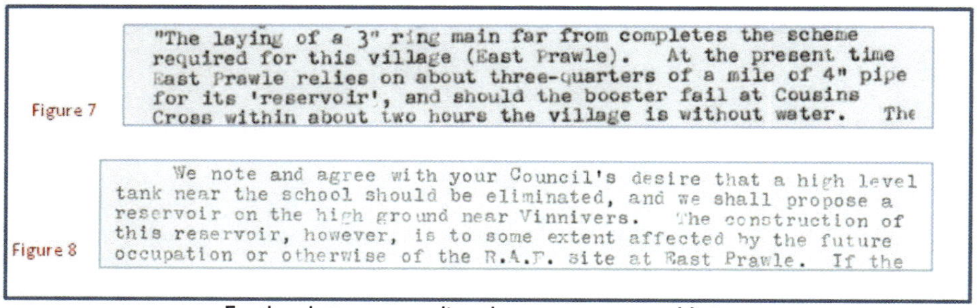

Figure 7

"The laying of a 3" ring main far from completes the scheme required for this village (East Prawle). At the present time East Prawle relies on about three-quarters of a mile of 4" pipe for its 'reservoir', and should the booster fail at Cousins Cross within about two hours the village is without water. The

Figure 8

We note and agree with your Council's desire that a high level tank near the school should be eliminated, and we shall propose a reservoir on the high ground near Vinnivers. The construction of this reservoir, however, is to some extent affected by the future occupation or otherwise of the R.A.F. site at East Prawle. If the

Further letters regarding the water tower at Vinivers

From Richard:

The tower came because there wasn't enough pressure to bring the water up here. They pump it from South Pool up into that tower and from there it goes to Portlemouth and East Prawle ... a couple of years ago we didn't have any water – the sensor out there had failed to come on and so the water drained off; there's also a sensor that switches on the pump at South Pool and it hadn't worked. So when it drained out, nobody had any water.

A Final Comment

There were a lot of papers I didn't particularly need for writing this book, but I felt it important someone from the village should be aware of their existence before they were sent to the Devon Records Office. So in March 2013 Roger Tucker and I went to Exeter one more time.

The night before, at 7 o'clock, Roger rang to say it was fine to go to Exeter but he had to take 35 of Richard's sheep to market and he would be on the green with them at a quarter to eight!

So that's what we did. We set out with a large trailer carrying the sheep and got to Exeter market at 9.30, which was great. Roger dealt with it – I just stood and watched. Afterwards we went to the farmers' café for an enormous breakfast and then on to South West Water to look at the documents. Parking proved interesting with a large 4x4 and trailer. We had to leave it outside the front entrance, which caused quite a stir.

Unfortunately, I didn't take a photograph of the truck and trailer on the day, but I did later, which you can see on the previous page.

Moorwell Pond

(undated) Moorwell Pond from Diana Shelvoke

2011 Moorwell Pond

Moorwell Pond – the duck pond on the way into East Prawle did not exist on the 1842-47 Tithe map of Chivelstone so its origin is uncertain, although there was a well at the back supplying much of the drinking water for the village. The pond is man-made with a limestone base.

From conversations with Derek and Richard, it is clear the pond was originally opened out for animals to drink and for traction engines to obtain water – Derek remembered frequently taking the horses and cattle to drink at the pond.

Richard explained:

I think they made the pond for the horses to drink but mainly to fill the water butt for the traction engines. The engine drove the mobile threshing machines so they could go out into the fields right beside the rick to do the threshing. That saved a lot of work.

A Square

The first time I heard of a 'square' was in the recollection by Ethel Ellis in Stephen Pedrick's *A Century of Memories*.

….We used to have to go down across two fields to fetch water for Mother's washing. We had two large buckets and we used a 'square', so you didn't feel the full weight of those buckets: it's easy as pat to pick up those two buckets using a 'square'.

I had no idea what a square was and had been unable to find anything about it on the internet. However, Winnie knew exactly what it was and said: 'A square is just a square of wood that you put on the two buckets ... to stop the water splashing against your legs.'

In another conversation with Winnie:

... Village people got their water from the well down Around Castle and in every village there's what you might call somebody a little bit – not stupid but not quite with it, and he used to fetch water for these people, using a square ... he would fetch the water with a bucket, carry it up to the top of the hill for people. I suppose they'd give him perhaps a penny.

circa 1925 Iris Brialey (née Hannaford) and her father with a square on the wall

The distance from the well at Around Castle to the top of Providence Hill is quite a distance when carrying buckets. Derek used the square to take buckets of water from that well up to his sister-in-law, Betty Partridge, at the top of Provi Hill.

I left the matter of the square there without totally understanding it. Several months later when looking at old photographs with Richard, including the one above, he asked me if I knew what the square wooden frame hanging on the outside wall of the cottage was – it was a 'square'! Richard's explanation answered all the queries so that I could understand it.

A few weeks later when I saw Winnie and her daughters Gill and Elaine, we experimented with a square and two buckets. You stand inside the square and hold it and the bucket handles together, making it impossible for the buckets to bang against your legs. Easier said than done. Richard very kindly made up a square and Jane, his wife, took a photograph of him.

Richard Partridge with his Square

Thought to be Sid Wood, described as Devonshire watercarrier (from Stephen Pedrick)

Schooling

Little education took place until the late 19th century. Illiteracy was common in those days. An X marked the signature for many baptism and marriage certificates.

Cora Mann said she had an old aunt born in 1864 and her grandfather was born the year before; neither of them could spell. Before the village school was built they used to have lessons in the Methodist Chapel for Sunday school and they were taught for a penny a week.

Ashley Ford told me about his grandfather, Philip Putt (born in 1869, in what is now known as Allington Cottage, down towards New Houses). He told Ashley he went to a 'Dame' school which cost 2p a week also in the Methodist Chapel. This was run by a distant cousin who was born with only one hand. Unfortunately, little more is known.

A **Dame school** was an early form of a private elementary school in English-speaking countries. They were usually taught by women and were often located in the home of the teacher.

The School at East Prawle

As a result of the Elementary Education Act of 1870, a School Board of five members was formed on October 30, 1874. In 1878/79 a mixed board school was set up in East Prawle, at a cost of £325, at the northwest edge of the village, catering for pupils of all ages. It was built for 100 children. The act extended the compulsory age of attendance at school until the age of ten. I understand the schools at East Portlemouth, South Pool and East Prawle were all built about the same time, which is likely, given the Elementary Education Act of 1870.

The school building in 2011

Through the East Prawle History Society I have received a document on the 'East Prawle Board School' compiled by David Welch. He was working at the Coombeshead School Resources Centre in the 1970s, based at the Field Study Centre – the old school building – in East Prawle. The document is based on the first Log Book from the school (sadly now missing). It has information about the quality of teaching, the attendances and the teachers.

The report from H M Inspector received in July 1879 was described as a 'hanging' report:

The general state of this school is very bad. The attainments throughout are discreditable, the style of instruction defective, and the discipline and tone perfectly unsatisfactory. There is no evidence of method or intelligence. The infants are neglected...the children are fully capable of profiting by instruction.

By 1882 the Report was highly commendatory: 'Tone, discipline and instruction excellent... results in this remote school are in all respects equal to those in the best town schools.'

For more details of David Welch's report on the schooling at East Prawle and for the description from the Millennium Book, please visit www.katejenningsprawle.co.uk.

There is differing information as to the attendants of the school: from Kelly's Directories the average attendance between 1888 and 1893 was 40; by 1902 attendance was 47, in 1906 it was 63 and in 1914 it was 72. Whereas David Welch's information from the original Log Book was as follows: 1883 above fifty and rising; as many as 82 were recorded in 1888; from 1896 to 1902 the average was around fifty and then a marked and rather surprising increase up to a maximum of seventy-five in 1908.

Under the Local Education Authority the East Prawle school became a Council School as a result of the 1902 Act. In 1947 the seniors were transferred to Kingsbridge, and the school closed in 1968 when the juniors were transferred to a new school at Stokenham.

Below is a list of head teachers from both Kelly's Directories and David Welch's list.

Date	Head
1877-1879	Frederick Ware
1879-1887	Miss Thomas
1887-1889	Ellen Hill
1890-1895	Emily Cawsey or Elizabeth Cawsey or Elizabeth Cawley
1895-1930	Caroline Eliza Langdon
1930-1932	Irene Isabella Crees
1932-1936	Mrs Gertrude Emily Lapthorn
1937-1938	Florence Elizabeth Legg
1938-1942	Miss A Wrigley
1942-1956	Miss N Basnett (Mrs Tabb)

Caroline Langdon was the head mistress for 35 years and taught in Winnie Easterbrook's time, also teaching Winnie to read music as well as play the piano. Miss Langdon lived in View Charmenté and rented from Ern Rendle. Miss Bessie Wotton and Mrs Ella Ford were helpers. At some point Margaret Sawtell helped teach (date unknown) and later Mrs Nellie Tabb, who continued teaching at the school until it closed in 1968.

Winnie Easterbrook's class at Prawle School in about 1920

Back row: Ivy Gordon, Evelyn Logan, Lily Cole, Dorothy Partridge (Tripp)*, Ethel Pepperell, Chrissie Putt, Amelia Arthurs, Betty Trout, Marjory Putt

Middle row: Mona Cudd, Helen Arthurs, Edith Trout (Logan), Gladys Putt (Logan), Felicia Putt (Logan), May Hannaford (Shepherd), Dorothy Putt, Doris Rogers

Front row: Florrie Tabb, Lilian Arthurs, Dulcie Weymouth, Phoebe Elliott, May Putt(Penwell), Gracie Thornton, Winnie Tucker (Easterbrook), Lucy Stone, Winnie Putt, Eliza Putt *Married names in brackets

In the Woodleigh Deanery Magazine of January 1901 the report on Miss Langdon:

On December 10th and 19th, Miss Langdon gave her annual school entertainment for the distribution of prizes for good attendance and progress. The greatest credit is due to the admirable way the children sang, acted and danced. The dresses were very pretty, the 'frog dance' by boys who looked as though they had just hopped from the marshes was exceedingly telling. Not less than twenty-one children received prizes for making every possible attendance throughout the year. We regret Miss Langdon was not favoured with better weather, and hope her friends will not allow her to suffer financially on that account.

There is a similar report in January 1902, ending with 'Miss Langdon is heartily congratulated on the very successful result of all the pains and time she has devoted to the welfare of Prawle school.' And in December 1902: ... 'School work in our remote villages requires and deserves encouragement and we hope all friends of Prawle school will do their best to make the prize giving entertainment as successful as usual.' These reports continued for many years.

One assistant's record of service outlasted even that of Miss Langdon. Bessie Wotton started in June 1907 and she was still teaching when the first Log-book ended nearly forty years later.

Memories from the students

Ashley Ford, born in 1929:

During my time there the head mistress was Miss Wrigley who I think was a North Country lass. The second mistress was Miss Wotton, always referred to by locals and pupils as 'Teacher Bessie'. She was Prawle born and bred and lived with her sister and a handicapped brother in the bottom cottage of the row opposite what used to be the Providence Inn. I doubt she was qualified in any modern sense but was a first class infants' teacher. There were just the two of them and they drilled us well in the three Rs: in my time four of us got scholarships to Kingsbridge Grammar School and another to the Royal Hospital School, Holbrook. They did a good job. 'Teacher Bessie' also ran the Church Sunday School which was held in the school building.

The toilet facilities were primitive well into the forties. Buckets were the order of the day; particularly vile in the summer's heat. Mains water and sewers arrived in the village with the RAF, I think in 1941, and it took several years to spread through the community as a whole. Mains electricity arrived 1951/2. As I recall the school provided no hand washing facilities of any sort, but I recognise now that we were all pretty grubby by today's standards. The great benefit for those of us who survived has been a robust immune system!

My mother attended the school which she left in 1915, aged fourteen. For many years she was the caretaker there and I spent many an evening giving her a hand cleaning the place. In winter the coke fired 'Tortoise' stoves had to be lit every morning in time to warm the building for the 9am start. There were two stoves, one in each class room, which she would prepare the night before and light next morning around 7 am. I can still see them glowing red in very cold weather. During my years there a school doctor examined us annually and needy children were given free milk to counter malnutrition. My brother and I never qualified, much to my mother's irritation. The school doctor did, however, find that I had flat feet and hammer toes and said 'he'll never get into the army with those feet' to which my mother replied that would be no bad thing (both my parents lost brothers in the First World War trenches). Whatever her reservations regarding the military she enforced a long exercise regime which in due course allowed me to pass A1 into the army, for which I was very grateful. There was also the school dentist who in the course of time pulled several of my milk teeth. There was little real poverty in the village but I do remember one boy coming to school in a pair of ladies high heel shoes miles too big for him. Even at that early age I felt his misery and shame.

There were no canteen facilities, most children went home for lunch, those who couldn't brought sandwiches, doorsteps with tomato, beetroot, onion, cucumber filling (only one item at a time), all basics from the garden and very occasionally a slice of cheese or corned beef. Mother, looking back a further twenty years, remembered children walking to school from Chivelstone and South Allington and outlying farms with nothing to eat at lunch time. They would often disappear and return with a turnip pulled from a nearby field. That was their lunch.

Alice Stone born in 1930:

Alice was in hospital between the age of two and three; from three to six she went to Treloar Hospital for Disabled Children in Hampshire and at eight went to East Prawle School for one year. Alice had to leave because war broke out, after which she had homework but never saw any teachers. When Alice was nearly thirteen she went to The Girls Heritage Craft School at Chailey Common in Sussex until aged sixteen.

Christopher Trinick born in 1934:

The girls and boys playgrounds are separate. There are outside toilets and also air raid shelters. There was a bell over the porch to tell the children when to come in. The walls are very thick and there are high ceilings and sills (to stop you from looking out). There were 'Tortoise' coke stoves with an oven above to heat pasties etc. that the children brought to school for their lunches in the days before school meals. (Meals were supplied from Kingsbridge from 1944 and cooked at Prawle School.)

Christopher also recalled Mrs Ford's father (Ashley Ford's grandfather, Philip Putt) remembered Prawle School being built.

Brenda Jeffery born in 1939:

I started Prawle school a couple of weeks before I was five and I stayed until I was 12. As my birthday was in September, I couldn't leave in the summer as the others did, but had to stay until Christmas.

Prawle school had two classrooms, one for the beginners taught by Miss Bessie Wotton and the older ones in the other classroom taught by Mrs Nellie Tabb. We had the usual lessons the same as today. Sometimes we would go out for a nature walk finding flowers etc and finding out the names. Miss Wotton would take us for PT and we would walk down to the Assembly Room next to the Providence Inn, where we would wear our shirts and black knickers. We had to take out our hankies, blow our nose and tuck the hanky up our knicker leg and we were not allowed to use them again until the lesson was over.

We had little bottles of milk each day, but there was a law you only had them up to a certain age. School dinners were brought out from Kingsbridge each day. Mrs Pat Farleigh, then known as Putt, came and served out the lunch; each Christmas she would give every child a present. I have still got mine, a blue hanky sachet. I will always treasure it, I only told Pat, a few weeks before she died, I still used it.

Richard Partridge born in 1941:

I started at Prawle School aged 4 ½. Mrs Nellie Tabb taught the older children and Miss Bessie Wotton taught the younger children. At about 11am, we were all given a small bottle of milk to drink. I went home for a mid-day meal. After I left, a kitchen was built on the side of the school, to enable meals to be cooked on the premises. Mrs Peggy Presley was in charge of the cooking.

A fire was lit in the middle of one of the rooms, with a chimney going up through the roof. The older boys would fetch coal from the shed and would stoke the fire to keep it going. I think Mrs Ella Ford would clean the school and light the fire before we went to school. The fire was a similar model to the ones used at the RAF Camp.

Elaine Trant born in 1950:

We had two class rooms, the Small room and the Big room, with two teachers, Miss Langridge (younger ones) and Mrs Tabb (older children) from 9am till 4pm. Meals were delivered from South Pool, until the kitchen was built, in about 1958. Occasionally, during the summer, if the weather was nice, we would have lessons outside in the playground. Once or twice we all walked down to Horsley for a swimming lesson.

Heating was a tall round iron stove, with metal railing guard. To start with boys and girls had separate play grounds, but while I was there the corrugated metal sheets were removed, and we all mixed together. Gill remembered the ice cream van stopping outside, once a week .

Sarah Trinick, born in 1964, did not go to Prawle School, but was one of the first pupils to start at the new Stokenham Primary.

Margaret Mitchelmore remembered that shortly after she left school she used to teach swimming down at Horsley Beach, because Nellie Tabb couldn't swim. They had a rope which the children couldn't go beyond.

From 1945 for seven years, Pat Farleigh, the postmistress, ran the school dinners during her lunch hour from the post office. Her father was the 'correspondent' for the school and so if there was a problem with staff, Pat helped out. The food was sent out from Kingsbridge in large containers.

Pat told me:

I had to dish up and wash up. I was supposed to do two hours a day from 12 to 2. We had to put oil cloths on every desk and I had to wipe them off and put them on top of the piano. And all the cutlery was horrible – you had to clean it every day, all the containers. I washed the dishes in an ordinary bath, a roundy bath with handles. There were 39 children and they had milk then, free milk, and they were supposed to wash the mugs, but they'd leave them all for me to wash, as well as all the dishes.

Getting to School

For most people getting to Prawle School was a relatively simple case of walking. Journeys to Kingsbridge School were a little different.

I have already mentioned Margaret Mitchelmore told me that as a child, her mother used to walk Margaret and her brother, Bill, over from Lannacombe every Sunday to stay with her grandparents at No 1 Sea View. They went to the village school from Monday to Friday and walked back to Lannacombe again for the weekend.

Ashley Ford about the journey to Kingsbridge Grammar:

It was a hell of a journey to get to school at Kingsbridge. First, we cycled to East Portlemouth, where we left our bicycles at the farm below Rickham Farm. We then walked down the steps to the ferry, crossed on the ferry to the Salcombe side, walked up to the bus station near the Salcombe Parish Church; bus to Kingsbridge, where we stayed all day, until it was time to repeat the journey home again. We went in all weathers and our wet clothes were dried out in the boiler room. If it was very rough the ferry man would point to us to go towards South Pool – Ditch End – the ferry man could run down the river in the swell but couldn't come straight across. It would be dark but we had lights - we were as hard as nails.

Ashley told me that he passed his driving test at the age of 16 and from then on he and his brother, Elwin, would attend Kingsbridge Grammer School on Ashley's motorbike. He also remembered in 1944 that the private Twyford School for Girls closed down. Devon District Council in their wisdom then allowed the girls to attend the Grammar School - a disaster academically as far as Ashley was concerned...

Sarah Trinick remembered her father, Christopher Trinick, telling her how he travelled to school at Kingsbridge, about three years after Ashley, in almost exactly the same way. Whether he had a bike or had to walk Sarah wasn't sure.

Richard told me, to get to school in Kingsbridge, Johnny Green used to ride his pony, Trigger, up from Prawle Point to Uncle Jack's at Locks Farm, where he left the pony. He went to school in Kingsbridge on the school charabanc, came home and rode Trigger back again. In winter Trigger was kept in one of the Nissen huts at Prawle Point.

Apparently records of the School Managers' Minutes 1903-1935 were found in a recycling skip at Tor Quarry, and taken to the Cookworthy Museum, Kingsbridge, in August 2000. They were given to the Devon Record Office in August 2001. (D 6121)

Leaving School & Out to Work

Until the last forty years or so, most children left school at an early age, sometimes as early as 12. As a general rule boys worked on the farms and girls went into service. The cottages where they lived were small and as soon as the girls were old enough they went into 'situations' – 'living-in service' – to make room for the younger children. Unless there was a lot of dairy work, daughters were not at an advantage and for at least a hundred years, country girls in the South Hams had been going off into domestic service.

Ashley Ford's grandfather, Philip Putt born in 1869, left home and school aged 8 and went to Lower House Farm to 'live in'. In 1877/1878 his first job was harvesting with scythes. It was very hot work for the farm workers and part of their emoluments was free cider. He was allowed to lead the donkey, with panniers of rough cider on either side, to and fro back from the harvest field to the cellars where their own brew rough cider was stored. All the men had kegs (small barrels) and he kept them supplied from the donkey all day long.

Miss Langdon wanted Winnie to stay on at school and become an assistant. However, after her parents bought the shop in Dartmouth, Winnie's mother used to stay in Dartmouth during the week, and Winnie, aged 15, had to give up school in order to run the home and look after the family.

The following children left school at 14: Pat Farleigh (née Putt) to work in the post office; Phyllis Wotton (née Partridge) to work on her father's farm; Maurice Putt went to work at Lower House Farm; Nancy Richards (née Hayman) first worked for the Reverend Adams at Ferndale and from 16 ½ helped her mother run the Chivelstone post office for 33 years.

Derek Wotton also left school at 14. During the war while still at school, he was able to get dispensation permits for time off school in order to help with the farming. 'We had so many days off on a card, to say where you were working and what you were doing. …. We were going to stay home anyway!'

Brenda used to help her Auntie May at Ferndale House, South Allington, while still at school. She left school aged 15 on 17 December and started work on Saturday 18 December, for Mr Fred Tripp at Garlands Farm, South Allington. She worked for him for 30 years until he died, doing everything from domestic work to picking potatoes if help was needed. Brenda also remembered that during the war, if you worked on the land, you weren't called up.

Many local people worked at South Allington House for Squire Pitts. The Pitts family were in residence at South Allington House for more than 100 years. Gladys Login, born in East Prawle as Gladys Putt (Margaret Mitchelmore and Bill Login's mother) kept house for Squire Pitts for many years.

Shops

Shopping in East Prawle

There has been a shop in East Prawle since the late 19th century, although many of the villagers' requirements were also met by local butchers, bakers and travelling salesmen with their pots and pans.

From the History, Gazetteer & Directory of Devon, 1850, the shopkeeper was N Edwards in East Prawle. Also in 1878-79 Thomas Pile, Mrs Charlotte Torring Edmonds, and possibly, Joseph Park were the shopkeepers. From Kelly's Directory in 1888, 1889, 1893 and 1902 the shopkeeper was Mrs Sarah Adams. By 1906 it was Mrs Frances Emma Stone. There is no mention of shopkeepers in Kelly's Directory from 1906 until 1935 when Mrs Mary Trout is mentioned. Winnie Easterbrook remembered Mary running the shop (she had five girls and a boy).

However, Richard Partridge has a letter from his grandmother to someone, perhaps renting Rosario, dated 21st June 1919. The location of the shop is still unknown.

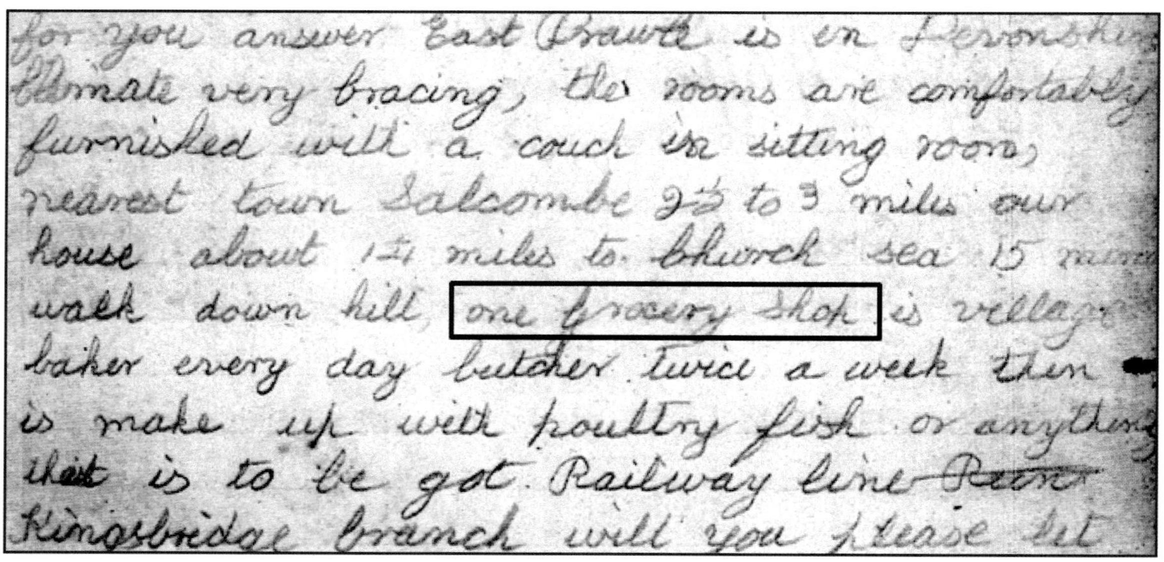
for you answer East Prawle is in Devonshire
Climate very bracing, the rooms are comfortably
furnished with a couch in sitting room,
nearest town Salcombe 2½ to 3 miles our
house about 1¼ miles to Church sea 15 min
walk down hill one Grocery Shop in village
baker every day butcher twice a week then
is make up with poultry fish or anything
that is to be got Railway line
Kingsbridge branch will you please let

Winnie (born in 1912) was insistent there were two shops, one run by Miss Paige (she also played the organ in the chapel). 'Miss Paige just had the little shop. You never went in. You had to stay out in the porch, while she went into what must have been a little kitchen, to fetch what you wanted. The other, run by Mrs Putt, was more of a shop and had a counter.' The shops were in the two houses on the green, now known as Kittiwake and Windfall. Miss Paige was in Kittiwake and Mrs Putt in Windfall. Mary Jane Paige was a shopkeeper in the 1911 census.

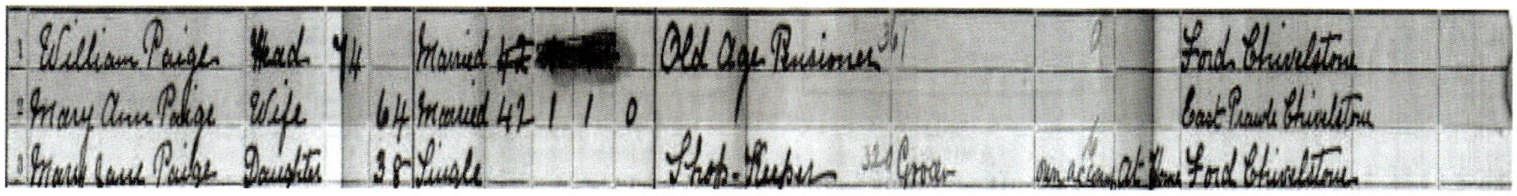

1 William Paige	Head	74	Married	Old Age Pensioner		Ford Chivelstone
2 Mary Ann Paige	Wife	64	Married 42 1 1 0			East Prawle Chivelstone
3 Mary Jane Paige	Daughter	38	Single	Shop Keeper Grocer	own account at Home	Ford Chivelstone

The 1911 Census

In a later conversation I asked Winnie why she went to Miss Paige rather than Mrs Putt. She replied that she would go to either one, but particularly remembered standing in the porch, giving her bit of paper, and Miss Paige weighing up inside. 'She would be in there cutting - cutting the currant in half. You didn't know what she was doing.'

Winnie Easterbrook also said:

In Prawle we had two shops, two public houses, a dressmaker, a shoemaker … and, of course, we had travellers come with pots and pans, and paraffin oil. …. Two bakers came from Frogmore and East Portlemouth, and the butchers three times a week. Everything brought to the door then. People couldn't afford cars, many people only went to Kingsbridge once a year, for Kingsbridge Fair.

Nancy Richards doesn't ever remember going to Kingsbridge as a girl: 'You didn't really need to because there was Noyces used to come around with oil and all hardware stuff and you used to get two or three bakers, and the fruit man from Plymouth ... we had two drapers used to call, and butchers – so we didn't have to go shopping, it was so different.'

It is interesting that Derek Wotton, Richard Partridge, Brenda Jeffery, and probably many others, remember that although there were two shops in the village, one was up on the southside, in Vue Charmanté (it later became the Pottery) and the other in Windfall (but not Kittiwake). These villagers are all between 19 and 35 years younger than Winnie, which perhaps explains the discrepancy. In questioning Winnie further, she told me the shop in Kittiwake closed when Miss Paige died.

A document from Wilf Login with the names of people who lived in East Prawle in 1935 confirmed Mr and Mrs Putt and family as 'wheelwright and shop owner'; and Mr and Mrs Trout and family as 'shop'. A further document by Richard Albert Partridge, Richard's grandfather, concerning a Chivelstone Parish assessment indicated they were both still the shopkeepers in 1939.

Brenda told me that it was her aunt Emma Putt who ran the shop with the counter (known as 'Putts' shop). Alice Stone remembered spending ages choosing her allowance of sweets there. Michael Partridge told the story of his brother Bob buying peppermints for his great-grandfather, who would give him a bit extra to buy some for himself. If the weight wasn't right, Mrs Putt would cut the sweet in half.

Emma's husband, Harry Putt, was one of the village carpenters and undertakers, working from the same building.

Harry Putt making cart shafts on the village green; John Henry Putt's workshop in the distance; no telephone box or lavatories but there is a telegraph pole.

Postcard of the two shops on the green

The 'Putts' shop and the carpentry shop

Brenda thought the shop closed in about 1953 because they moved into the council houses at that time, and her Granny Putt (sister to Emma) moved next door about six months later, by which time the shop was closed.

Derek remembered they used to get all their groceries from the village shop, delivered from Kingsbridge and never had to go out of the village. Everything they needed was there.

Miss Mapplebeck ran the shop on the south side (Vue Charmanté), sometime between the late 1940s and 1950s.

After Miss Mapplebeck, Harry and Mary Ashen bought the house and shop in 1957/58, followed by a Mr Convrey, who sold to Joy and Jim Corley in 1962 (their son Michael married Gillian Easterbrook). The shop closed after a year, and Barbara Caudery bought it and divided it into two dwellings, selling the shop to Robert and Rosemary Melville, who ran it as a pottery.

The current shop location, Piglet Stores, was originally part garage, part stables and part pig house. John Henry Putt (father to Pat Farleigh, the postmistress) used to house his animals there.

The building on the right, in both photographs, has become the village shop,

Derek told me:

The building was a little garage belonging to the Pigs Nose, where they used to sell oil and petrol. The petrol pump was just beside the pub. The tanks were taken out as they were probably dangerous. They weren't very big tanks but I can remember going there, well before I left school, I used to drive an old banger around here.

Elaine Trant remembered that Larry Wootton, who ran the Pigs Nose in the sixties, had a little shop where the pool room now is. 'He'd sell petrol and then go in and cut off a hunk of cheese if it was needed.' Later this moved across the road to the present shop. In 1966 Larry got permission to convert the store into retail shop premises.

The Ashens (see the shop at Vue Charmenté on the previous page) followed Larry Wootton in running the Piglet Stores. Colin Fowle ran it for several years and sold to Lindsey Linley in 1986. It remained closed until Vic and Ranah Day bought it in 1988. They sold it to Viv and Chris Lally in March/April 2006, who still run the shop and café (open in the summer months), and much appreciated by the village. Today (2017) in East Prawle we have one pub and the shop and café.

Apparently there used to be a shop where Bella Rundle lived (Rundle's Cottage) at the top of Provi Hill. Bella told Alice Stone there were cubby holes right up to the ceiling for storage. Alice didn't know whether it was Bella who ran the shop or someone before her. Bella Rundle was born in 1905 (seven years before Winnie), and so far, we have no further information.

Bert Stone, cousin to Winnie, who was the shoemaker (inherited from his father Bill Stone - Uncle Bill), lived at Rock Cottage with a little building on the side, known as the Cobblers. Bert was wounded in the First World War. As well as the villagers' shoes and boots, he repaired all the shoes for the servicemen at the RAF camp during the Second World War. Richard remembered going down there to get his shoes mended.

Diana Shelvoke told me it was important to call Bert Stone the shoemaker, not cobbler.

Early postcard of Rock cottage

Charlie Yalland was the blacksmith. He was Pat Farleigh's great-uncle and his blacksmith shop was converted to the Post Office in June 1983 where Pat Farleigh continued to run the Post Office until she retired in December 1993. (See more about the post office in East Prawle on page 79.)

According to Richard:

Charlie was called Charles Augustus Yalland and lived at Higher Borough as a boy, where his father farmed. Charlie Yalland became the blacksmith. He was still working when he was nearly 90. I've got a bill here from him to Uncle Jack and I think I worked out he was either 88 or 89.

We know from the 1911 census that he was 40 in 1911 and we also know he died on 7 April 1960. So Richard is correct in his assumption.

The Pannier Market in Dartmouth

Pannier Markets are so called after the wicker baskets or panniers used by farmers' wives to carry their wares to market.

Winnie's father (W R E Tucker) went to Dartmouth market every Friday to sell vegetables on the market square. They set off at 6 am with pony and trap. On Dartmouth Regatta days, Winnie went with her twin brother, Jack. On the return they slept in the back in potato sacks.

The three horses, Molly, Polly and Punch would pull a covered wagon – the third pony was required to help get round the steep corners on the hills at Chivelstone. 'I remember going to Dartmouth with two horses in the trap, and the fore-horse was called Polly; she must have known every blade of grass on the way.'

Winnie said they took every type of vegetable which grew on the farm: carrots, potatoes, turnip, cauliflower, cabbage. They also used to collect butter and eggs from the locals around. On the Thursday they went to East Portlemouth to Mrs Goodman at Holset Farm. They collected from Chivelstone Barton from the Weymouths, South Allington from Miss Fowler, and Woodcombe Farm.

From about 1918 until 1955, Richard Albert Partridge and his two sons, William Albert and John Henry (Jack) also delivered vegetables and farm produce twice a week to Dartmouth shops on Tuesdays and Fridays. Later Derek would go with them on Fridays and would stand on the square to sell the left-overs. Later his carrots for the Dartmouth market were grown in the fields down towards Maelcombe House.

W R E Tucker, an Early Farm shop?

In 1922 William Richard Ernest Tucker, Winnie's father, rented a shop in Smith Street, Dartmouth, until 1955. The shop front has hardly changed. Sadly, there was a fire on 28 May 2010 in which the shop and the surrounding buildings were badly damaged.

Frances Ann Tucker (Winnie's mother) and Freda Caudell

Freda Caudell who helped in the shop

The T Ford and Dartmouth Market Square

Winnie's father later bought a T Ford car, chopped the back off and converted it into a van. The picture above shows him in Dartmouth Market Square unloading his produce. He weighed everything on the scales on the box to the right.

Cauliflowers for Newton Abbot

Newton Abbot

In the late 1940s Winnie went with her brother Jack to Newton Abbot every Wednesday with a van load of cauliflowers, all of which sold.

We went there every Wednesday, go to Dartmouth, cross on the Higher Ferry, and go to Newton Abbot. Stand outside the market doors to sell the cauliflowers (only cauliflowers). We'd bring back fish and chips and sit and eat them in the front of the van.

This caused many complaints from the shopkeepers and write-ups in the local papers.

Dressmaking

This book cannot be complete without mentioning Alice Stone, severely disabled at the age of two. I heard from several people about Alice's prowess as a seamstress before I first went to meet her in February 2011. Alice's story is extraordinary, because in the days before there was much help for disability, she overcame hers and grew up to be a seamstress and mistress of the art of dressmaking.

At 19 Alice went to St Loyes College in Exeter for the disabled – she was there for a year from March 1949 to March 1950, where she learned dressmaking. On returning to East Prawle she took over the dressmaking from Miss Wotton, the school teacher. Alice made wedding dresses, bridesmaid dresses, party dresses, loose covers and anything that was asked.

Alice started with a sewing machine loaned by Remploy, but they hassled her because they felt she wasn't making sufficient money – not an easy thing to do in such a small village. However, Jane Shadbolt said of Alice that she was far too generous and never charged enough.

Alice is tiny and had to balance on her crutches while laying out a pattern. Tall people had to kneel to be fitted – although she had a big table on which she was able to lay the designs.

Alice stopped dressmaking in the early 1980s when her arthritis made it impossible.

Remploy was established in the 1940s with the objective of providing employment opportunities for people with a wide range of mental, emotional and physical disabilities.

Communication

The Post

I doubt many of us today would think the postal system in the UK has improved, although with the advent of internet shopping, delivery dates are much better. However, before the post was standardised, in 1840, it was somewhat haphazard.

It is well documented that before 1840 the British postal system was complex and expensive. Letters were charged by distance and the number of sheets of paper. Normally the charge was paid by the recipient, not the sender. As a result people often 'cross-wrote' their letters to save money. However, a large number of items travelled free, in particular letters to and from Members of both Houses of Parliament.

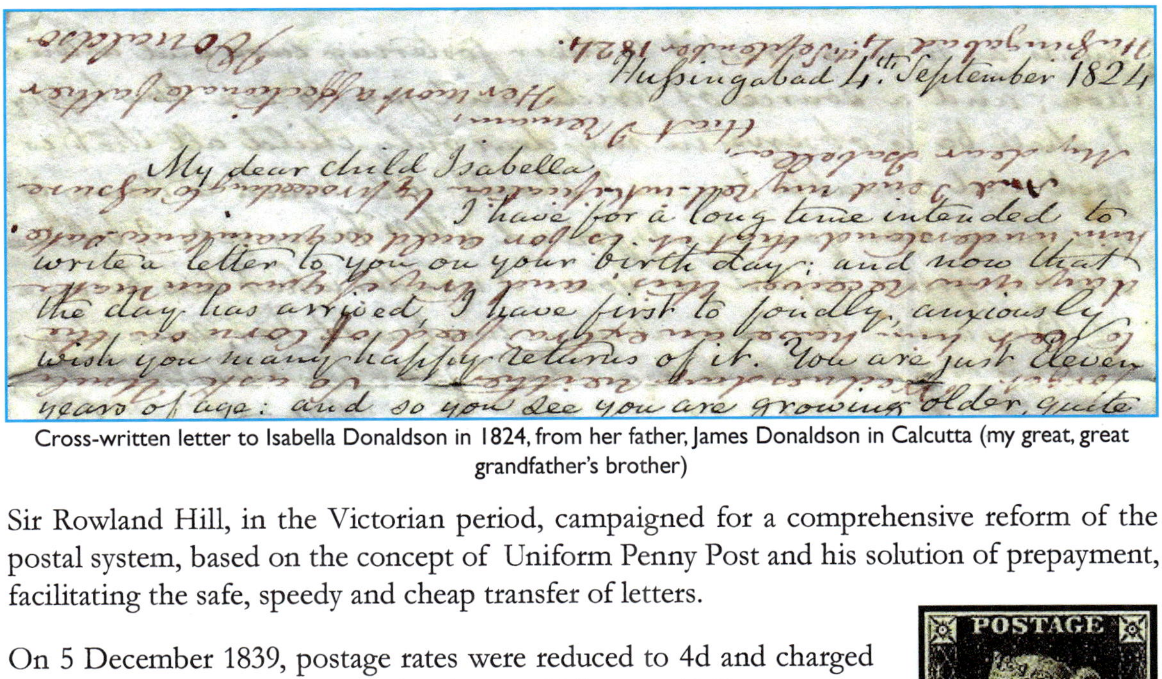

Hussingabad 4th September 1824

My dear child Isabella,

I have for a long time intended to write a letter to you on your birth day; and now that the day has arrived, I have first to fondly, anxiously wish you many happy returns of it. You are just Eleven years of age: and so you see you are growing older, quite

Cross-written letter to Isabella Donaldson in 1824, from her father, James Donaldson in Calcutta (my great, great grandfather's brother)

Sir Rowland Hill, in the Victorian period, campaigned for a comprehensive reform of the postal system, based on the concept of Uniform Penny Post and his solution of prepayment, facilitating the safe, speedy and cheap transfer of letters.

On 5 December 1839, postage rates were reduced to 4d and charged by weight. This proved so popular that, on 10 January 1840, rates were further reduced to 1d for half an ounce and all free privileges were abolished, including that of the Queen.

The Penny Black, which was issued in England in 1840, was the world's first adhesive postage stamp. The stamp has a portrait of

Queen Victoria (as this was the most difficult image to forge successfully), is primarily black in colour and cost one penny, hence known as the Penny Black.

Because it was the first postage stamp, the Penny Black did not show a country of origin. Today, British stamps are still the only postage stamps not to do so.

Postcards

The first postcards were produced in 1870. There was great demand for a cheaper postal service and in September the halfpenny postcard was introduced. These were plain cards, front and back with a pre-printed stamp and published by the Post Office. No other companies were permitted to print postcards at this time. In 1894 the first picture postcards were issued in the UK and permission given to other companies to publish them. They had a picture (or photograph) on the front with the address written on the back. In 1902 the Divided Back postcard was introduced, which allowed people to write messages on one half of the back of the card and an address on the other.

In 1906 the fashionable Photo and Lithographed cards made by Eastman Kodak, entered the marketplace by making an affordable camera called the 'Folding Pocket Camera'. The public was now able to take black and white photographs and have them printed right onto postcard backs.

Margaret Mitchelmore's grandmother Mrs Hilda Putt, daughters: Gladys, Margery and Nora

Caroline Langdon, Headmistress of East Prawle School

Postcard sent from East Prawle Post Office, unfortunately the date isn't legible

In the early 20th century, postcards became a popular method of sending short missives. Postcards of family portraits were very successful.

Foss Cottage has a wonderful *cabinet postcard album* with postcards kept by the Miss Fosses between 1904 and the 1930s. Most of the postcards were just short missives with expected arrival times, no worries about the postcard not getting there in time.

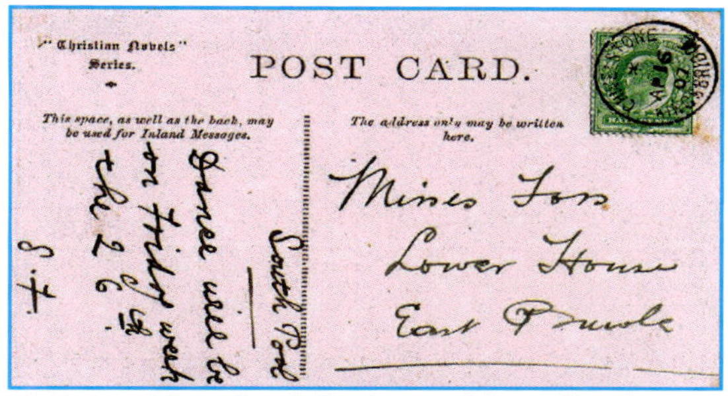

Addressed from South Pool, posted from Chivelstone, Kingsbridge, April 16 1907
'Dance will be on Friday week the 26th S F'

There are some delightful comments on these postcards:

- December 25 1904: 'Very many thanks; it was delicious six can testify to this statement. F.P.F. Xmas-Day';
- March 22 1906 11.45 am: 'I shall be delighted to have primroses only in bunch as the blown ones do not revive. Sending tea cloths Thursday';
- December 10 1908 at 5 pm from Salcombe: 'I have arranged with Mrs Turner to school on Saturday will meet you same place & time if wet Saturday Monday is fixed';
- 'Hope to be with you tomorrow somewhere about 4.0pm – shall be delighted to see you again'.

There are many more in a similar vein.

The Post Offices

We no longer have a post office in East Prawle or Chivelstone, although one operated in both villages for more than a hundred years.

East Prawle

According to a survey of Post Offices by an independent researcher, Ken Smith, on behalf of the British Postal Museum and Archive, the East Prawle post office was established in 1890 and had Money Order and Savings Bank facilities and an Annuity & Insurance Office at least by 1905. Kingsbridge and Salcombe alternated as its nearest post towns. It is not mentioned in Kelly's Directory until 1902 (see the table of Directory listings of the post offices at Chivelstone and East Prawle in Appendix I).

circa 1924: No 1 Corner Cottage, the building on the left, Photograph from Iris Brialey (née Hannaford)

In Kelly's Directory of 1902 William George Samuel Beer was the sub-postmaster for East Prawle, although it is known that it was his wife, Carrie Beer, who ran the post office.

The East Prawle post office was in what is now known as No 1 Corner Cottage on the village green.

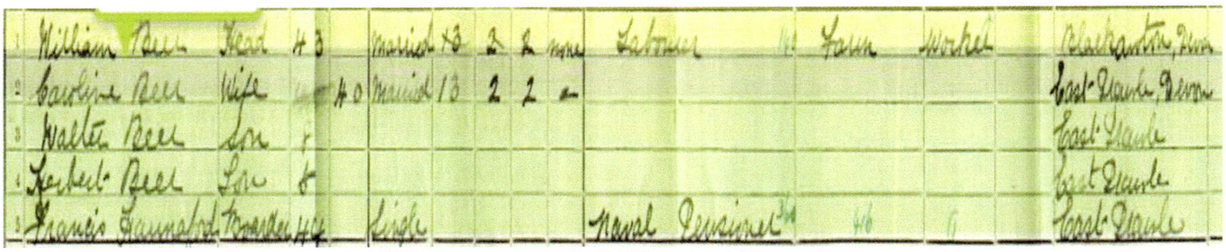
William Beer	Head	43		Married	13	2	2	none	Labourer Farm Worker	Blackawton, Devon
Caroline Beer	Wife		40	Married	13	2	2	–		East Prawle, Devon
Walter Beer	Son									East Prawle
Herbert Beer	Son	8								East Prawle
Francis Hannaford	Boarder	44		Single					Naval Pensioner	East Prawle

1911 Census record of William and Carrie Beer

In 1915 the post office moved to the cottage on Fore Street which belonged to Granny Fanny Hannaford, a widow. She brought up seven children of her own and four orphans, including Emma Wood. From 1915 Emma Wood took over running the post office and her daughter Pat joined her as soon as she was old enough.

Quoting Pat Farleigh, born in 1924, from Stephen Pedrick's *A Century of Memories:*

I've done for the Post Office for fifty-five years, so that's a good service. I was twelve years as Assistant to my mother, and forty-three and a half years as the postmistress. My mother had taken the Post Office over in 1915 from Mrs Beer and I took it over from Mum in 1950, so it was in our family all that time, seventy-eight years!

In June 1983 the post office moved to a cottage on the green that had been converted from Charlie Yalland's blacksmith shop, and finally closed in 1993.

1921 Post office, Fore Street, with public telephone sign

1980s the post office on the Village Green

Chivelstone

From the British Postal Museum and Archive we know that the Chivelstone Post Office was opened on 20 March 1845 and was UDC (undated circular handstamp issued). There is little other information but we do know deliveries were made from 1850. The post office was housed in the first row of cottages on the road down towards South Allington.

Chivelstone Post Office on the way down to South Allington (Cookworthy Museum P1400.22.4)

Early deliveries and dispatches from White's Devon, Billing's Directory and Kelly's Directories:

Date	Post Office	Sub-Postmaster	Information
1850		W Lidstone	Post to Kingsbridge 1 aftn.
1857		W Lidstone	Mr W Lidstone, Sub-Master. Arrival by Foot Post from Kingsbridge 11.30 a.m. Despatch immediately afterwards, - the messenger waiting while the bag is made up, Money Order Office, Kingsbridge.
1878-1879	South Allington/ Chivelstone	Mr Edward Yabsley	Letters are received at 9.25 a.m. and despatched at 3.40 p.m. weekdays only, via Kingsbridge. Torcross is the nearest Money Order Office. Letters are received at Prawle at 11.30 a.m. from Kingsbridge. There is a WALL LETTER BOX here, cleared at 3 p.m. weekdays only. Salcombe is the nearest Money Order Office.
1888	Chivelstone	Mr Edward Yabsley	Letters by foot post at 10.50 a.m.; dispatched at 2.25 p.m. The nearest money order office is at Torcross & telegraph office at Salcombe.

See Appendix II for full detail of Kelly's Directories on the post offices and deliveries from 1889 until 1939.

Fred Gordon, Chief Officer Coastguard, ran the post office for a while during 1939. After 1939 it is unclear who ran it but it was in danger of closing. Nancy Richards (née Hayman) remembered in 1946 Mr Osborne from Woodcombe came to see her mother. He begged her to oversee running the post office until Nancy was old enough to take it over – Nancy was 16. She had a counter in the room which also had a Lidstone, and her mother would be cooking dinner while people came in for stamps. Nancy ran the post office for 33-34 years and closed it in the late 1970s. Apparently there also used to be a telephone exchange but before her mother's time.

For further information on the post office at East Prawle I have been allowed to use extracts from the Chivelstone Parish Council (the very first meeting of the Chivelstone Parish Council was held on 4 December 1894):

- On 29 June 1900 a meeting was held 'for the purpose of considering the advisability to petition the Postal Authorities for a Telegraph Office for the parish of Chivelstone'.
- On 18 January 1901 a further meeting was held to consider Postmaster General's conditions offered and also the term of guarantee of £25. It was agreed that the Postmaster General be asked if the sum for the guarantee could be somewhat reduced as the Parish of Chivelstone was a small one. Mr P Putt moved an amendment that the Postmaster General again be asked if the Telegraph Office could not be opened at the Coast guard station East Prawle.
- On 12 March 1901 the letter from the Postmaster General was discussed, which stated a reduction of £6 from the original sum of £25 thereby making the present sum of guarantee £19. The Post Office Authorities would be responsible for half that amount, viz £9.10s and the Chivelstone Parish Council to guarantee the remainder viz £9.10s. Again Mr P Putt moved an amendment that the East Prawle Post Office be made a Telegraph Office instead of Chivelstone.
- On 10 April 1901 'that according to the communication received from the Postmaster General no application for Prawle Sub-office to be established and that Chivelstone sub office could be established as a Telegraph Office'.
- On 26 April 1901 'As the Councillors have now agreed to become guarantors for the establishment of the Telegraphs, we now move a resolution to petition the Postmaster General for a second delivery of letters for Chivelstone and East Prawle, the letters being already sent to Frogmore a distance of 4, 5 or 6 miles, also that the postman may be sent with letters in the afternoon as the delay of a second delivery causes great inconvenience.'
- By 15 April 1902 this all seems to have been dropped for the time being, although discussion rumbled on regarding a reduction in the guarantee payments and lack of second delivery.

Delivering the Post

In *Kingsbridge and its Surroundings* (published in 1874), Sarah Prideaux Fox wrote:

The Post Offices at Kingsbridge, Salcombe, and Torcross, are, as is now usual, the receiving offices for messages. The mention of Telegraphs and Post Offices seems to take us back to the time when Kingsbridge letters were delivered by a woman, and that woman extremely deaf, and unable to read writing. How she managed to take the letters to their right destination is a kind of mystery; but she did so much better than could have been expected. When 'Jenny' became superannuated, a postman was appointed to succeed her, and he (as well as the letter carrier for Dodbrooke) is now attired in the orthodox livery of blue and red, which certainly does look more business-like than the black bonnet and little woollen 'turnover' of his predecessor.

The first postman I have been able to record for East Prawle is in the photograph, on the next page, with his pony and trap. For many months I had no record of when and who it was, but the road round Moorwell Pond clearly already existed. However, in September 2010 when Stephen Pedrick, author of *A Century of Memories*, looked at the photograph on the right he knew it was Jim Putt from Frogmore, Stephen's mother-in-law's grandfather! Apparently he was given the pony and trap when he could no longer walk from Frogmore to East Prawle with the post every day. We know this was in the 1920s because Bob Partridge remembered as boys they used to throw stones at him, Postie Putt. So that's the end of the mystery. Jim Putt was born and bred in East Prawle. His grandfather and father were carpenters. He was a Chief Petty Officer in the Navy, and then he joined the Coastguards. On retirement he became a postman, walking from Frogmore to Prawle and back every day.

Postie Jim coming up from Moorwell Pond: Photograph from Iris Brialey (née Hannaford)

In Stephen Pedrick's second book of local memories *Daishels and Figgy Duff*, Sylvia Putt, Jim's daughter, is recorded as saying:

> They came back here to Frogmore in 1911, when my father took on with the Post Office. My father walked from Frogmore to East Prawle posting, for twenty years. At one time we lived at South Pool, so he had to walk down here first, before he started work – then he went back to South Pool and up to Chivelstone, South Allaton [sic] and all up round Prawle and Lannacombe.

A story about Jim Putt the postman: Winnie remembered being told that Jim came with a telegram about her cousin Bert Stone, who was in the First World War, with the message that Bert was believed dead. However, another telegram came through immediately after and they said Jim couldn't get back quick enough with the good news to say Bert was found, but wounded.

Sylvia took over some of the rounds in 1925. We know they lived in a little dark cottage (now pulled down) next to the Globe Inn.

For a period of time, certainly between 1926 and 1930, the postal address used to be East Prawle near Salcombe, not Kingsbridge. (See the table of Directory listings of the post offices in Chivelstone and East Prawle in Appendix II.)

Winnie recalled: 'The postman used to come across on the ferry boat from Salcombe. He kept his bike in a little hut at East Portlemouth and would cycle over with all the stuff.'

Derek remembered Bill Budd also came from Salcombe across to Rickham, High House Farm, as far as New House Corner, then down to 10 (via Wood Lane) and back again.

Nancy said the post for Chivelstone was brought from Kingsbridge at 7.15 am and George Rundle would cycle down from Prawle and, while the rest of the post was being sorted, deliver the Chivelstone letters. He delivered the post to Woodcombe, Lannacombe, South Allington, Borough, and Start Point on his bike, using the back roads to Kellaton. He'd come home to building work all in a day. Bobby Partridge did the journey once but on a pony and thought it a very long trip. When George was on holiday Nancy had to do the rounds on an old bicycle. When George retired, Nancy's father, Percy Hayman, took on the delivery, but he walked round.

A amusing story introduced to me by Celia Strong, leader of the Kingsbridge U3A History Group from Ken Williams and Dermot Reynolds *The Kingsbridge Branch*:

On Sunday our band of friends decided to have a day out at Torcross. They hired a wagonette from the Anchor Hotel and set off at 8 o'clock on their journey. However, they came to an abrupt stop outside the Inn in Frogmore and the horse refused to go any further. The licensee and his wife watched the proceedings with great amusement and then let the travellers into the joke. The horse normally worked for the Post Office and this was a regular stopping point for the postman to deliver mail whilst the horse was given a bucket of beer. A drink all round – including the horse – resolved the situation so off they set again. Stopping at each pub they arrived at the Torcross Hotel just in time for lunch at 1 o'clock.

Tim Blyth found the article on the right in the Western Morning News dated 27 August 1934 regarding the speeding up of the post.

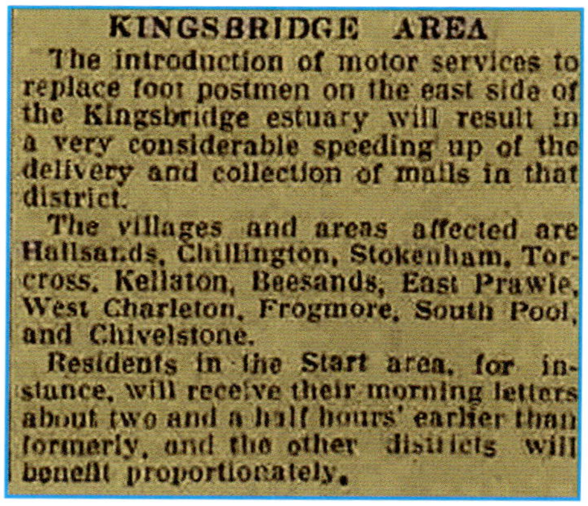

KINGSBRIDGE AREA

The introduction of motor services to replace foot postmen on the east side of the Kingsbridge estuary will result in a very considerable speeding up of the delivery and collection of mails in that district.

The villages and areas affected are Hallsands, Chillington, Stokenham, Torcross, Kellaton, Beesands, East Prawle, West Charleton, Frogmore, South Pool, and Chivelstone.

Residents in the Start area, for instance, will receive their morning letters about two and a half hours' earlier than formerly, and the other districts will benefit proportionately.

The Telegraph and Telegrams

S P Fox wrote at length about the telegraph in *Kingsbridge and its Surroundings*:

About the middle of 1865, The United Kingdom Telegraph Co. extended their line from Totnes to Kingsbridge, the wires being carried along the turnpike road between the two towns; the receiving office being at Mr G P Friend's. Towards the end of 1868, Sir William Mitchell, the proprietor of the Shipping Gazette, also carried a wire from that office to his signal station at Prawle, thus being enabled to supply his paper with early shipping intelligence. This line was worked with a single wire; the return current being obtained by 'going to earth', as it is termed. Sir William Mitchell's station at Prawle, and that of the Messrs. Fox, of Falmouth, at the Lizard, Cornwall, are, perhaps, two of the most important on our coasts.

The Telegraph Act of 1870, nationalising the telegraph companies, resulted in a huge increase of telegrams being used, which helped to reduce rural isolation.

The Second World War meant a hectic era for the Prawle post office, particularly when the RAF moved to Prawle. Telegrams were delivered to the post office in East Prawle and then by hand around the village. Pat Farleigh remembered a telegram was three halfpence to deliver down under the hill (in particular to the Miss Fosses at Foss Cottage), a penny for the village, three pence to Prawle Point, and 1/10d to cycle to Hallsands and Start Point Lighthouse (on Wednesdays when Chivelstone post office was closed).

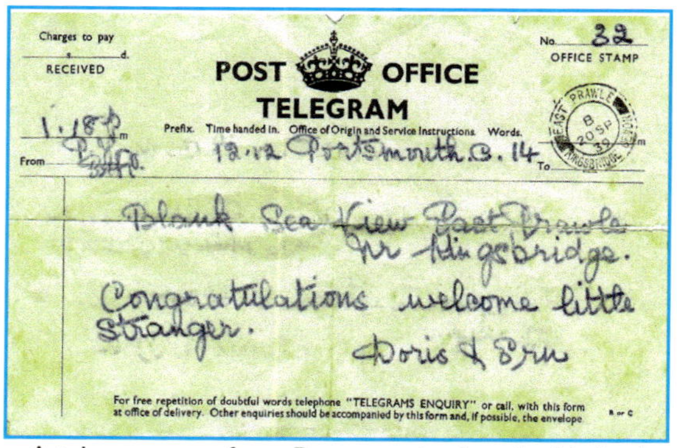

Charges to pay s. d.
RECEIVED
POST OFFICE TELEGRAM
No. 32
OFFICE STAMP
Prefix. Time handed in. Office of Origin and Service Instructions. Words.
12.12 Portsmouth B. 14
From To
EAST PRAWLE 20 SP 39 KINGSBRIDGE
Blank Sea View East Prawle Nr Kingsbridge.
Congratulations welcome little stranger.
Doris & Ern
For free repetition of doubtful words telephone "TELEGRAMS ENQUIRY" or call, with this form at office of delivery. Other enquiries should be accompanied by this form and, if possible, the envelope

A telegram sent from Portsmouth after the birth of Brenda Jeffery (née Blank) on 20 September 1939 and delivered by Emma Putt, Pat Farleigh's mother

Pat said that, for a wedding at Hallsands, she cycled out there eight times with telegrams! Hard work on an old bicycle without gears. Nancy remembered her 'sister Mary used to deliver telegrams all over the place – Hallsands, Scoble, South Pool – also on a pushbike. She'd get to South Hallsands with a telegram and by the time she got back there'd be another one.' Sometimes she was able to borrow a pony from Mr Fowler at South Allington.

Telephones

Pat told me the first telephone in the village was installed up at the little post office, her Granny Hannaford's cottage (on Fore Street). Her father, John Henry Putt, had to build a very big sound proof box for it. It was the only telephone for people to use and Pat worked out how much they owed. She took the money, filled in a form and sent it off with their balance every week.

The first mention of telephone numbers at East Prawle in Kelly's Directory in 1935 is the Providence Inn as Chivelstone 8, The Union Inn as Chivelstone 9 and William Richard Ernest Tucker, farmer and market gardener as Chivelstone 4. By 1939 Welle House, boarding house was Chivelstone 211 – a 2 had been added to the front of the other numbers.

Elaine remembered:

When we had the telephone first, which was in the early 60s, we shared a line with Miss Leonard. You would pick up the phone and she'd be there talking. And then of course she didn't put the receiver back and I would run over to Miss Leonard and ask her to check the phone, because we couldn't use it until she did.

Charlotte Lewis (née Trinick) from Bonaventura also said they shared with Miss Leonard, and Arnie Mann remembered long distance trunk calls taking forever:

I know it was a long winded process to try and make a phone call. I remember when I was staying for school holidays with my grandparents in South Allington and phoning home to say I'm going to be on such and such a train, it would take probably 25-40 minutes to be connected to Hatford in Hertfordshire.

BT Telephone Box Saga

From *This is Exeter* on Friday 30 January 2009:

A SOUTH Devon village, which staged a telephone box protest 'stand in' three months ago to try to stop BT carting their prized kiosk away, has been victorious in its battle to win the traditional red box back.

Although East Prawle has its kiosk returned, it comes minus a telephone, but villagers reckon at least it will be 'handy' by acting as a kind of street lamp for nearby residents.

East Prawle hit the headlines more than a year ago after it was revealed mobile telephone reception is so bad the only way locals or visitors can contact the outside world is by standing on a village green bench and waving their telephones in the air to catch a signal.

Roger Tucker, Louise Emberton, David Hampden-Smith and Tim Blyth

There is some good news for villagers still trying to make mobile telephone calls. Mr Tucker has deposited a two-foot high block of stone dragged out of one of his fields to give callers somewhere to stand instead of climbing on the village bench [which was being damaged]. He used a JCB to haul it to the village green were it has been deposited next to the bench, not far from the village's only other telephone kiosk, which does have a phone.

Transport

Nowadays we take transport for granted, although perhaps not so in East Prawle: the Coleridge Bus comes once a week on a Wednesday to go to Kingsbridge for a morning's shopping.

I struggled with this topic until I realised that transport is a constant throughout the book: the postman, driving to Dartmouth, horses and tractors etc.

Roads

John Fairweather-Tall in the his article *Travel by Water* wrote:

Country roads throughout were often in what has been described as 'a parlous state', and perhaps worse than when the Romans had left them. For centuries the deep narrow lanes with high banks had been pounded by horses' hoofs, the solid wooden and iron wheels of wagon and carriage had deeply rutted them and, 'livestock droves turned them into ribbon dungheaps'. Their hazardous state therefore comes as no surprise. Generations of cattle droves and pack-horses and donkeys made them almost impassable.

Even as late as the early 20th century, one report described the country's roads as still 'filthy', adding that cars 'progressed through a sea of mud over surfaces of the most sodden and heavy going character'.

Movement within the South Hams was very restricted and people relied on foot or horse for moving about. The first passenger coach service in Devon started in 1658, taking four days for the journey from London to Exeter. Its average pace probably did not exceed three miles an hour.

The first [local] coach service began in 1824 operated by Robert Foale of Kingsbridge, departing from the King's Arms (to Plymouth). With the opening of the South Devon Railway in 1848, these coaches met trains at Kingsbridge Road Station (Wrangaton). A steamer service began in the 1860s operated by the Kingsbridge Packet Company running twice weekly to Plymouth calling at Salcombe. Later, a daily coach service ran between Dartmouth and

pre 1916 Dartmouth Coach, three horses & passengers Torcross to Stokenham (Cookworthy PO518)

Kingsbridge (Anchor Hotel) connecting the Kingswear trains running three times a day.

Robert Waterhouse wrote:

In 1824, Dartmouth and Torcross were linked by the construction of a turnpike or toll road. This was followed in 1845 by a connection to Kingsbridge which passed through Stokenham and Chillington.

This turnpike road provided a direct dry-land route from Stokenham parish to other parts of the district for wheeled vehicles for the first time. Its effect on local communications cannot be underestimated.

Kathy Tanner wrote in her *Coaching Days*:

We do not know when the coach route from Kingsbridge to Dartmouth was started, but it may have been after 1842 when the road from Stokenham to Dartmouth was improved by the Transport Trust. By 1858 Robert Foale was running a coach from the Kings Arms to Dartmouth twice weekly in winter and three times a week in summer.

Ellen Luscombe in 1861 wrote about a trip from Salcombe to Torcross:

... Frogmore, which perhaps is a delightful place to those who reside there, though it seemed so dreary to us. There seemed to be some little traffic in the village, as we observed several malthouses or cider stores built by the side of the river for the convenience of the water carriage; there was also a rather good bridge across the river, but beyond it there was no navigation.

A bit later on: 'As we proceeded, some parts of the road became agricultural and common place by comparison.'

circa 1914 Torcross Hotel and Dartmouth Coach (Cookworthy PO830i)

Toll house on the A379 towards Plymouth

Coach and Horse	1 shilling
Horse and Cart	5d
Bullock	2d
Pedestrian	1d

The Motor Car

The general traffic on the roads would have been very quiet when Winnie Easterbrook was a child. The roads were dusty in dry weather and naturally very muddy in wet weather. There would have been farm machinery, carts and wagons, pony traps, carriers' vans (horse driven), bakers' carts, perhaps a few bicycles and of course people on horses or donkeys. Many people walked to their destination, however far. Only a few cars appeared after the First World War, with tractors and mechanisation coming to Prawle during the Second World War.

The earliest vehicles had solid tyres, with imaginable consequences for passengers' comfort. When pneumatic tyres first followed the solid sort, they often proved too fragile and were liable to be punctured on the rough, unmade roads. When they escaped punctures, mechanical parts such as axles broke as a result of violent jolting.

Building the Roads

East Prawle Green with first car belonging to Dr Webster and stones on the green for road building

Many thanks to Tim Blyth who found the *Surveyors Account of Money Expended on the Highways of the Parish of Chivelstone* at the Devon Record Office (renamed to Devon Archives and Local Studies). The accounts were weekly reports from 1839 to 1856 and make absolutely fascinating reading.

Although there are many labourers' names and the work they carried out, I have used the example of a Mrs Gunn below. There were two Mrs Mary Gunn, one at Bowhay House and one at Ford, although it is not clear which Mrs Gunn did the work. The example below is in 1853:

Day labour & location 1853	Date	No of Days	Daily Rate (d)	£	s.	d.
Filling in ruts South Allington to Lannacombe	11-16 April	6	6		3	
Filling ruts Chivelstone to Penny Hill	18-23 April	5	6		2	6
Breaking stones and filling holes from Ford to Cousins Cross	30 May-4 June	4	6		2	6
Breaking stones and filling ruts from Penny Hill to Chivelstone	20-26 June	6	6		3	
Filling holes Prawle to Chivelstone Cross	4-9 July	5	6		2	6

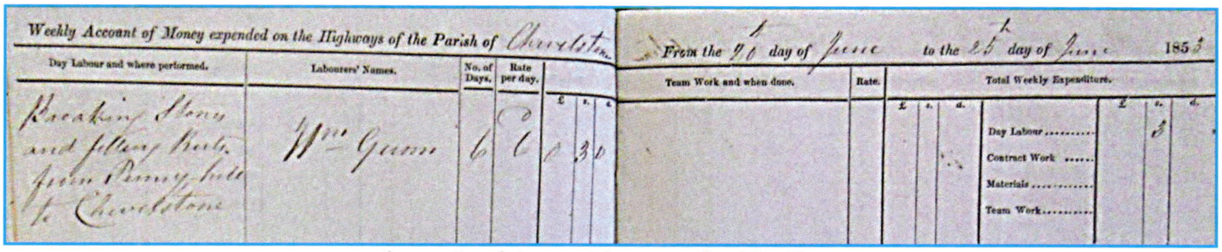
Weekly Account of Money expended on the Highways of the Parish of Chivelstone — From the 20 day of June to the 25 day of June 1853

Day Labour and where performed.	Labourers' Names.	No. of Days.	Rate per day.	£	s.	d.	Team Work and when done.	Rate.	£	s.	d.	Total Weekly Expenditure.	£	s.	d.
Breaking Stones and filling Ruts from Penny hill to Chivelstone	Wm Gunn	6	6	0	3	0						Day Labour		3	
												Contract Work			
												Materials			
												Team Work			

A sample of the weekly report for Mrs Gunn

Roger Tucker said that in 1855 William Tucker lent his horse and wagon to repairing the road to Stover Lake. Some stones were brought from Sharpers and the fields around, the rest came from Winter Pool Quarry (on the way to South Pool). Amongst the surveyors' accounts is evidence of Mr Tucker's wagon and two horses for one day, as well as carts and two horses from Mr Foss and Mr Hutchings. They were repairing roads with stones from Ford Hill to Chivelstone Cross and loading stones from Winter Pool Quarry.

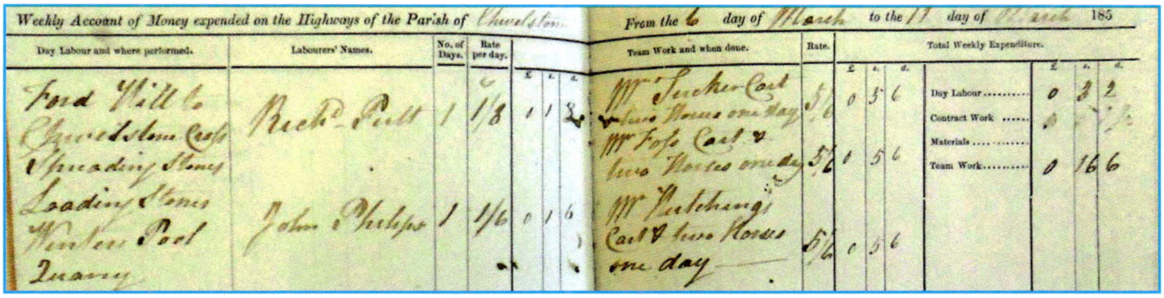
Weekly Account of Money expended on the Highways of the Parish of Chivelstone — From the 6 day of March to the 11 day of March 185

Day Labour and where performed.	Labourers' Names.	No. of Days.	Rate per day.	£	s.	d.	Team Work and when done.	Rate.	£	s.	d.	Total Weekly Expenditure.	£	s.	d.
Ford Hill to Chivelstone Cross Spreading Stones	Richd Pull	1	1/8		1	8	Wm Tucker Cart two Horses one day	5/6	0	5	6	Day Labour	0	3	2
							Wm Foss Cart & two Horses one day	5/6	0	5	6	Contract Work			
Loading Stones Winter Pool Quarry	John Philips	1	1/6	0	1	6	Wm Hutchings Cart & two Horses one day	5/6	0	5	6	Materials			
												Team Work	0	16	6

A sample of the weekly report for the work carried out by Mr Tucker, Foss and Hutchings with two horses per day

Roger also told me his grandfather took the horse and cart to Dartmouth by going past Stover Way to Woodcombe, up to Higher Borough, then down to South Allington and up round by Northern Town. Roger's brother, John, wrote 'the grandparents would bring back any packages/parcels from the train to East Prawle. In frosty weather they had the horses reshod with long nails sticking out the bottom for extra grip to get home - Chivelstone Hill would be icy,' but Uncle Bill told Richard they would get the blacksmith at Stokenham to put longer nails in the horses' shoes, on their way to Dartmouth. They probably did both.

The first East Prawle Parish Council was held at Prawle School on 4 December 1894, and on 6 November 1896, after a lengthy discussion it was decided to write to the District Clerk in reference to the bad condition of the roads in and around the vicinity of East Prawle, as below:

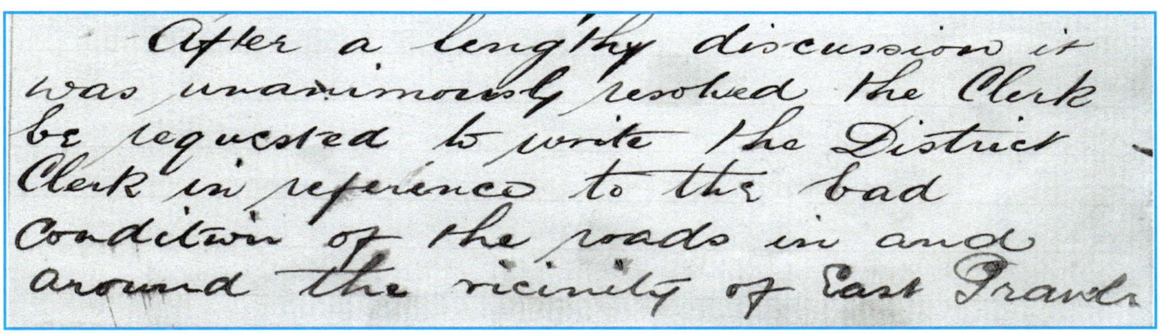
After a lengthy discussion it was unanimously resolved the Clerk be requested to write the District Clerk in reference to the bad condition of the roads in and around the vicinity of East Prawle

In the early 1900s Roger's grandfather also had the contract to maintain all the roads in East Portlemouth, Chivelstone and South Pool parishes. Stones and limestone rubble were brought by barge to Goodshelter, Frogmore and South Pool. They were loaded into carts at low tide (the stone came in by barge at high tide), pulled by two horses, with a third horse to help up around the steep corner at Goodshelter. The stone was taken and tipped into heaps beside the road where it was needed.

Collecting limestone from the shore at Frogmore by the bridge - note the building by the bridge that is no longer there

Roger told me they would bring the stones, some earth and limestone and spread that out. Small stones in low spots, earth on top, damped down with a bucket of water. Then horses with a very large roller would smooth it all out.

Winnie remembered that Jim Stone (father to Alice, the dressmaker in Prawle, wounded in the First World War), helped to build the roads when he came home. Jim sat in the lay-by where the recycle bins are now on Broad Road. He would be there every day breaking up the stones, wearing goggles made of wire, with no glass at all.

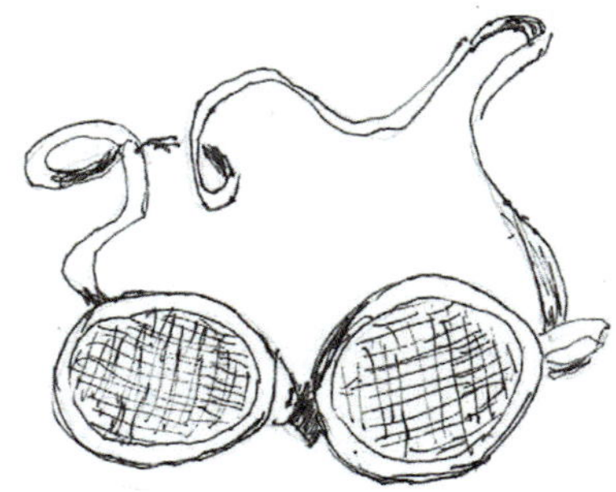

Tarmacking the Roads

It is not really clear when the roads were tarmacked. It was usual to spray the tar, followed by the chippings. At the time John Henry Putt looked after the roads. From Richard Albert Partridge's diary (Richard's grandfather), it is clear that in 1930 his horse and cart were used for 'drawing chippings' for John Henry Putt on three days in July:

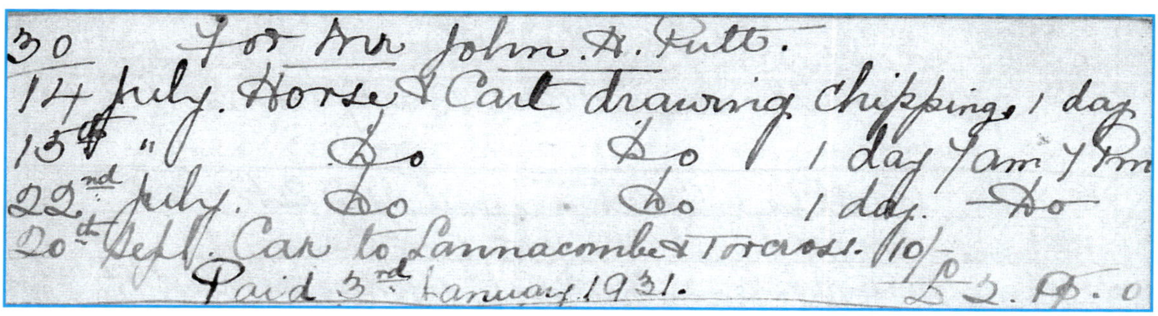

30 For Mr John H. Putt.
14 July. Horse & Cart drawing chippings 1 day
15th " Do Do 1 day am & pm
22nd July. Do Do 1 day. Do
20th Sept. Car to Lannacombe & Torcross. 10/-
Paid 3rd January 1931. £2. 15. 0

Looking at some of the photographs on the East Prawle History Society database, where the roads were still stones, it looks likely that tarmacking came to the village somewhere in the late 1920s. Although the road down towards Prawle Point seems to have been treated either before or during the Second World War.

A story from Michael Partridge on the road to Prawle Point:

I was riding with Charlie with a load of dung and we came down to that gateway at Higher Holloway. They were tarmacking the road for the first time. It took several weeks of tarmacking, because it was rocky all the way down. We came down around in sight of Holloway Gate with a load of dung with this Massey, and in the middle of the road was one of the workmen with his wheelbarrow. Stood in the middle of the road just lighting up his pipe. Charlie come round the corner 'Get out the way I can't stop' made him drop his pipe and baccy and pushed in the gateway.

Carriers

East Prawle is at the far end of everywhere and travelling around was never easy. Some things could only be bought in Kingsbridge.

According to Roger Grimley in his booklet 'Carriers from Chivelstone Parish':

The first known carrier was Louis Bowhay who farmed at Prawle, in 1870, with his horse drawn vehicle to Kingsbridge and Dartmouth.

By the late 1890s William Tucker (Roger's grandfather) was running a service to Dartmouth every Friday with his horse drawn van going through Chivelstone, Torcross, Strete and Stoke Fleming en route. The journey took about 4 hours collecting farm produce from Woodcombe and Chivelstone (butter, eggs, cream, carrots, potatoes, etc.). A few passengers were also carried.

In 1920 Richard Albert Partridge (Richard's grandfather) was running a horse drawn vehicle carrying passengers, parcels and produce to and from Kingsbridge on Wednesdays and Saturdays, but in 1923 he turned to motor transport and bought a Ford touring car.

John Henry Putt (Pat Farleigh's father) was also a carrier and taxi man from about 1920, and in 1926 the Woodleigh Deanery Magazine added a note 'Mr Putt runs a motor bus from Prawle to Chivelstone Church on Sunday evenings. Will you please use this bus as much as possible in order to make the venture possible from the point of view of cost'. He was also a carpenter and farmer.

Jack Partridge and Richard's father also ran a carrier business and had taxis in the mid twenties to take people to church and weddings. Richard has many examples of his grandfather's handwritten diary where he kept a detailed account regarding his motor hire:

1925

- 15 Nov 2 trips Portlemouth Motor 6/-
- 13 Dec 2 trips Portlemouth 6/-

1926

- Mr Chandlier Grammar School Motor Cycle 2/-
- Hire of car to Kingsbridge 12/-
- 16 May G Stone car to Buckfastleigh 45/- Paid
- 19th May Ton Van to Buckfastleigh 45/- Paid

Cattle 1931

- 7th Jan Bought Heifer Cow K. Market £29.10.0
- 13th Feb Heifer to Bull Tolchard. 40 wks 20th Nov 1931
- 13th March Heifer re Bull Tolchard 40 wks 13 Dec 1931

Note: one car is left hand drive, the other right hand

Richard told me:

They also had a van in which they used to collect people as well when the picture house opened in Kingsbridge. They were busy, especially in the winter time, ferrying the Beesands fishermen; when they couldn't go to sea in winter, they'd be in the cinema. They took them in the van and were running back and forth all day long taking them in for different showings of the film in Kingsbridge.

Diana Shelvoke remembered everything was done by carrier: for three pence Jack Partridge returned their library books to the Boots Library in Kingsbridge and brought back the next book on the list.

In talking to Stephen Pedrick in 2003 Harry Jervis remembered:

Me uncle used to run the crabs from Hallsands to Kingsbridge twice a week; he used to go down with a horse and cart, the old hay cart. I often used to go with him, we'd leave at about seven o'clock in the morning ... it would take about four hours to get there .... unload the crabs at the Station, give the horse a break, then come down on the Quay, and if any of the tradesmen had any parcels for Hallsands they'd bring them down and put them in the cart. Then we'd go out to where the 'Crabshell' is now, that was a coal yard, load up with coal to fill the cart which made the journey worthwhile ... take the coal back to Hallsands and he used to deliver it to the fishermen's cottages before he went home – all in a day's work!

Other Ways of Getting About

I have mentioned before that Winnie, born in 1912, used to walk to St Sylvester's Chivelstone for the service and then walk on to lunch at South Pool with Wilf's parents. She would then walk back to Chivelstone for a further service and on home to Prawle.

Iris Brialey, born in 1922, as a very young girl remembered coming down from London on the train, coach to Salcombe, across on the ferry, walk up the steep Portlemouth steps, carrying her suitcase. Iris thought it was five miles to East Prawle (in fact it's only about two). They would walk to Prawle where they stayed in what is now known as No 1 Corner Cottage (the one on the end at the top of the green), where her aunt Carrie Beer lived. (Carrie used to run the post office with her husband until 1915.)

Iris remembered:

If we wanted to go out we used to get up early in the morning and pick up the lorry which collected milk churns from the barns. He would take us round, do all the collection on his way and then he'd drop us off at Kingsbridge.

Pat Farleigh was born in 1924 and talking to Stephen Pedrick:

I cycled to Kingsbridge for a long time, for music lessons. I started when I was eleven, until I was fourteen. ... I think it used to take me forty minutes to go in; I used to cycle out Ford way and come back through Stokenham; but it used to take me longer coming home 'cause I had to push up all they hills, and I only had an ordinary bike, you see, no three speed or anything.

Railways

The great railway engineer, Isambard Kingdom Brunel, first proposed to bring a railway to Kingsbridge in 1836, when he surveyed possible routes between Exeter and Plymouth, but a line was not completed until fifty-seven years later. Lack of money and rows over the route of the line were responsible for the delay.

S P Fox wrote:

Kingsbridge people now will not care much which line is made: they want railway accommodation, and how it comes they will not greatly care. Whether any of the present generation will live long enough to see locomotive engines bustling in and out of a railway station at this place, remains to be proved.

On 5th April 1848 Wrangaton Station was opened on the Great Western Railway adjacent to the new main route to Plymouth. The name was changed the following year to Kingsbridge Road Station, to reflect the fact that travellers to the Kingsbridge area alighted here to catch the stagecoach for their onward journey. ... In 1895 following the opening of a branch line from South Brent to Kingsbridge through the Avon Valley, the station reverted to its original name.

The line was completed to Kingsbridge only and opened on 19th December 1893, the company having been absorbed by the GWR ten years earlier. Nationalisation in 1948 brought few changes, the route becoming part of the Western Region of British Railways. Traffic continued to diminish and both freight and passenger services ceased on 16th September 1963, although Brent remained open for a further year. It was a lovely old line that 'Primrose Line'; it was a beautiful ride.

Kingsiridge Station and Dartmouth Coach (Cookworthy Museum PO849a)

Kingsbridge Station (Cookworthy Museum PS3454)

Dr Beeching, chairman of British Railways, became a household name in Britain in the early 1960s for his report The Reshaping of British Railway, commonly referred to as 'The Beeching Report'. This led to far-reaching changes in the railway network, popularly known as the Beeching Axe.

Sadly the railway to Kingsbridge was axed at this time and there is little left to show for it. By 1982 the station yard became an industrial estate. The main station building survived but was demolished finally in 2009, leaving only part of a platform.

The Salcombe and East Portlemouth Ferry

I have been unable to find the exact date when the ferries started between Salcombe and East Portlemouth, but I suspect a long time before the information I have managed to find below.

Abraham Hawkins in 1819 wrote:

The breadth of the harbour (Salcombe) in the narrowest part is scarcely two furlongs. The East side is in the parish of Portlemouth. Betwixt these shores there are passage-boats. For a horse the charge is three pence (but double on Sundays); and for a man a penny.

Ellen Luscombe mentioned 'going over the ferry to my friend at Portlemouth Rectory' in *Myrtles and Aloes* published in 1861.

James Fairweather in 1912 wrote: 'The ferry is taken to Portlemouth. ... Soon a lane is seen on the left descending to the foreshore, which is known as Higher Passage Way, and it is here where horses and carriages conveyed across the harbour by the horse-boat attached to the ferry, are landed and embarked.'

The ferry is not mentioned in Kelly's Directory of 1888, but it is mentioned in 1906.

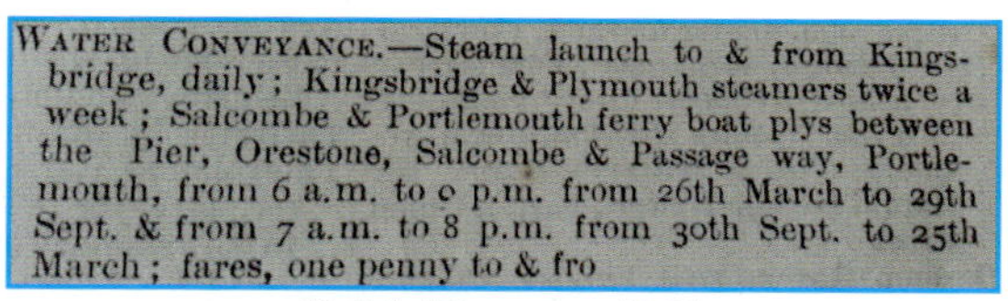

WATER CONVEYANCE.—Steam launch to & from Kingsbridge, daily; Kingsbridge & Plymouth steamers twice a week; Salcombe & Portlemouth ferry boat plys between the Pier, Orestone, Salcombe & Passage way, Portlemouth, from 6 a.m. to 9 p.m. from 26th March to 29th Sept. & from 7 a.m. to 8 p.m. from 30th Sept. to 25th March; fares, one penny to & fro

Kelly's Directory 1906

The first motor ferryboat plying between Salcombe and Portlemouth 1911. (Cookworthy Museum P0126)

East Prawle Public Transport

Again from Roger Grimley I learnt:

The first ('proper') bus (rather than carrier's van) came to Prawle when the Great Western Railway opened a Road Motor Bus service between Torcross and East Portlemouth on 13th July 1925. Passengers from Portlemouth, Prawle and Chivelstone changed buses at Torcross to continue their journey to either Kingsbridge and Plymouth or Dartmouth.

From 26th November 1925 some buses ran through from Portlemouth to Kingsbridge Railway Station but as from 9th July 1927 this ceased and it was again necessary to change at Torcross.

As from 1st January 1929 the GWR road motor services and those operated by the National Omnibus & Transport Co were merged into a new company, Western National Omnibus Co Ltd. They took over the route to Portlemouth and numbered it 110.

During the winter the bus for the service was kept at Harry Sanders garage at Torcross but in the summer it was garaged in a building belonging to Mr W F Harding at East Portlemouth.

In October 1934 the service comprised:-

A journey from Torcross at 9.30am to East Portlemouth

Returning at 10.35am to Stokenham where there was a seven minute wait for the bus to Kingsbridge or ten minutes for Dartmouth.

In the afternoon a bus waited at Stokenham for the 5pm Kingsbridge – Dartmouth and ran out to Prawle and Portlemouth.

Travel by Road!

SOUTH DEVON AREA
(No. 2)

1st to 31st AUGUST, 1938 (inclusive)

110 KINGSBRIDGE, TORCROSS AND EAST PORTLEMOUTH 110

Weekdays only.

		am	am	pm	pm
Kingsbridge (Station)	dep	9 15	11 0	2 20	6 35
Torcross (Post Office)	dep	10 15	11 50	5 20	7 40
Stokenham	..	10 20	11 55	5 25	7 45
Dunstone	..	10 31	12 6	5 36	7 56
Chivelstone	..	10 41	12 16	5 46	8 6
East Prawle	..	10 48	12 23	5 53	8 13
Rickham Lane (for Gara Rock)	..	10 54	12 29	5 59	8 19
East Portlemouth (P.O.)	arr	10 59	12 34	6 4	8 24

		am	am	pm	pm
East Portlemouth (P.O.)	dep	9 0	11 5	3 5	6 20
Rickham Lane (for Gara Rock)	..	9 5	11 10	3 10	6 25
East Prawle	..	9 11	11 16	3 16	6 31
Chivelstone	..	9 18	11 23	3 23	6 38
Dunstone	..	9 28	11 33	3 33	6 48
Stokenham	..	9 39	11 44	3 44	6 59
Torcross (Post Office)	arr	9 44	11 49	3 49	7 4
Kingsbridge (Station)	arr	10 45	12 54	4 58	8 9

Bus Timetable in 1938

Both journeys operated every weekday. The fare from Portlemouth to Stokenham was one shilling.

Some buses used on the Portlemouth service had bonnets that projected beyond the radiator and this gave the appearance of a snout. As a result they were referred to as 'Flying Pigs'.

The Coleridge Bus

For the past 30 years, when the service began with a bus on loan, volunteer drivers have brought people from the rural surroundings of Kingsbridge into the town - picking up in different locations each morning from Tuesday to Friday every week.

The service is self-supporting - not grant aided; 30 years of fund-raising have kept the Coleridge Bus independent. It is regulated and bound by legislation in the same way as other public transport services. All the volunteer drivers hold PSV licences which qualify them to drive anything from a small bus to a double-decker. The challenges of the narrow, twisting South Hams lanes dictate the size of the Coleridge Bus.

The Coleridge is probably the longest running community bus in the South West and, as far as we are aware, is the only operating on a full bus company licence and operated by volunteers.

As I mentioned at the start of this chapter, the Coleridge Bus comes to East Prawle on Wednesdays to take people to Kingsbridge for their shopping.

Religion

The Twentieth Century

I am a churchgoer, not a regular churchgoer but, now we live in East Prawle, we support the fund raising events to raise money for St Sylvester's Church, at Chivelstone, which is always desperately in need of money. I am donating the profits from this book to the church.

150 years ago the church was at the centre of village life. Religion in one form or another was the focal point of Sundays in particular. There were several services on a Sunday. For example, quoting from the Woodleigh Deanery Magazine of April 1919, during the Easter period on Good Friday: Mattins [sic] and Liturgy 11 am; Devotional Service 2.30 pm; Evensong and Sermon, 7.30 pm. Easter Day: Holy Communion 8.30 and 11 am; Mattins 10.30 am; Children's Service with Prize-giving 3.30 pm; Evensong 6.30 pm – this at St Sylvester's alone. On normal Sundays St Sylvester's had two services a day, one at 11 o'clock and one at 6.30, until it was reduced to one 11 o'clock service. The Chapel also had two services a day, one in the afternoon and one in the evening.

There was the Methodist Chapel at the top of Providence Hill and St Sylvester's Church at Chivelstone. The church people went to St Sylvester's and the chapel people went to the Methodist Chapel. Although sometimes the church people went to the Methodist Chapel, it was rare for it to be the other way round (the Chapel was in the village and easier to get to). The exception was weddings and funerals because the Methodist Chapel had no licence to perform these functions and so they took place at St Sylvester's in Chivelstone.

The end of the First World War probably saw the beginning of the decline in church going – now Sunday attendance is the exception rather than the rule. There is still a weekly service at St Sylvester's, and our present vicar, the Rev Pam Kemp, oversees seven parishes and is kept very busy. She came to this area in June 2011 and by February 2012 had held 22 funerals – a sign of the times around here.

Winnie remembered, when she was young and sang in the choir on Sunday mornings and afternoons, she would cycle or walk with two girlfriends to St Sylvester's:

We'd go in the afternoon walking, and take our tea, and in the summer we'd sit just on the steps to the right, up around the church. We'd sit there, we girls ready for the evening service, but when it was winter, the church was always heated by the coal boiler. You can see the pipes outside if you look up. So in the winter we'd sit around there and have our tea, ready for the evening service at 6.30.

During the war she walked to Chivelstone to church and, after a service there, she walked on to have lunch or tea with the Easterbrooks, her husband Wilf's parents, in South Pool. She then walked back again for a further service at the church and back to Prawle for an evening service at the Methodist Chapel. She remembered the lovely little lanes, full of primroses in the summer, and no traffic. In those days the road was still a track.

When Winnie and Wilf were first married they also went sometimes to the Chapel if they didn't have time for the church service, particularly once Winnie started playing the organ there:

That's when they only had one service at Chivelstone. They'd have one in the morning and the Chapel had one afternoon and evening. I was always free to go to both. In the middle of the Chapel, where it parted from the Sunday School, was the pulpit for the parson – it was a proper religious place.

Elaine Trant, Winnie's daughter, remembered going to a Methodist service in the Chapel. Mr and Mrs Rundle were always in the front pew, with Winnie and Elaine in the one behind and Osmond Moore beside them. When it came to the sermon either George Rundle or Osmond Moore would pass a boiled sweet back or forth (one for Mrs Rundle as well) – a lot of sweet paper rustling took place throughout the sermon – they couldn't sit without having a sweet!

St Sylvester's Church, Chivelstone

S P Fox in 1874 wrote: 'The church at Chivelstone is an ancient one, dedicated to St. Silvester; this is the only church named in his honour in all England. The old rood loft remains, and the pulpit is formed of a solid block of wood.'

According to the *History of the Priory of Totnes,* the Chapel at Chivelstone was listed amongst its property in 1288 and it became part of the property of the Priory of Bisham, Berks, in 1495. Joined with Stokenham, Chivelstone was taken by the Crown at the dissolution of the monasteries.

John Stabb in his book *Some Old Devon Churches* (1908):

The church consists of chancel, nave, north and south aisles, south porch, embattled west tower with five bells, and is mainly Perpendicular in style. The oldest part of the church is the chancel, which was erected early in the

14th century, the aisles were added a century or more later. There is a fine rood screen of the Dartmouth type, extending across nave and both aisles. The groining is gone and the spandrels are filled with the remains of the old carving. There are painted figures of Apostles and bishops on the lower panels of the chancel screen, in the aisles the panels are decorated with arabesque patterns. There are north and south parclose screens. Special notice should be taken of the pulpit. It is all in one piece, being hollowed out of the trunk of a large oak tree; the outside has been shaped into octagonal form, and is richly carved and painted to match the screen. The living is a chapelry annexed together with the vicarage of Sherford to that of Stokenham. The registers date from 1630.

Kelly's Directory of 1939 stated:

The church was restored in 1897 and affords 200 sittings. The register dates from the year 1684. The living is a rectory annexed to South Pool, joint net yearly value £435, and residence in the gift of the Lord Chancellor (two turns) and Col. W. Parker (one turn) and held since 1931 by the Rev Bernard Norton Adams BA of Selwyn College Cambridge.

It is believed that the country was divided into ecclesiastical parishes by around 1200, in the case of Chivelstone the parish was focused on the church with its dedication to St Silvester, the only such dedication in the country. However, the medieval dedication was to St Mary, Silvester not being recorded until 1742.

The Screen dated 1460

There is a note beside the screen: This beautiful screen dated 1460 is made of Spanish Chestnut. It had much of its tracery outlined in brilliant colours. Unfortunately over a century ago it fell into a sad state of ruin, but in 1979 the centre section was dismantled and restored in the workshop of Herbert Reed & Co. Exeter. Before being replaced, a plinth was set into the floor. The centre panels were cleaned.

The Pulpit

Looking towards the Altar

Probably no one knows much about church attendance in the old days. However, from the 'Chivelstone Parish Heritage Appraisal' we know that 1851 saw the country's only religious census, taken on 30 March:

The parish church of St Silvester recorded 48 adults at the morning service and 38 children at the Sunday school, with 140 adults and 39 children at the afternoon service. At the Bible Christian Bethel at East Prawle village, erected in 1848, there were said to be 100 at the afternoon service and 80 at the evening service, while at the Independent Chapel at Ford (then said to have been erected around 1750) about 20 attended the morning service and 65 the afternoon service.

For full details of the Episcopal Visitation Returns in 1744 for Chivelstone, go to the website www.katejenningsprawle.co.uk. Visitations were the means through which Anglican bishops could gather information about their diocese and monitor the performance of the parish clergy.

The Organ

Winnie told me that at Chivelstone they had an American organ (thought to be given by Mr H Foss in November 1915), until on 1 December 1950 Miss Emma Foss presented the organ that is still in the church today. The organ was dedicated by the Rt Rev The Lord Bishop of Exeter. When the American organ was replaced it ended up in the belfry until it fell to pieces.

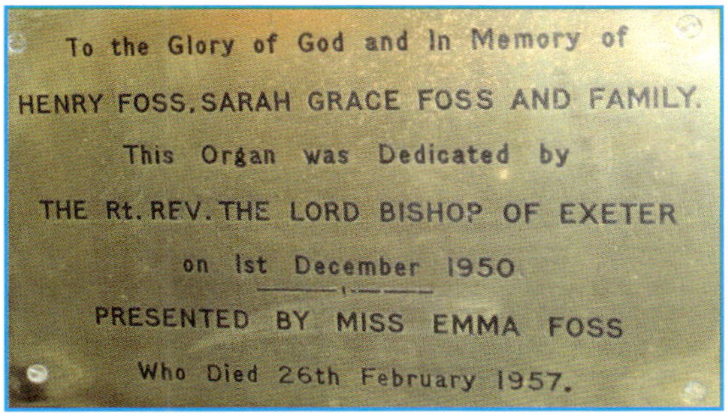

The dedication and organ of St Sylvester's

Winnie Easterbrook playing the chapel organ in the Community Hall

For the chapel services Winnie played the chapel organ that was stored in the Chivelstone Parish Community Hall, and is now in the church.

Winnie said she played at Hugh Helby's funeral at Chivelstone, and Miss Rosemary, his sister, said: 'Wouldn't my brother be thrilled to know you played at his funeral.' (Hugh Hunter Hasler Helby born June 1902, died June 1990.)

Organists

The Methodist Chapel	Chivelstone Church
Miss Polly Paige, who also ran the shop in the house now known as Kittiwake, up to the 1930s. Blanche Partridge/Moore née Tucker until her death in 1980. From 1980 Winnie Easterbrook continued even when it became the Community Parish Hall.	Miss Thomas and Miss Foss (in 1887). Miss Langdon for many years (resigning in December 1915). Miss Bessie Wotton, the under teacher at East Prawle School, up to the 1960s. Mrs Relle in the 1970s. Winnie Easterbrook, regularly until 2004. From 2004 shared between Jane Bickle, Jeanne James, Hillary Jarrett.

Funerals

In medieval times, each parish had a burial guild, which supplied bearers to carry the corpse; the coffin, however, was parish property, so the corpse was buried in its shroud, the coffin being taken back for re-use. Although it isn't known if this happened in Prawle, in the listed thatched cottage in Chillington, Living Waters, the right hand end of the rear wall of this room is a coffin-shaped recess reputedly housing the village coffin while not in use. Only the very rich could afford a separate casket in which to be buried. At the end of the graveside service, once the corpse was removed for burial, the coffin was returned to its niche in Living Waters ready for next time.

Coffins were made of wood. Nowadays they can be made of cardboard or, locally, even willows. Tradition was that a corpse must be carried feet first, whether inside a coffin or not. For funerals at St Sylvester's Chivelstone, there were two sets of coffin bearers who walked the coffin from the village to the church, a distance of two miles.

There were two undertakers in East Prawle, brothers Philip and Harry Putt. Philip Putt was carpenter and undertaker for the Church people, and Harry Putt was carpenter and undertaker for the Methodist people. Everyone was buried at Chivelstone, whether Church or Methodist.

I had hoped to have finished this book while Winnie Easterbrook was alive. Winnie died on 13 February 2012 just three weeks before her 100th birthday. Her funeral was held at St Sylvester's Chivelstone on 24 February 2012 where she is buried next to her beloved Wilf.

We all returned to the Community Hall where masses of food had been provided. At the end of the afternoon Jane Bickle played the organ Winnie always used to play. It was a rare sight to see three Tucker brothers gustily singing hymns along with the rest of us. I felt honoured to be part of it. As children they sat at the back and sang as loudly as they could to outdo Uncle Bill Putt, the Steward.

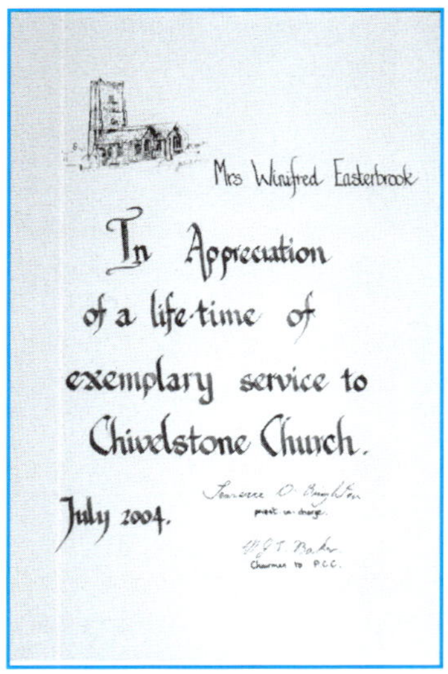

Certificate of appreciation

John Tucker recalled in his diary:

Jane Higgins (Bickle) played the Harmonium which Aunt Winnie always played. We finished up by singing a Methodist hymn, Roger and Vicky, William and myself. It was Blessed Assurance, the chorus is 'this is my story, this is my song, praising my saviour all the day long, this is my story, this is my song, praising my saviour all the day long' or words to that effect. It was a fitting end to Auntie Winnie's life for her favourite word was always 'lovely'. Everything was 'lovely'.

Memorial cards are a lasting and befitting tribute to a departed loved one and certainly one hundred years ago the practice was very common. There were no telephones for easy communication.

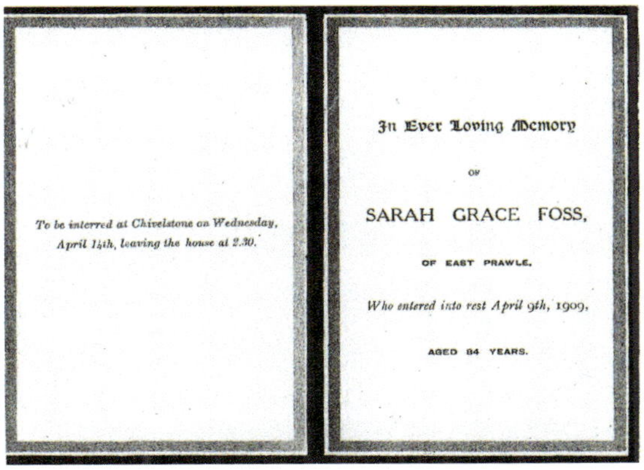

In Ever Loving Memory
of
SARAH GRACE FOSS,
of East Prawle,
who entered into rest April 9th, 1909,
aged 84 years.

To be interred at Chivelstone on Wednesday,
April 14th, leaving the house at 2.30.

The Graveyard

The church is set into the slope of the hill and the graveyard runs up the hill at the back. In 2013 the East Prawle History Society mapped out the graveyard and was able to document 366 graves; 1712 is the earliest found. There are several gravestones for sailors who died as a result of shipwreck (see more information on page 161). There are also many locals buried here.

St Sylvester's graveyard

Another view of the graveyard

Sunday School

There is no longer any Sunday School in East Prawle but in the past it was very different.

The Methodists had Sunday School in the Chapel and St Sylvester's had Sunday School at eleven o'clock in the Assembly Room, once it was built. Once a month they would go to the church service. Before then Winnie thought that as a child she would have gone to Sunday School in the chapel, but she wasn't sure.

Uncle Bill Putt and Aunt Bessie

Bill and Bessie Putt, always known as Uncle Bill and Aunt Bessie, were the Steward and

Stewardess at the Methodist Chapel and they also ran the Sunday school. (Uncle Bill's father ran the Sunday School before him.)

Both religions would join together and sometimes go by bus to Plymouth. Richard Partridge has a record of his grandfather's diary 'taking a motor van and motor car to Torcross and return with children.' The diary is dated 1924. Sunday School was important in the Prawle Fair Whitsun celebrations (see Festivities on page 110).

From the Woodleigh Deanery Magazine of August 1907:

The Choir and Sunday School had tea at Lannacombe, on Saturday afternoon, July 20th. We hope everyone enjoyed the lovely weather, and the excellent tea provided by Mrs Quick. The Coastguards were very kind in taking the children out in a boat.

In 1910 the outing appears to have been at Sherford, and the Prawle children went in wagons; and in October 1918 at Mill Bay:

Mill Bay was the delightful rendezvous of our Sunday School children on Thursday, September 12. Mr Baker, of South Allington, kindly provided a wagon, and we all went for a ride, at least as many of us as the wagon would hold; the rest getting to the beach on 'Shanks pony.' And what huge fish we caught. And what beautiful sand-pies we made! ... Never, we can say, has a group of children behaved better, never has more generous good feeling prevailed.

In January 1919:

Our Sunday School, consisting of about twenty scholars, forms one of the most promising features of our work at present. Most of the children are very regular in attendance, coming considerable distances in all winds and weathers. They are well-behaved and attentive, they are interested in their lessons, and sing quite heartily. It would do their elders good to look in upon them occasionally on Sunday afternoons; they would always be welcome.

Sunday School outings, probably in 1924

The Choir

From the Woodleigh Deanery Magazines in about 1907 to at least 1922, it is clear that the choir of St Sylvester's played an important role. As mentioned above in August 1907 the choir had tea at Lannacombe with the Sunday School.

In March 1908:

The choir, ringers and other Church officers spent a pleasant evening together, in Prawle Schoolroom, on Friday evening, February 7th, as the guest of Mr Churchwarden Pitts and the Vicar. Mrs Rendle spared no trouble, and provided a most excellent supper, which was thoroughly appreciated by all, the table and room being beautifully decorated by Miss Langdon and other kind friends.

A similar meeting took place in April 1909, and again in February 1912. From the January 1922 Woodleigh Deanery Magazine:

The Choir sang carols the week before Christmas at Kellaton (Tuesday), Larnacombe [sic] (Wednesday), S.Allington and Chivelstone (Thursday), and Prawle (Saturday). The sum collected was £5.14s and is to be given to the Sunday School. ... We believe Mrs Pitts is giving the children a tea, Mrs Helby is supplying a Christmas tree, and the sum raised by the carols is to be spent on loading the tree with presents for the children. We thank Miss B Wotton and the Choir and congratulate them.

The Church Bells

Originally the church had five bells and it is thought that the sixth bell was added in 1892, for the wedding of a Miss Prettyjohn to a Mr Pitts. The original five bells were rehung with timber from Diptford in 1896 specially for the wedding of Miss W Harris-Pitts.

A further bell was added in 1952 and was presented by Miss Emma Foss. I discovered this recently when Elaine Trant, Winnie's daughter, was clearing out and found the dedication on the right.

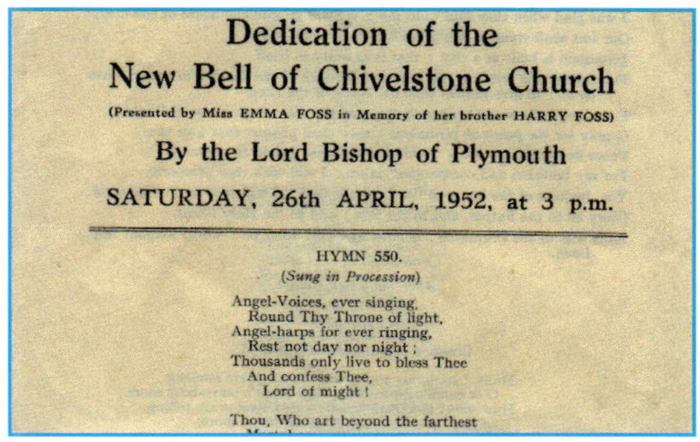

Dedication of the
New Bell of Chivelstone Church
(Presented by Miss EMMA FOSS in Memory of her brother HARRY FOSS)
By the Lord Bishop of Plymouth
SATURDAY, 26th APRIL, 1952, at 3 p.m.

HYMN 550.
(*Sung in Procession*)

Angel-Voices, ever singing,
Round Thy Throne of light,
Angel-harps for ever ringing,
Rest not day nor night;
Thousands only live to bless Thee
And confess Thee,
Lord of might!

Thou, Who art beyond the farthest

From an unidentified source I have the following information regarding the five bells:

The Church Goods Commissioners in 1553 found at:

Chenellyston iiii belles yn the tower theire.

Ellacombe recorded five in 1865, of which he reported that: 'the first is broken, the second cracked.' Of these the 1st, 2nd, and 5th, appear to be of the same date, the other two later. They are most elaborately inscribed, as follows:-

1. Musich is not worth a groat.
2. But yet the music wont agree
   Unless tis seconded by me 1710
   William Dyer, Esqr, Nicholas Came deputy warden,
   & Richard Partridge warden.

3. William Sumpter & Nathaniel Hawkins C.W. 1798 C.P. S.P.
4. Thomas Cornish: John Chope C.W. SP:CP: WP: 1779.
5. Yet all is a confused noise
   Without my last commanding voice.
   Richard Came: Edward Luscombe: 1710.
   John Crouch: Crispin Collins: Frederick Barker Vicar. Joshua Crane.

This last bell bears the stamp of John Stadler of Chulmleigh, who may be assumed to have cast the three bells dated 1710. He cast seventeen bells in this Diocese, but does not appear to have put his quaint rhymes on any but these.

In the Woodleigh Deanery Magazine of November 1919 it was noted that new ropes for the bells were needed. By January 1920 the new ropes were in use and the bell ringers spoke well of them.

The Hand Bells

I have only been able to find a fragment of information concerning the hand bells, which still exist and are used on a fairly regular basis. From the Woodleigh Deanery Magazine of June 1923 the fund raising tea for the bells is mentioned.

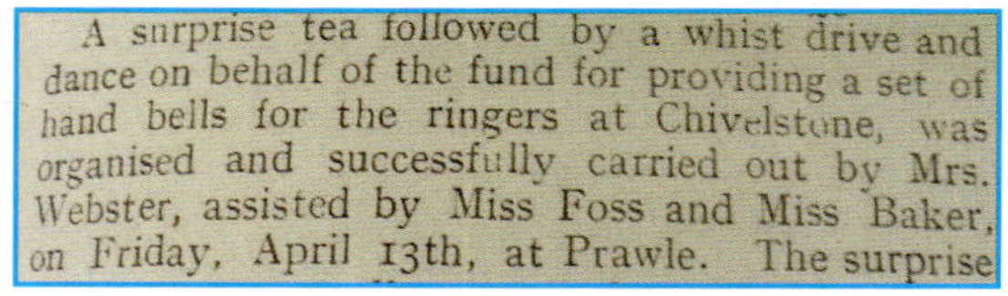

A surprise tea followed by a whist drive and dance on behalf of the fund for providing a set of hand bells for the ringers at Chivelstone, was organised and successfully carried out by Mrs. Webster, assisted by Miss Foss and Miss Baker, on Friday, April 13th, at Prawle. The surprise

June 1923 Woodleigh Deanery Magazine

In September 1923 the Magazine stated that the Rev Maurice R Bailey will be very grateful for £5 further donations towards the set of hand-bells before they can be bought.

Nancy Richards, in the 'Chivelstone Parish Millennium Book', was a regular attendant of Sunday School. She learned hand bell ringing and at Christmas there used to be about 20 people who went round to the outlying district ringing the hand bells. Although considerably younger, Sarah Trinick also remembered going round the villages with the hand bells at Christmas.

Lighting

From the Woodleigh Deanery Magazine of January 1937:

Chivelstone Church has now a much brighter and warmer feeling on the dark winter evenings, as it has been lighted with five hanging Aladdin lamps. Mrs Webster and Miss Foss were instrumental in providing three of them. Miss Braine-Hartnell kindly provided another and the fifth was provided out of the reserve Church fund.

Chapel of Ease

During the medieval period, wealthy landowners often owned private chapels of ease for their personal use and chapels were also provided for the use of remote communities by religious institutions. The chapels at Sherford and Chivelstone, founded by the late 13th century, attached to Stokenham, eventually became parish churches in their own right in the 1530s.

We know from W A Roberts that in 1547:

The churchwardens of Stokenham pay … 12d for a chapel and associated building near Hallsands and 12d again for a chapel and associated building near to Prawle.

It may be speculated that these chapels at Hallsands and Prawle … their presence immediately on the coast may have something to do with the availability of sea transport. A funeral procession travelling from Prawle or Hallsands to Stokenham churchyard by the narrow pack horse lanes, rocky in summer and deeply muddy in winter, could otherwise have a difficult and distressing journey.

From the New Venture newspaper for the Exeter Diocese dated June 1979:

It has long been a source of discontent that Chivelstone should be attached to another parish. Although attached to Stokenham, apparently Chivelstone had always elected its own Church Council and controlled it own affairs. It also had a resident curate. At that time independent status was not to be and in 1931 the chapelry was moved from Stokenham and attached to South Pool.

Use it or Lose it

In the 1970s the church at Chivelstone was so poorly attended they were thinking of closing it, however, the parishioners formed the Friends of Chivelstone Church. The Sunday School was restarted, coffee mornings, country fairs and concerts took place and a choir was formed.

Roger Tucker recalled that on impulse, returning from delivering cauliflowers up the country, still in his working clothes, he called in on the Bishop of Exeter in an attempt to create the parish of Chivelstone rather than being tied in with South Pool. In 1977 the Bishop of Plymouth came to Chivelstone and held the first Confirmation Service there that anyone could remember.

On 1 April 1979 H M The Queen having signed the Order in Council, Chivelstone obtained independent parochial status within the new united benefice of East Portlemouth, South Pool and Chivelstone. On 22 May the Bishop of Exeter came to Chivelstone Church to preside over the institution and induction of the first incumbent of the new benefice (the Rev John Taylor).

Jane Cater's wedding, the first after the change, 26 June 1979 at Chivelstone Church

At a meeting in late December 2016 with Robert Waterhouse (now Field Archaeologist at Société Jersiaise, but used to live locally) he gave us the following information regarding the church:

The main part of the church dates from somewhere between 1536 and 1549. The tower and the chancel predate this, but the nave and aisles were rebuilt at that time, replacing an older structure which probably had no aisles, but might have had a transept. The rood screen was built for the original church (around 1500 in his opinion), hence the fact that it doesn't fit perfectly in the new structure. There were probably wooden casements around the pillars to hide this. This means that the outer sections of the screen are slightly later (1536 -1549). They don't have saints depicted on them as this was in the early days of the reformation and papist adornment was no longer acceptable. They have arabesques painted on them.

The painting on the roof may well be a Victorian renovation, painting over older paint beneath, but the roof itself is original with some renovation. The bosses on the roof are largely original, but one or two may be Victorian replacements.

He suspects that the 'crypt' is not actually a crypt, but a vault dug at a later date.

The font is just post reformation as it has no decoration at all. Originally the church was a chapel of ease so was not allowed to carry out baptisms (or marriages), hence it did not have a font at the beginning. The pulpit is carved out of one piece of wood and the base is Victorian. The roof in the porch is interesting because 'wagon roofs' in porches have rarely survived.

Bible Christians and Methodists

From the Millennium Book:

On 10 May 1848 an indenture was granted for 1000 years at a cost of one shilling per year. It was granted between William Nicholls of the first part, Mary Chope of the second part and William Richards, John Weekes, George Burgoyne, Peter Hannaford, Thomas Lee, John Godwood, James Godwood and Robert Burgoyne of the third part. Together they built a meeting place of cob and local stone with a slate roof. This was for the Early

Bible Christian movement, which had come to East Prawle from North Devon. These buildings were said to be called Providence Halls. The Bible Christian Movement became the Methodist Church, and regular meetings and services were held in the Methodist Chapel until its closure in the 1990s.

In 1907, the Bible Christian Church in England was amalgamated with the United Methodist Free Churches and the Methodist New Connexion, to form the United Methodist Church. Richard has a document listing the Trustees for the Chapel in East Prawle at this time.

The Methodists in East Prawle were deeply religious. Uncle Bill Putt never read anything but the Christian Herald on a Sunday and was shocked if he found anyone cutting a cabbage or picking peas; there were six other days of the week. Children were only allowed to play quietly. From *Sisters Against the Sea:* 'Children were not allowed to go out to play on Sundays. They had to amuse themselves as best they could without being noisy or getting dirty'.

During most of the twentieth century local chapels were well attended but congregations gradually dwindled, and eventually both the chapels at East Prawle and East Portlemouth closed in the early 1990s.

The building that was the Methodist Chapel and is now the Chivelstone Parish Community Hall, was a meeting room on the Tithe map of 1842-47 and then opened as a chapel in East Prawle in 1848. It was a low square building with hipped roof, shown on the First Edition Ordnance Survey 25-inch maps (published 1867-1890) as 'Bible Christian Chapel'. The chapel closed in 1996 and was bought by the Parish in 1997, then renovated with heritage lottery money as well as other grants and donations. It opened on 19 August 2000, continuing the building's life as a meeting place for local people. The hall is well used and enjoyed and is an enormous asset to the community.

2011 Providence Hill and the Chivelstone Parish Community Hall

19 August 2000 from the left Vicky Tucker, Winnie Easterbrook, Phyllis Wotton and Professor Smith (taken at the opening of the Millennium Community Hall)

St Brendan

There has been much research into the existence of a chapel dedicated to St Brendan (the Navigator) located in East Prawle but there is no firm documentary evidence and no surviving structural evidence. St Brendan (one of the early Irish monastic saints circa 484-577) was ordained by Bishop Erc, Bishop of Kerry, and sailed around northwest Europe spreading the

Christian faith.

Historians have referred to the chapel but it is not known how long it had been in existence. Anne Born writing about the Celtic influence mentioned St Brendan and the clifftop chapel at Prawle Point. W G Hoskins wrote that there was a medieval chapel at Prawle, dedicated to the 6th-cent. Irish Saint Brendan, now quite gone and he mentioned 'St Brendan, the navigator, rounding the foaming Start and raising a chapel on the headland of Prawle.'

Jeanne James, who lived in East Prawle, wrote in 'Devon & Cornwall Notes & Queries' that:

> The medieval chapel of St Brendan at Prawle (Southpralle) is first documented on 24 June 1421, in the register of Edmund Lacey, Bishop of Exeter. Being pre-Reformation, it would have been a Catholic chapel. The vicar of Stokenham was granted licence for divine service there.

Robert Waterhouse in his 'East Portlemouth Heritage Appraisal' also wrote about a chapel dedicated to Saint Brendan. It still existed at Prawle during the 15th century. The 'Chivelstone Parish Heritage Appraisal' noted that in the 1750s there was said to be a former chapel at East Prawle, by then converted into dwelling houses. This is thought to be the three houses on the right after Higher Farm as you enter East Prawle – the fields behind known as Chapel Park (numbered on the Tithe apportionments of 1842-47), and Chapel Lane leads up to the houses.

It does seem more likely that the chapel was in the village itself. Richard, whose family dates back at least to the 16th century in East Prawle, has spent many hours researching this, and thinks that the site of the chapel is where the cottages adjoin the field called Higher Chapel Park – again mentioned in the 1842-47 Tithe apportionments and map of Chivelstone parish.

Richard noted that Jeanne James had been delving into chapels on the coast and thought the chapel was somewhere else in the village. However, he has also received details where it mentioned 'chapel houses burning down and new houses being built'. He thought that's why Jeanne couldn't find anything about the chapel; because the houses were burnt down in 1700s and subsequently new ones were built.

In the 'Devon & Cornwall Notes & Queries' of August 2014, Jeanne James has written a further article entitled 'New light on the site of the medieval chapel at Prawle' confirming her agreement.

Recently Richard was given a copy transcript of an indenture dated 1869 which refers back to a 'certain term of three thousand years commencing on or about the 1st May 1597.'

Extracts from Richard Partridge's transcript of the indenture of 1869 are on the next page.

Thomas Perrett - of one pt and sd Thomas Perrett of or pt in conson of natural love and affection wch sd William Perrett had and bore towards his son sd T. Perrett the dwellinghouses heredits and premes with appurtenances thrinar descbd were (inter alia) assigned by sd William Perrett to sd Thomas Perrett his executors administrators and assigns for all the then residue of a certain term of Three thousand years commencing on or about the 1st May 1597.

of 2 dwellinghouses formerly called Chapple Houses and wch were originally burnt down TOGETHER with the gardens belonging to same and held therewith all wch sd premises thrinbefe descbd were for the ppse of identification only and not by way of limitation more parlarly delineated on the Map or Plan attached thrto and thron coloured pink and green respectively.

ALL THAT dwellinghouse or houses and other bldgs many years since erected by one John Blank on the site of two dwelling-houses formerly called Chapple Houses formerly burnt down with the Plots of ground and rickplace walled in thrunto belonging situate lying and being at East Prawle in psh of Chivelstone in sd Coy of Devon formerly in posson of sd John Blank his

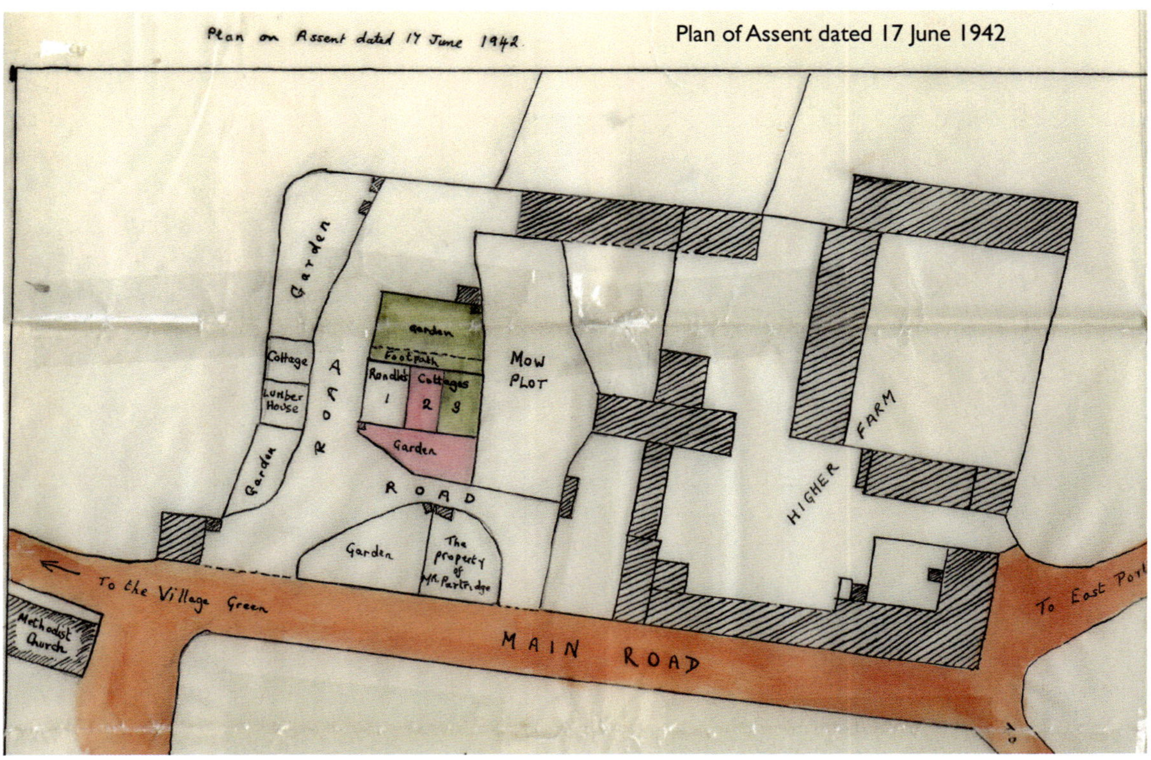

Plan of Assent dated 17 June 1942

Festivities

Prawle Fair and Whitsun

Markets and fairs have existed for centuries – for the buying and selling of animals and produce, often with amusement stalls, sideshows and rides – hence fun fairs as well.

The first fairground rides appeared in the eighteenth century. These were small, made of wood and propelled by gangs of boys. In 1868, Frederick Savage, an agricultural engineer from King's Lynn, devised a method of driving rides by steam. His invention, a steam engine mounted in the centre of the ride, transformed the fairground industry.

Whitsun

Pentecost is part of the Moveable Cycle of the ecclesiastical year. According to Christian tradition, Pentecost is always seven weeks after Easter Sunday; 50 days after Easter (inclusive of Easter Day). The feast is also called Whitsun, especially in the United Kingdom.

Winnie Easterbrook told me Whit Sunday was always to do with the Methodist Chapel. The children would say scripture pieces in the chapel (which is now the Chivelstone Parish Community Hall). There was a platform – Winnie remembered being on it herself. The school children would each be given a scripture, or text, to say. One year it was the Creation and then, Harry Putt would ask the question 'Who created the world?' Up would jump one of the boys, say 'God', and so on.

The Methodist Chapel in 1961

Much later, Richard Partridge, Alice Stone and Brenda Jeffery also remembered the children would recite pieces of poetry and little extracts from the Bible. Brenda remembered:

We used to do it Whit Sunday and Whit Monday. Mum used to buy us our new dresses and you'd go up and they'd have a platform there for all of us. Miss Wotton used to do the church Sunday School, and she would come down with her children. Uncle Bill Putt (the Methodist Chapel Steward and my grandfather) always took the Christian Herald and we would be made to learn verses from it and take it in turns to stand up and recite them.

Alice Stone remembered she used to be put in one of those basket chairs her mother had and they would lift her onto the stage.

All the children would go around the village singing hymns on the Monday afternoon to raise money for both the Chapel and the Church. Then the children and some of the grown-ups would have a tea party in the Sunday School room, attached to the Chapel, before the evening service. They also remembered that an organ was placed on a wagon pulled by a horse, and the children then went singing. Mary Blanche Partridge (Winnie's elder sister and Richard and Michael's mother) played the organ.

Prawle Fair in the 1970s

Prawle Fair

Prawle Fair is a major annual event nowadays here in East Prawle, but its history is somewhat confused. References can be found in Directories dating back to 1847 and it is possible this custom was a Christianised version of an older festivity associated with Spring and marriage.

Prawle Fair 1973

In the 1878 Kelly's Directory a fair was held on Whit Tuesday, but there are no other references. However, we know Prawle Fair took place in 1912 because Pat Farleigh's parents (Emma Wood and John Henry Putt) met there.

Prawle Fair 1980

Prawle Fair was always held on Whit Monday, as part of the Whitsun celebrations – organised by the chapel but all religions joined in. Winnie remembered before the Second World War they used to come with swing boats – different from the ones Alan Blyth now brings each year.

Prawle Fair 2002

Winnie recounted in Stephen Pedrick's book:

We used to have Prawle Fair on Whit Monday and Miss Pritchard used to come from Kingsbridge with her pony and trap, and all her 'fairing' and glorified 'ice-cream'... custard and all that and well... a sixpence would buy more than you wanted, 'cause farthings counted as well. In the evening there would be a 'kiss-in-the-ring' in one of the fields. They'd come from Beesands, all around, and then somebody would come and knock you out... you'd go running and when they caught you they'd kiss you...'course you could easily slip up in a cow dab as you was going around!

Winnie also recalled that people came with swing boats: 'not like you get now. They were little things to ride on.'

I have talked to several people born and bred in the village and it is a mystery why Prawle Fair stopped. There was a long period when Prawle Fair did not take place, perhaps because of the Second World War. It was started again in 1972/3 by Roger Tucker and Robert Melville and then stopped again the year Roger had to deal with a field of hay as a matter of urgency (and which in the end he lost). However, moves were made to restart it and so it recommenced, certainly by 2002 and continues to the present day; a very successful event.

The Raising of the Glove

Kingsbridge has had a long association with the Abbots of Buckfast, who were originally lords of the manor of Churchstow when Kingsbridge parish formed part of the manor. The then Abbot obtained the right to hold a weekly market in Kingsbridge in 1219 and later the Abbot John Matthew applied for a royal charter to hold an annual fair in the town. This was confirmed in 1461.

The Raising of the glove Prawle Fair 2011

The link with the 1461 charter is continued at the glove hanging ceremony on the Wednesday evening of every Fair Week, when the charter is read by the town mayor and a stuffed and garlanded glove is hoisted on the Shambles in Fore Street, to show that the fair is in progress and to signify free trade and clemency for its duration.

Although it is a Kingsbridge custom, it has also become a Prawle Fair custom. Vicky thought the original reasoning was that the ladies wore gloves with a posy to put up to their noses – a nosegay – to ward off the farm animal and general fair smells. This seems very likely!

Christmas

The history of Christmas traditions changed enormously in the 19th century, when most of the familiar components of the modern Christmas including St. Nicholas, Santa Claus, and Christmas trees became popular, as did decorating the house and tree with holly and mistletoe.

The Christmas tree first gained popularity in British and American society thanks to the husband of Queen Victoria, the German-born Prince Albert. He installed a decorated Christmas tree at Windsor Castle in 1841 and woodcuts of the Royal Family's tree appeared in London magazines in 1848.

Victoria and Albert gathered around the Christmas tree with their children

Robin Stanes wrote:

Christmas was a great feasting time, the 12 days of Christmas really meant 12 days holiday. The cows were mostly dry, the ewes had not started to lamb, wheat and rye were already sown, barley and oats could wait for the spring, most of last year's harvest was still in store and the hard days of February, March, and early April, when supplies of food and corn and hay and perhaps firewood ran low, were yet to come.

Winnie's candle holders

Winnie remembered they didn't have a fir tree but a piece of holly and Elaine, Winnie's daughter, remembered they had candles that they lit on a peg – you could only light them for a few minutes before they fell off.

Winnie talked about having turkey at dinner time, always with sprouts, turnips, carrots, parsnips and potatoes. The vegetables would all be boiled, even the potatoes. Then at tea time it would always be savoury, a boiled ham perhaps, followed by the cake. If they had supper it would be around nine, ten o'clock at night. Winnie remembered one year they had roast rabbit.

John Tucker talked fondly of Christmas at Lower House Farm in the 1950s. Christmas started in February 'with the geese making their big strong nests on the other side of the pond in old dustbins laid on their side.' His mother would collect the eggs and put them in the dairy on a grapefruit tray and turn them every day. 'Is there any broody hens, I will get the cellar ready to sit them'. They would be put in the cellar in the nesting boxes and a few weeks later lovely goslings hatched, yellow and fluffy. 'Mum would bring them in as they hatched and put them in a box and wrap them up in a woolly jumper by the Aga or Lidstone. All great fun. When strong enough they would go in a coop in the front garden, getting them ready for Christmas.'

John also remembered they 'had turkey for dinner and tinned peaches with bread and butter for tea. Auntie Winnie spread it so thin it was supposed to be better for you.'

Roger recalled, when he was young the Tucker's, Easterbrook's and Partridge's all went to Town Farm for Christmas Day.

Richard also remembered:

I hung a stocking up on Christmas Eve, but cannot remember having many presents, perhaps a book or two !! Always a lump of coal, an orange and some sweets in my stocking. Until I was about 11 years old, all Granny and Grandad Tucker's family would meet at Town Farm for a Christmas Dinner, always about 1pm. My father would always dress up as Father Christmas and give out presents to the children after the meal.

Easter

For some reason Winnie and I never really discussed Easter. All I know is that everyone went to church; the ladies in their Easter bonnets. I have asked various people but it is clear Whitsun seemed to be a much bigger village event.

Harvest Festival

Although the number of church goers has declined, harvest festival is always well attended.

In Britain thanks have been given for successful harvests since pagan times. The celebrations on this day usually include singing hymns, praying, and decorating churches with baskets of fruit and food in the festival known as Harvest Festival. We must all be familiar with hymns such as 'We plough the field and scatter' and 'All things bright and beautiful'.

From 1900 in the Woodleigh Deanery Magazine we learn that Prebendary Churchward took the Harvest Festival services for more than 30 years. His death is recorded in the January 1917 magazine. In the Kelly's Directories from 1888 the Rev Marcus Dimond-Churchward, MA, vicar of Northam is described as one of the principal landowners in East Prawle. He owned Higher Farm and Lower House Farm. His niece, Miss Ellie August Sarah Braine-Hartnell, inherited the farms and she first appears in Kelly's Directory of 1919.

According to early Woodleigh Deanery Magazines tea after the Harvest Festival was always arranged in the barn at South Allington owned by Mr Pitts. Later Mr Baker's barn was used, and sometimes Mr Tolchard's. Certainly when Winnie was in her twenties, she remembered there was a service for Harvest Festival at Chilvestone followed by a tea down at South Allington in one of the barns there.

Elaine Trant, Winnie's daughter remembered produce was brought to the Methodist Chapel where an auction took place. When the chapel closed, the auctions stopped. The Church held them in the Providence Inn until it closed, and then moved to the Pigs Nose, where it continues to be a popular annual event.

Farming

'I have been in all the counties of England and the Devonshire husbandry is the best'

These were Oliver Cromwell's words spoken in company at Hampton Court in 1658 and recorded by John Aubrey.

Introduction

This isn't about farming – I am no farmer, only a farmer's daughter. Earlier I mentioned my mother bought a farm in Warwickshire during the Second World War. She wrote two books about her experiences and a further one on milking and one on British Agriculture. I am quoting her on some of the topics later in this chapter.

It is possible that most of the farms date back to Saxon times, although evidence is lacking. The 1086 Survey recorded three manors in what was to become Chivelstone parish, all assessed at one hide and all owned by Iudhael of Totnes ... Chivelstone had its full complement of three ploughs, which were worked by three villeins and three smallholders, along with three acres of meadow and six of pasture, and was valued at 15s.

Both Prawle and Woodcombe possessed commons, enabling the cottagers to survive by grazing a few animals. The commons were stinted - numbers of beasts were restricted - as indicated by the occasional reference to someone exceeding his quota, as well as encroachment onto them.

A survey on the available corn was carried out in 1623 because of failed harvest the previous year. This survives for Stanborough and Coleridge hundreds and at Chivelstone records the 12 principal farmers whose households contained an average of just over nine persons. (See more population details in Appendix I on page 178.)

From the end of the eighteenth century until the First World War, most farmers in the South West were tenants with leases of seven, 14 or 21 years. At the time of the Tithe map (1842-1847) the Rev Marcus Dimond Dimond-Churchwood, vicar of Northam, owned Higher Farm and Lower House Farm which were rented out. His niece, Miss Braine-Hartnell, inherited the farms and continued to rent the farms out for many years.

Kelly's Directory of 1919, 1926, 1930 and 1935 cite Miss Braine-Hartnell as one of the principal landowners in East Prawle. Little is known about her but Winnie Easterbrook, Derek Wotton and Richard Partridge remembered hearing her name as landlord. It is thought she lived in Totnes and died at the age of 90.

Farming has changed considerably in the last hundred years. In the past many men were needed to work on the farms, with ploughing, harvesting and threshing, managing the horses, and other tasks. Machinery has replaced much of the need for manpower and of course horsepower. Farms which in 1851 employed up to 18 workers now use only casual labour and at that date the parish population was almost double what it was in 2001.

Until relatively recently farms were small - before the Second World War there were 50 acre farms, usually mixed farms: cattle, sheep, pigs, hens, crops etc. The main crops were wheat, barley and oats. However, between the wars, tenants were able to buy their farms and there has been a steady decrease in the number of farms. Roger Tucker told me that the land they now own used to be 23 land lots.

From Robin Stanes in *A History of Devon*:

Farmers paid great attention to their banks and hedges. Hedges had to be cut and laid when the field took its turn to be ploughed. Corn ground needed a good stock-proof fence, and around the grass fields a bank and hedge gave good shelter to outwintered stock. Faggotwood and cordwood were also valuable products. The height of the Devon bank can be as much as six feet, on top of which is the hedge; the core of the bank may be stones, boulders and tree stumps from the time when the land was cleared. Some banks are at least a thousand years old.

Woodland was also important to the countryman. Firewood and peat were the only local sources of warmth before the 18th century. The undergrowth of woodland was coppiced – cut to ground level – every 15 years or so, and the produce sold for firewood, tanning or charcoal. Timber trees were preserved in the hedges and woods by landlords, and cattle excluded from woodland, which was too valuable. Furze or gorse was also used as a fuel. It was burnt or singed before cutting to remove the prickles, and then made into faggots of 'black sticks' for firing the household boiling coppers. Uncut, it could also provide useful winter fodder for cattle.

Green Lanes

The English countryside was once covered by a network of green lanes, in use from prehistoric times. They were the routes for Roman legions, mediaeval travellers, tradesmen, drovers, and miners with their wares. Some go back to Iron Age and Bronze Age times, being routes used by farmers to drive their animals to market or between upland and lowland pasture. Such footpaths, bridleways and long-distance trails are part of our living history.

Anne Born quoting Westcote in 1630:

Devonshire is full of hills and valleys … very uneasy for travellers and their horses. Before human beings could ride through it all they had to clear away some of the dense forests. Waves of immigrants arriving at the coast could penetrate inland only along the high ridges of the hills, and thus were marked out the prehistoric ridgeways still followed by 20th century roads. They follow driftways and cattle routes inland and may date from before the Bronze Age.

From the 'Chivelstone Parish Appraisal':

There were occasional references to trussways and sandways. The former appear to be packhorse routes that were to become known as green lanes, while the latter enabled farmers to carry sand and seaweed from the beaches to fertilise their fields. At Woodcombe in 1577 John Pounde 'wrongfully ploughed up a path called a Sande Waye and a Trusse Waye' and was required to reinstate it.

Animal Droves to Dartmoor

The first time I heard about cattle droves to Dartmoor was at a talk by Robert Waterhouse at South Pool in about 2008. Since then I have discovered that this was a yearly occurrence in East Prawle. And it is clear that animals have been grazing Dartmoor since the Bronze Age.

In historical times the 70,000 acres of moorland were divided into quarters, North, South, West and East. These quarters would be rented by 'agisters' or 'moormen' who would then organise the grazing and welfare of the cattle in his charge or sub-let parcels of land. The farmers who owned the cattle would then pay a fee to the agister for his services. The practice of pasturing cattle on the moor was known as 'agistment'.

For grazing purposes the high rainfall and the moisture holding properties of the peaty soil have meant that in dry summers when the lowland grazing would have dried up, the moorland grasses continue to grow and provide fodder for the cattle.

Robert Waterhouse referring to Ford in the Domesday Book said this was a prehistoric fording point of a small stream on an important north south route. It was almost certainly a drove road used in transhumance, from the coast at Prawle to the moors around Stanborough, and further towards Dartmoor.

Also: 'Transhumance, the practice of grazing stock in different places (often some distance apart) in the summer and winter, seems to have been widely practised in the South Hams before the Norman Conquest.'

When the cattle were being moved onto or off the moor it was described as the 'Red Tide', because most of the cattle were of a red colour and there were so many of them in the droves.

Animals were taken to Dartmoor in order to free up the fields to make hay for horses. Cattle can eat straw, although they also eat hay, but horses – the most important and hard working animals only eat hay.

Derek said: 'Yes. Cows ate the hay as well – they didn't all have straw. However, they had to move the cattle to get enough land to grow the crops on. They weren't big farms, a lot of these farms now were three or four farms. I mean they were family farms years ago, not big farms.'

Derek remembered taking the cattle to Dartmoor several times, and Richard remembered that he once went as a young boy. They went with Father Partridge, Derek's father-in-law and Phyllis and Richard's father. They left East Prawle with about 18 animals, some having come from East Portlemouth. They went down to South Allington to pick up Fred Tripp's cattle. From there they walked through Ford and Kernborough, where they picked up Farmer Helmer's cattle. By this point there were 50 to 60 cattle. They carried on through Tanpits Lane to Chillington, up to Coles Cross and on to East Allington where the cattle would spend the night at Lower Coombe Farm.

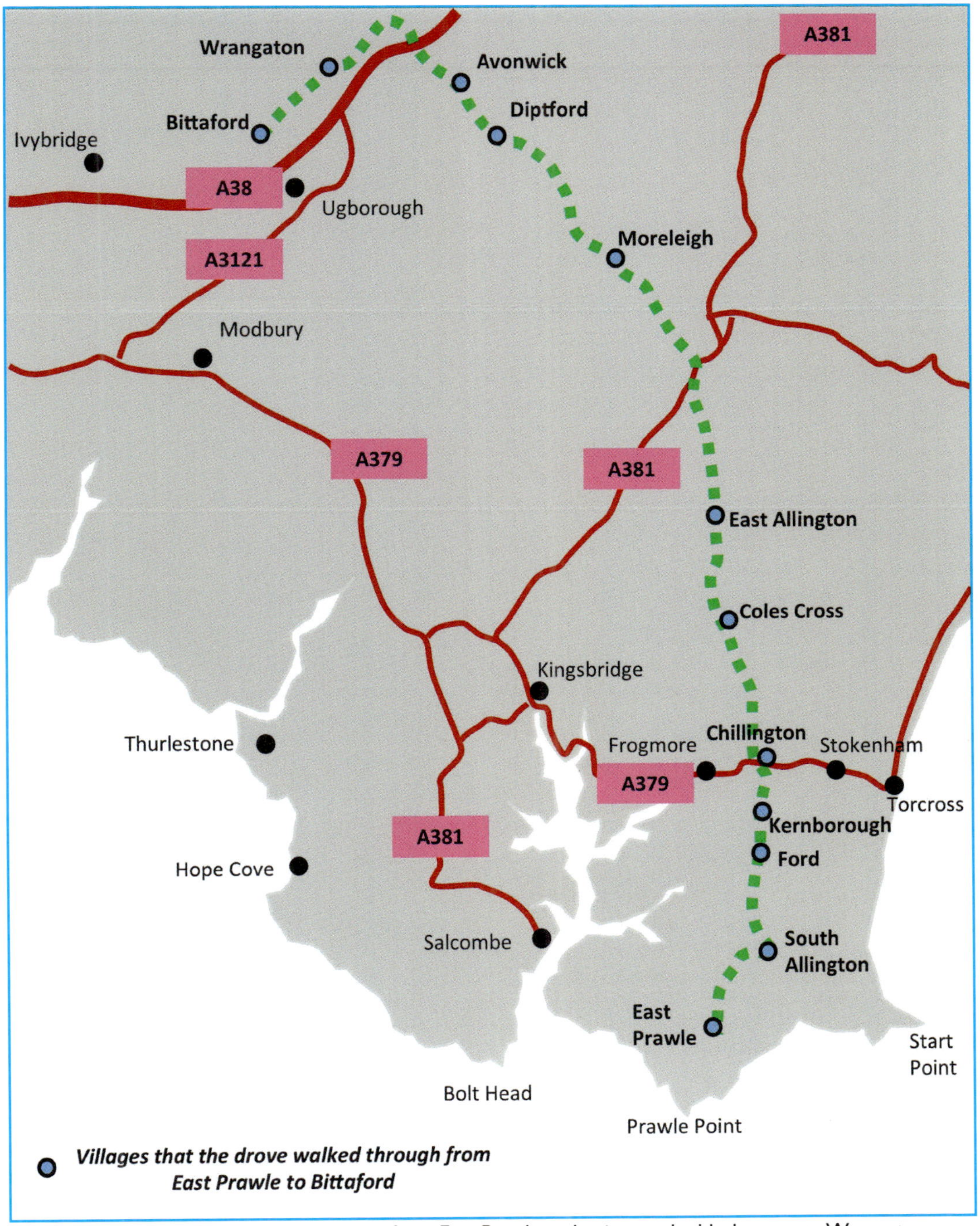

Driving cattle to Dartmoor starting from East Prawle and going up the black route to Wrangaton

The next day they would travel from East Allington up through Moreleigh to Diptford, Avonwick and finally across the main road to a farm at Wrangaton. The farmers there took over looking after the animals on Bittaford Moor. It seems incredible to have achieved this in just two days – nearly 20 miles. However, in those days there was only the occasional car.

Derek also remembered they would have people standing in gaps in the road and entrances to houses all along the way. One time the cattle were straggling for about three miles long in the narrow roads – and somebody reported them!

A herd of cattle walking through Chillington, photograph donated to the Cookworthy Museum by Rosalind Page in 2009 (PS2830)

The cattle's return journey also proved interesting. If the animals were out on the moor, they had to be rounded up. There weren't any tags or numbers on the animals. Some would have branded horns and some brand marks on the rump, P for Partridge or T for Tripp. It was quite a feat to sort the animals out.

Michael Trant, whose parents used to farm at Northern Town, South Allington, said that Luscombe and May used to hold auctions at the Kings Arms in December, known as the 'winter keep sale'. Farmers from all around, but mainly from the Moors, would come and buy swede and kale fields for winter keep.

A remnant of medieval times is that many moorland farms have Common Rights attached to the farms. This gives them the right to graze a specific number of animals on their local moor. The Manorial System means that Livestock can only graze on the piece of Moorland belonging to the Manor in which the farm is situated. Some farms have Venville Right. This is a right to graze on the 'Forest of Dartmoor'. This dates back to the time when the Duke of Cornwall was given the bulk of Dartmoor by his father, the King, as a hunting Chase, but primarily as an opportunity for the young Duke to gain experience in man management in preparation for when he became King in due course.

It isn't clear when this arrangement ceased, but probably in the early fifties. The combination of foot and mouth, the military use of the moor and far more traffic on the road made it unfeasible. Tractors and lorries were replacing the need for horses and the long journey to the moors.

Diana Shelvoke remembered that her grandfather, Richard Sawtell of Higher Farm, had a shepherd who used to take sheep to Dartmouth market. Dartmouth was too far to go in one day and so the shepherd arranged to put them up overnight at a farm en route. The shepherd, whose name she can't remember, wouldn't stay at the farm even though there was a bed for him. He walked back to Prawle for the night and was back again early the next morning.

Dartmoor has a long connection with the Duchy of Cornwall. Edward Plantagenet (The Black Prince) became the first Duke of Cornwall in 1337.

Horses

From *Traditional Farm Buildings of Great Britain* by R W Brunskill: The horse was the prince of animals; providing mobility for the knight in war and for the gentleman in peace. It was for many centuries spared the labours of the farm. The ox was the draught animal. The horse was expensive to buy or rear, temperamental in use, tending to fragility in health, expensive to feed and requiring a special diet, including oats. The horse also required special grooming and was almost worthless when dead. The ox, on the other hand, was correspondingly cheap to rear, stolid and docile in the yoke, hardy, not prone to sickness, easy to accommodate, undemanding in food and providing valuable meat and skin when a useful life came to an end. But the ox was slow and far from versatile, and so from the seventeenth century onwards was gradually replaced by the horse.

Horses have been essential to man's livelihood, hence 'horse power'. They were necessary for country life and farming – they did all the work a tractor now does. They also created a lot of employment for people: blacksmiths, saddlers, coachmen, horsemen, grooms etc. Before the coming of the railways, the speed of the horse dictated the speed of life - it was leisurely.

Horses continued to be important for agriculture until the Second World War when pressure on food production became greater. Although the Fordson tractors were available, the first mass-produced tractor, the Fergusson, manufactured in Coventry, did not start production until 1946.

Jane and Richard Partridge told me about George Tabb, Derek's cousin, who used to work at Woodcombe. He walked to Woodcombe in the morning, worked behind the horses all morning – ploughing or working the fields. At midday he'd tie the horses by the side of the hedge and put a nosebag on each of them, so they fed while he walked to Prawle for his dinner. He returned to Woodcombe, and worked on into the evening before walking back to Prawle for the end of the day.

1930s William Albert Partridge (Richard's father)

Shoeing a horse was a regular event. Charlie Yalland was the last blacksmith in East Prawle and he was still working in his late 80s.

At the Forge - Philip Putt, with grandsons Ashley and Elwyn Ford. Behind is Charlie Yalland (Great uncle to Ashley & Elwyn), village blacksmith 1937

Michael Partridge told a wonderful story about Charlie Yalland: 'if you had a broken chain, or broken equipment, and brought it back from the fields before Charlie's lunchtime, he would repair said object before having his lunch and leave it outside for you to collect on your way back to the fields from your lunch.'

Derek on Bill beside Captain

Derek told me, aged between 6 and 8, he was put on a pony with a cart and he went from High House Farm (towards East Portlemouth), down Holset Lane to Goodshelter where he'd collect a couple of bags of coal. The coal was put in the cart for him, Derek gave the money and turned the pony round to return. The pony knew where he was going because he'd been there before! That could never happen nowadays.

Bullocks

'Every good farmer loves a bullock. Show him a bunch of good bullocks and he will take out his pipe, rest his elbows on the gate and settle down for the afternoon.'

The definition of bullock – a gelded bull, steer, or mature castrated male bull destined for meat production.

In the 18th century bullocks and sheep were sold at Dodbrooke market and fair, with those cattle bred on the commons said to be smaller than those reared on the farm.

Winnie's memories of bullocks:

The bullocks which went to market were kept in the barns at Torrings to fatten them up. They had mangers from which they fed rather than running around – they'd be eating all the time to get fat.

Wilf Login in Stephen Pedrick's *A Century of Memories*:

There was a barn where they used to fatten the cattle in the winter, and they was tied up in there: they'd never come out, they'd be stood in that shed for about four months. They'd just get mangolds and hay and straw ... and to tie them they had a chain around their neck, down through a loop and a block underneath so they couldn't pull it through. That chain used to go up and down and what a clatter! Cor like thunder! ... right next to my bedroom. At about eighteen months they would be taken to market, walking all the way to Kingsbridge.

Bullock chain from Geoffrey Tripp

I can't resist quoting my mother, in charge of her bullocks:

A bullock that is doing well should merely eat or lie down. For some time ours had very little chance of lying down because when we were not feeding them we were peering in to discover whether they had lain down. The first sign that a bullock is really beginning to fatten is a little lump of flesh on the pin bones of either side of its tail. Next, meat begins to appear on the shoulder and it begins to sweat slightly. Then you can be sure it is doing well.

Philip Putt told his grandson, Ashley Ford, how, at the age of eight, when working at Lower House Farm he was put in charge of feeding the bullocks in Shadycombe Valley down at the Linhay. After the last meal of the day, he had to go down to feed the bullocks. He was terrified and said he tried once and was so scared he couldn't do it. He hid away with the lantern and crept back. However, in daylight he roughly timed how long it took to get down to feed the bullocks and gave them a double feed the next morning. Apparently he got away with it.

The Linhay at the bottom of Shadycombe Valley

Bullocks on Horsley Beach (from Didi Caudery)

It is a well known suspicion that for some people, ghosts lived in the Shadycombe Linhay, and for others it was a lovers' tryst. Ashley, who died in January 2017, believed he was conceived in the loft above, and has asked that his ashes be scattered there – to take place later in the year.

Mangolds

In the past, mangolds (short for mangel-wurzel) were a staple feed for dairy cattle and emergency food for farming families. If you had livestock or poultry, this was great animal feed, but it is no longer grown. (Nowadays it is sugar/fodder beet, which is much easier to grow and to store.)

A comment from Harold Widger on pulling mangolds:

Pulling mangold: that was alright if 'twas dry ... but cor, if they was wet they wouldn't twist, and wouldn't it try your hands! You weren't allowed to have a hook to cut 'em because it would spoil the top. The mangold used to be put in a 'cave' up against the hedge, and covered in with straw and all the broil: that's the parings from the hedges – that would keep them, or the frost would spoil them and they'd rot in no time.

A mangold is a large coarse yellow-to-reddish-orange beet that grows up to two feet long and is grown chiefly as food for cattle. However, fed immediately to cattle they cause stomach upsets. They need hoarding for a while so a sugar change takes place. They hoard quicker indoors hence the tipping into special root houses. The tops were never fed to the animals because they were poisonous.

Mangolds (from Tim Blyth)

Sheep

At the time of writing about sheep (the middle of March 2015) lambing around East Prawle is such a delight to see – the mark of spring with little animals teetering and skipping about.

Early lambing is popular in the South Hams because of its mild climate and the finished lamb price is at a premium for these flocks.

In the early 1900s, the majority of income from a sheep operation was from the sale of wool rather than meat. Today, it is the other way around. While wool is still important on many sheep farms, lambs almost always contribute the majority of income.

In the 1940s my mother wondered why anyone would work with sheep:

Almost all the work connected with them is disgusting. First they have a not very attractive smell, secondly they carry a species of tick which leaps gleefully on to the clothes of anyone who goes amongst them, and, although it makes its presence immediately felt, can usually only be found when preparing for the bath, thirdly their diseases are legion, and one more repellent than another. If their feet are not constantly attended to they develop a complaint called foot rot which stinks to the heavens and involves the paring away of most of the foot. They have regularly to be dosed against an infestation of worms. Finally in the summer they are attacked by the ordinary bluebottle, which lays its eggs in their fleece to turn almost immediately into a maggot, which runs in its thousands all over the body of the wretched host, biting and tearing the skin and leaving a dark damp trail in the fleece to mark its passage. When they are first born their tails have to be cut off and, if they are males, they have to be castrated. How, one may well ask, can anyone be willing, even gratuitously, undertake such work as this?

On the counting of sheep she wrote:

If anyone has any personal reason for wishing to go quickly off his head, I recommend as a method the counting of lambs in the spring ... I can never remember exactly where I started or be sure that the trio on the hill have not moved and been counted twice; and just when I have decided that I have at last got it right I think 'Damn, I don't believe I ever saw the triplets', and I begin all over again.

My mother's first sheepdog:

The Sunday before Meg's arrival we had gone out to move the sheep. They were all over a big field bordered with bushes, and, riding ponies and pausing not at all, it had taken us exactly one hour and a half to do the job. With Meg I could do it single-handed in ten minutes.

Meg

Counting sheep

Robin Stanes told the story of a ewe he was looking after that would not 'take' her lamb but butted it away when it tried to suck. The lamb was getting weaker and so the farmer came over and recognised the ewe as having reared a lamb well enough the year before. Whatever we did, she still wouldn't 'love' the lamb. 'Get the dog in,' he said. I had no idea what he was about, but duly got my dog into the pen. The immediate reaction of the ewe was to defend her lamb against the dog, to protect it and 'love' it. Fear of the dog, mother love, overcame her rejection, and that did the trick.

Derek's Greyfaced Dartmoor

Derek told me that, aged about 14, the sheep got out along Broad Road and into one of Father Wakeham's fields. Derek had to go and fetch them, and as he was leaving Mr Wakeham said to him 'Don't let that happen too often young man.' He continued: 'and another thing young man, don't let the sun shine twice with sheep in the same field.'

Pigs

Although we had a few pigs when I was a child, I remember little about them. However, Winnie remembered that almost every cottage had a pig.

From Robin Stanes:

Almost every rural household kept a pig. Healthy and omnivorous they would be encouraged to scavenge in the farmyard and the lanes until they were ready to be fattened. They were happy in a hovel, under the framework of a rick, or in a pile of straw. They had to be rung through the nose or they would rip up any pasture, but given some rough land, pigs would reduce it to a cultivatable state pretty shortly. Pigs are intelligent, know their own interests very well, and are not frightened of human beings. It is said that a cat looks down on a man, a dog looks up to a man, but a pig looks him straight in the eyes! ...

Again from Robin Stanes: 'Most farmers fed their servants on fat bacon ... pigs were fed to a vast size; the West Country simile is not "fat as butter" but "fat as a pig". So fat were they that the resulting bacon was one eighth of an inch to an inch of fat.'

William Stone told Stephen Pedrick they always kept two pigs. His father said 'you must have two – one would eat faster and more than the other, and then they'd be fat quicker!'

Roger's grandfather had the contract to collect all the swill from the RAF camp – the leftover food; given the number of servicemen there would have been a considerable amount of waste.

He transferred this to the swill boiler:

First on the left hand side, in Town Farm Gate, there was a little flat bit of concrete and the swill boiler. It had a big fire box in the bottom and you stoked it up with coal. It must have been about 5-6 foot high and 3 foot wide. On top was a big round container which was fixed on two hinge points, one each side. You used to chuck all the food waste into the swill boiler and put the lid on, screw it down and cook it, so you re-cooked it to get rid of all the bugs. There was a handle on the side you pulled to tip the swill container on the top. It had a spouty bit on one side and it shot out into buckets, and then you'd take it down and feed the pigs in the troughs.

Pig Killing

Pigs were only ever killed to be eaten when there was an R in the month. From May to August pigs were rarely killed as the meat wouldn't stay fresh for long enough. Pig killing was not for the squeamish as it was impossible to escape the squealing.

Once fat, the pig was placed on a form, held down and the throat cut with a knife down into the heart. Boiling water was then poured over the carcass to make removing the bristles easier. It took three men to manage this.

Winnie's memories:

We had a pig's form, a proper wooden pig's form where they tie the pig. A wooden bench. We'd say 'pig killer's coming tomorrow'. And then he'd cut the throat and down at the barn at the bottom of the court they'd hang the pig up, cut it open. Squealing and crying … it was wicked and cruel, wasn't it?

Once dead the pig was hung up by its hind legs.

Samuel Friend, Granfer Tucker, George Farrier

Samuel Friend on left and George Farrier on right

Rose, my sister, aged about five remembered she had lunch early to go and watch. In the event she was nearly sick, and quite fairly traumatised. She said: 'I remember thinking ...and I hurried through lunch for THAT.'

Elaine Trant (née Easterbrook) remembered: 'Well I've never watched it. The noise of it. There used to be pigs at Shepherds Farm. When I was going home from school, going round that corner and you'd hear them squealing.'

Rabbit Trapping

Rabbit has been a staple food in Britain for centuries. During the Second World War rabbit pie was never off the menu because it was cheap and plentiful.

The season for rabbit trapping was from October to April and so it was a popular business among the fishermen during the winter months when the seas were rough. There were times when the farmers made more from renting out their fields for rabbit trapping than the rent they paid for the entire farm in a year.

George Tabb wrote in the Chivelstone Parish Millennium book: 'We once paid £60 for the trapping rights … when the rent for the whole farm was only £56'.

A typical gin trap in the set position

The word 'gin' is believed to be derived from the word 'engine', which was used centuries ago to describe any mechanical device, and indeed traps were referred to as 'engines' in literature from around the 17th century. Steel-jawed traps have been used since the 16th century to catch birds, mammals and humans. In 1827 a bill was passed in England banning the use of man traps but the manufacture and use of rabbit traps remained legal until 1958.

The traps were called gin traps and were extremely cruel. When used, the jaws were forced open and held down by springs. When the animal stepped on the plate, the pressure on the plate released the springs forcing the jaws shut and trapping the creature.

Diana Shelvoke's dog got caught in a gin trap and, in releasing the dog, she managed to catch her thumb in the trap ... she had to have a tetanus injection!

As a young boy, Derek helped set and pick up all the traps. They went out at night setting the traps and rescuing rabbits from the traps before the foxes got them. Richard remembered the traps were covered with very fine soil, which was sieved, and where possible they used mole hills, the soil being much finer. The traps were set near the hedges where the rabbits had their burrows. Set one day and collected early the next. They could catch 100 rabbits at a go.

Richard told the story of his elder brother Michael Partridge and his gin traps:

Uncle Billy was taking Mike trapping with him. Mike prepared these gins, whether they were new gins or not I don't know, but he oiled everything so they would work all right and be easy. Mike was so proud. Uncle Billy tealed up his gins, set them and covered them with fine earth. Mike also set his gins but unfortunately Mike didn't catch any – Uncle Billy's gins were full of rabbits. I suppose Uncle Billy must have told him afterwards, he probably said (in a whisper) 'What d'you do to they gins? You shouldn't have oiled them!'

Diana also remembered Unity and Jim Putt going off to set the traps. They used the field above Elender Cove, near Maceley, where as well as catching rabbits for the farmers, they also used to plant potatoes. Jim carried the bucket with the sieved soil but Unity had the heavy chains and gins slung over her shoulder, clanking along. Diana also remembered that she would be sent up to Unity at home to get some rabbits – these were always under the kitchen table.

Winnie remembered that her brothers, Willie and Jack, would trap rabbits around the farm.

A man would come every week from Kingsbridge called Tonkin to collect the rabbits and their skins. He'd be collecting hundreds of rabbits. In those days there was money to be made out of rabbits and their skins. The rabbits would also be sold in the Dartmouth shop as well as being sent up to London by train.

The traffic in rabbits was considerable and a loaded van was regularly dispatched to the Midlands. It is for this purpose that carriage label boards 'Kingsbridge-Birmingham' were made – on the Kingsbridge branch train.

Jack and Willie Tucker with rabbits

Circa 1900 Kingsbridge railway station. Platform with crates of rabbits (PS3554 Cookworthy Museum)

In addition to gin trapping, ferrets were also used. Winnie recalled that you'd put a net over the hole and the ferrets would be released into the holes to chase the rabbits out. She also said they escaped one time in the kitchen. Both she and Gladys were found on the kitchen table!

Rats tails were collected by the official rat catcher when he came to Prawle. Mike and Richard remember the rat catcher coming to the village during and after the Second World War. The reward was one penny for each tail. There were several ways to catch the rats: (i) A spoonful of poison on the end of a long stick put into the rat holes; (ii) Mike and Geoffrey Tripp (senior) caught and killed rats with dogs around the ricks; (iii) The gin traps were set close to the ricks (not inside the ricks) and were left overnight.

Growing Vegetables

Winnie said that before the shop opened in 1922, they would go to the market square in Dartmouth on Fridays. They sold cauliflower, carrots, turnips, potatoes, peas, beans, all sorts of runner beans, broad beans, everything grown on the farm. (See Shops on page 70 for more detail.)

From about 1918 the Partridges also went regularly to Kingsbridge and Dartmouth with their vegetables to deliver round the shops - much later Derek went with them.

Cauliflowers

Although cauliflowers came to England in the 17th century, they arrived much later to South Devon.

Captain Helby, of Maelcombe House, first saw cauliflowers in Roscoff, during his duties as Chief of the Coastguards for South West England, from Portland to Bristol, in about 1915.

He moved to Maelcombe House in the early 1900s and started market gardening. He brought cauliflower plants home from France, but he didn't know what to do with a mature cauliflower.

George Currie cutting cauliflowers

Roger's grandfather was already trading at Dartmouth Pannier Market and so he took these cauliflowers to Dartmouth to sell – they were very popular. As a result, he asked fishermen trading between Roscoff and Dartmouth to bring back packets of the seeds from French farmers, when he put the different varieties into numbered sugar bags – to ensure other people didn't know the variety. He was the first person in South Devon to grow cauliflowers.

Thereafter until about 1999 the Tucker farmers ploughed seaweed into the ground (as fertiliser) before planting cauliflower down at Horsley (fifteen acres) year after year. The cauliflower seeds were sown in seed beds in May, the plants pulled in July and planted out in the fields in July.

Milking

I have already mentioned ('In the Kitchen') that in the early 1900s there were several farms in Prawle and there were around 6-10 cows for milking and providing milk for the village. It remained much the same for many years.

Roger said they always milked by hand:

> You used to milk one or two cows, then the milk was scalded to pasteurise it. We lived on scalded milk and what we didn't drink or sell was fed to the pigs. Milk was only used for the family and calf rearing.
>
> In order to make use of a cow's full lactation, she reared her own newborn calf and an additional newborn calf until they were on solid food, when two more new born calves were added and finally one newborn calf, making a total of five. Nowadays the bought calves are reared by specialist calve rearers who take day old calves and feed them on dried milk.

c.1969 Cows going in for milking Lower House Farm, David Parkinson on the right

Derek loved milking, sitting down and hearing the milk go ting, ting, ting, 11 or 12 ten gallon churns a day from 15-20 cows.

And now the Wakehams milk their cows with the use of computers! (See the next page.) The cows have learnt exactly what to do and take themselves in and out of the barn as they wish. They queue up for milking, the equipment automatically attaches to their teats and the milk is processed. When done, they go out through a special gate which leads them to their next pasture, or they can go back inside in the warmth. It's an amazing bit of kit and most of the time works very well.

Inside the Wakeham's milking parlour on the left cattle feeding and on the right queuing up to the milking process

Sand, Seaweed, Lime, Guano & Dung

Today fertiliser is commercially purchased. Formerly, however, sand, seaweed and lime were extensively used on the land to improve the soil and also for buildings.

Sand: Harold Fox in his *Evolution of the Fishing Village* wrote:

Among the commodities which were gathered on the shore, sand itself probably gave more employment than any other. Sand lightened soils, and containing pulverized shells, it helped to counter acidity. When Richard, Earl of Cornwall, around the middle of the thirteenth century, granted that sea-sand could be taken freely from the coasts of the county, he not only provided what is probably the earliest written reference to the practice in the South-West, but also testified to a contemporary perception among farmers of the utility of sanding...

The typically south-western practice of spreading sand on the soil gave livelihoods to people living near the coast or river shore. Men with barges plied their trade up-river from the coastal beaches and dank mudflats which provided their sources of income...

Sand was carried to inland farms by ...packhorse. As a method of payment landlords took a toll from each packhorse which left a beach to begin its laborious inland journey along tracks known as sandways.

Ellen Luscombe writing in *Myrtles and Aloes* in 1861 when she visited Maceley Cove:

This little cove was frequented by people from a considerable distance for the sake of the beautiful white sand, which is so scarce an article on that coast; but it could only be brought to the top by donkeys, and it was wonderful to see how the poor creatures picked their way round the projecting pieces of rock which rendered the path so difficult, never stumbling.

Above the cliff the lane leading up to Merrymore Lane is still known as Donkey Path.

Ellen Luscombe continued:

'A little labour would have at least made a tolerable path for these willing animals; but as usual, what was everyone's business in this case was no one's business, and the poor beasts were allowed to spend double the necessary time and strength in their journey. Bad economy one would think.'

On the next page is a section of the Tithe map (1842-47) showing the lane from Woodcombe down to Woodcombe Sands, near Lannacombe, on which pack horses travelled back and forth.

Seaweed: has always been used as a fertiliser. Again we know from the 'Chivelstone Parish Heritage Appraisal' that: There were occasional references to trussways and sandways. The former appear to be packhorse routes that were to become known as green lanes while the latter enabled farmers to carry sand and seaweed from the beaches to fertilise their fields.

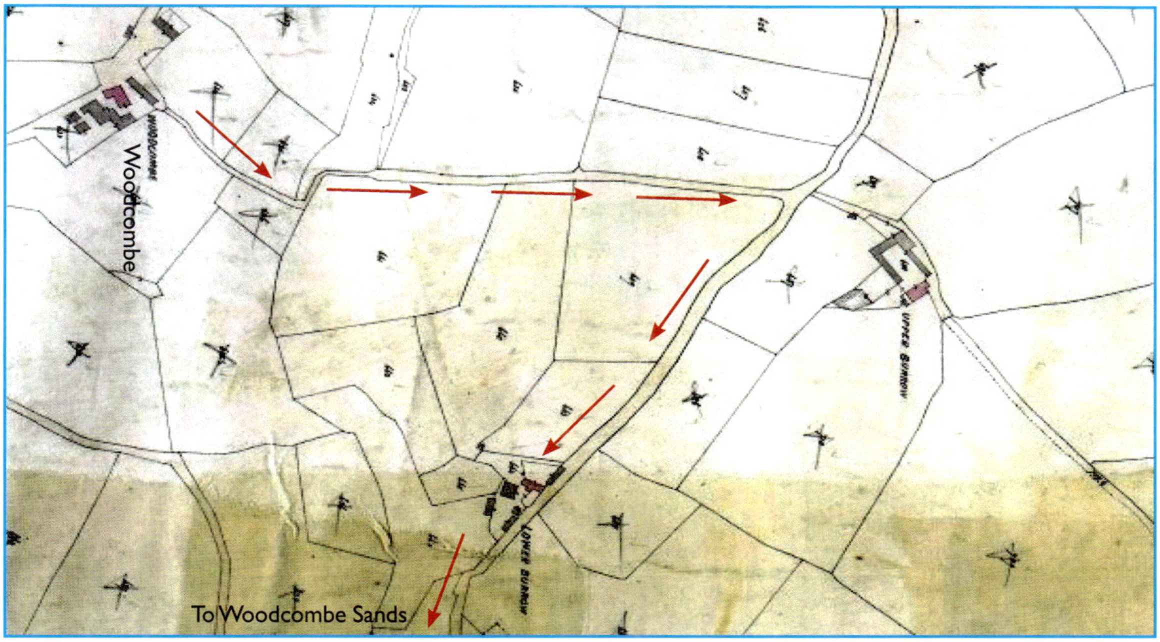

The Chivelstone Tithe map section from Woodcombe going towards Woodcombe Sands

For many years the Tuckers collected seaweed from the beaches, particularly Horsley for fertilising the cauliflowers growing down in the fields towards Horsley and the sea. (With the increase in the size and unwieldiness of modern tractors this has become impractical.)

Derek also remembered many years ago collecting sand from Mill Bay and seaweed from Horsley, no longer easy to get to with tractor and trailer.

William Tucker spreading seaweed above Horsley Beach

Collecting seaweed on Horsley Beach

Lime: A fourteenth century manuscript from Stokenham mentions the carrying of lime, and references to lime burning exist from 1630 onwards. At Frogmore where there were several kilns on the shore, limestone was shipped into the estuary and taken by horse or ox drawn sledge to the top of the kiln. It was then shovelled into the kiln in layers with wood or coal on a base of brushwood or gorse.

From Robert Waterhouse in his East Portlemouth and Stokenham Appraisals:

Limekilns began to be constructed alongside the tidal estuaries of Devon and Cornwall during the 18th century. Coal from South Wales and limestone from Torquay or Plymouth were brought by water and burnt in layers inside the kiln: a large conical shaft walled around with stone. The resulting lime could be used in mortar for building, but was more commonly used for reducing soil acidity in order to increase crop yields.

A 'burn' took from 3 to 5 days and, when completed, the lime was shovelled out from the kiln base. Great care was taken not to let the lime anywhere near water, on account of the violent chemical reaction this would cause, so this task would probably have been undertaken at low tide. Carts would take it to its destination, even if transport by water was faster: wetted lime could set a boat on fire!

In the early 1900s, Roger's grandfather had the contract to maintain all the roads in East Portlemouth, Chivelstone and South Pool parishes. This consisted of loading limestone rubble from Goodshelter, Frogmore and South Pool creeks at low tide (the limestone came in by barge at high tide), into carts pulled by two horses, with an extra horse to get round the steep corner at Goodshelter, and tipping it in heaps beside the road.

Limestone being delivered at Frogmore Bridge

Lime kiln in the Goodshelter area

Richard's grandfather, Richard Albert Partridge, kept a diary of all his dealings in the 1920s-1930s and there are detailed listings of the delivery of lime from Kingsbridge by horse and cart. He also took sand from Horsley, Lannacombe and Mill Bay to the builders in the area.

Anne Born wrote about buildings:

A curious phenomenon occurs in some old cottages on the Kingsbridge-Torcross road in the villages of Charleton and Chillington. Some of the broad chimneys lean markedly to the south-west from whence comes the prevailing wind. The reason for this is that the mortar – made of lime and sand – expands on the damp side away from the drying action of the wind and pushes the chimney towards the south-west.

Lime kilns eventually went out of use due to improvements in transport, such as railways, which enabled coal to be carried to large industrial kilns in limestone quarries.

Guano: Richard told me guano used to be imported from South America:

They'd bring it into Salcombe by boat. Maurice Putt remembered going with his father to Seacombe Sands: there was a barge loaded with fertiliser. They picked up the fertiliser off the barge and brought it to Prawle.

They used the sacks and bags for all sorts of things. Old men used to tie a West of England sack as an apron around their waists or over their shoulders to keep them dry. You would see Jack Hannaford, the fellow who used to work our horses, with a West of England sack around his shoulder, with a bit of string through the corner tied around there and also around his trousers as an apron!

Guano, or bird droppings, had been accumulating on the coastal islands of Peru for hundreds of years The realisation that seabird excrement (guano) had excellent properties as a fertiliser transformed western agriculture. For over a century the sale of guano was the single greatest source of income in Peru but, by the turn of the twentieth century, reserves had been nearly exhausted.

Dung: came in all sorts and was all mixed together. Winnie remembered the contents of the chamber pot were thrown onto the muck heap in the yard, and in turn spread upon the land.

In a *General View of Devon* Robert Fraser wrote:
In the greatest part of this district, the land thus prepared, is manured with a compost of earth, lime, and burnt ashes. ... In the southern part of this district, they are at a considerable distance from lime, and they therefore make use of sea sand as a substitute for lime ... which they mix with earth, the scrapings of the lanes, mud from ponds, bottoms of the ditches, etc. and above all, when they can collect it, with rotten dung ... all of which is generally carried on horses backs: on account of the country being hilly, carts are very little, or not at all, used, for the purposes of agriculture. The best farmers spare no expense, to collect these different manures, and mix them with each other with great care. This compost of dung, mud, and sea sand, is reckoned a most excellent manure, and more lasting than the composts with lime. This is practised, in great perfection, by the Messrs. Cornishes, at South Allington, whose farms would do honour to any country, and by all the farmers near the coast.

Threshing

There are several reasons for wanting to include a section about threshing. The first is that as a farmer's daughter I knew nothing about threshing.

In the early years of my mother's farming she was told:

You cut wheat when the grain is hard. You can bite it to find out. You cut oats when you squeeze it and find the milk has gone out of it. And you cut barley when the heads have dropped.' This is when to cut it. Then you need to store it and thresh in winter, or if you have a combine harvester straight away in one process.

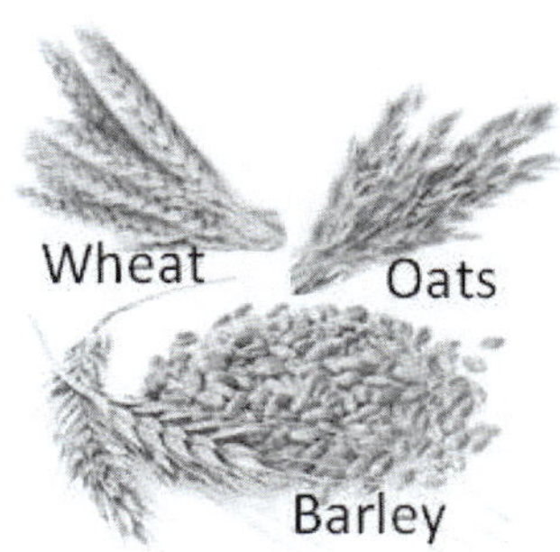

Threshing barns were characterised by large double doors in the centre one side, a smaller one on the other … The wind blew through and blew the chaff out one end. The design typically remained unchanged between the 12th and 19th centuries. The large doors allowed for a horse wagon to be driven through, the smaller ones allowed for the sorting of sheep and other stock in the spring and summer. For thousands of years, grain was separated by hand with flails, which was laborious and time-consuming. Mechanisation of this process took much of the drudgery out of farm labour.

Robert Waterhouse wrote in the 'Stokenham Heritage Appraisal': 'Horse engines, driving threshing and other labour saving machinery were a notable addition to many farms between 1841 and 1885, a relatively late modification in comparison with other parts of England.'

The second reason for wanting to write about threshing is that we now live in the modernised threshing barn of Lower House Farm in East Prawle - Sea Rocket Barn.

2013 Lower House Farm Threshing Barn (Sea Rocket Barn)

Richard once asked me if the round house was still there. I didn't know what he was talking about, but looking through our records when we bought the barn I found the diagram below:

The mechanism in this round house was to drive the threshing machine in the barn. The horse had to step over a bar going through, a metal bar that was turning and driving the mechanism. Later sometimes the machinery was above, so the horses didn't have to step over it. The shaft went above the horses and into the barn. The number of horses in use depend on what you were doing – cutting chaff only needed one horse but threshing all day three or four were needed.

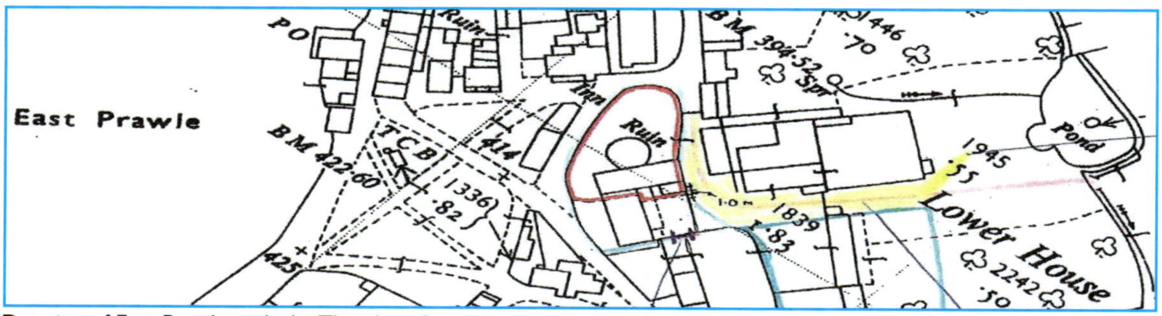

Drawing of East Prawle with the Threshing Barn and round house (long knocked down) marked in the red area, where the horses walked around to drive the mechanism working the threshing machine

Michael Partridge recounted his brother Bob's memories: 'the drive shaft revolving went into the barn down on the ground and the horses knew to stride over it. They never tripped over it.'

And in a later conversation with Richard I asked how the steam engine was used:

The steam engine drove the threshing machines, the mobile threshing machines. Early on they had threshing machines in the barns but they were small and it was difficult to store all the corn in the barn. This meant they had to build the ricks in the field, and then cart them into the barns to thresh, creating a lot of extra work. When the mobile threshing machines came around they were driven by the steam engines, and they could go out in the fields right beside the rick. That saved a lot of work.

There are many references in *A Century of Memories* to threshing and harvesting and how it was handled before combine harvesters. One in particular by Bill Widger was about traction engines and their use:

Goodman's had four traction engines, four sets: that's threshing-machines and engines. Their depot was out Holset, East Portlemouth. … The thresher used to go around to different farms and he'd have, say, four ricks. He'd pull the thresher in between them and thresh them all before he moved on. It was a dusty job sometimes, but it needn't be if it was picked up in good condition.

Postcard. Threshing machine powered by traction engine, travelled from farm to farm and required 11 men to operate

Built in 1904 Steam Traction Engine photographed at Avon Mill Autumn Fair 2010

Winnie on harvesting:

Mother used to make big currant buns, rock buns, sandwiches and all that, and take out 'drinkings' for the men. They called them 'drinkings', and I've still got the big copper kettle here, the copper kettle where you put a potato in the spout to save it splashing out. Mother would line a basket with a nice white cloth and put in cups, and I would go out and pour out the tea. We'd go to any field where they made a rick.

1946: Harvesting - Coolings Farm
Mary Blanche Partridge, Maureen Putt, Harold Hannaford, George Rundle, Jack Hannaford, Bob Partridge, Ern Putt, friend of Ern's, Ron Putt

Farmers' wives were expected to produce roast meat and apple pie dinners on threshing days, when neighbours came to help; and at harvest they appeared in the fields with jugs of tea and cut rounds, cream and jam and currant cake, all in wicker baskets covered over with white napkins.

Note: George Rundle, a villager, helped out at harvest time. Ern Putt, born in the village, moved away, but came back to help with harvest for several years. Ern Putt's daughter, Maureen also helped. Ern Putt's friend used to come on holiday to help with harvest. The others worked at Coolings Farm. Observe the kettle filled with tea in the front of the photograph (by the arrow) with a potato in the spout. to stop the tea spilling out.

I have said that my mother bought a farm in the war:

Threshing was a significant part of it: right until the end, that is until July 1943, threshing days remained a nightmare … Everything always went wrong on threshing days. Every man jack on this farm had a job to do connected with stock before breakfast, so it was never possible to start threshing until afterwards. My whole energies were given up to trying to ensure that we made a good start then. But we never did. Something would always go wrong. The belts would slip or the baler would get bunged up with straw and stop the lot, or it would rain and we would have to leave the rick we had intended to do and move into cover under the barns. … Of all the things I would rather not do, threshing takes first place.

My sister's comments on threshing:

My childhood was spent watching corn being harvested; first with cutters and binders drawn by tractors. Later in the winter, in the barns where the straw had been stored until it was needed, with threshing machines which mechanically beat or 'threshed' the corn seeds out of the straw. Then, in about the fifties, came combine harvesters which cut and threshed in one go and spewed out a line of straw while a baler followed behind. We used to ride on the side of the balers, watching as they gathered, compacted and tied up the straw into bales for storage. Nowadays great rolls covered in plastic appear in the fields and so I deduce that harvesting technology has moved on from the days of my youth.

Stephen Tucker combining in 2010

Roger Tucker's single furrow plough, now in St Sylvester's churchyard at Chivelstone

The combine was socially devastating: it undoubtedly saved time, but it isolated farmers and farm workers, and destroyed at a stroke the conviviality of harvest-time, the enjoyment of local cider and one of the building blocks of rural community life. Nevertheless, the introduction of tractors and combines and the departure of farm-workers were only the preface to the real story of modernisation.

Flowers

Flowers, or rather cut flowers, were an important resource in Prawle. Granfer Tucker grew Arum lilies in Town Farm garden and Uncle Bill Tucker grew chrysanthemums indoors in the greenhouse at Town Farm, and again in front of the greenhouse. Roger remembered they grew cultivated Devon violets down the valley in a big patch every spring. The women used to pick them and the flowers would go to the shop in Dartmouth. They would also go to Kingsbridge Station or Dartmouth and be sent up to Covent Garden. Narcissi and daffodils were grown along Ash Park in Under Torrs field. Geoff Tripp grew anemones and Fred Tripp primroses.

Diana Shelvoke remembered that she used to earn pocket money from Geoffrey Tripp. She would pick the anemones that grew down in Lower Holloway and then bunch them up. Fred Tripp down at South Allington grew primroses and anemones.

John Tucker remembered: 'They grew daffodils in the flat field on the cliff top, in the old cliff gardens and as children we had to pick them and bunch them ready for the shop in Dartmouth'. John also remembered they planted gladioli outside Sunnyside: 'a splendid sight for all to see'.

Prawle Point Birds and Birdwatching

Prawle Point is a birdwatcher's paradise. Prawle Point is the most southerly point in Devon and because of this, it is both the departure and arrival point for many migrating birds and butterflies. Butterflies including painted ladies, red admirals, and clouded yellows arrive here. They can be seen along with many other species of butterfly during the summer months, particularly along the lanes, which act as 'rides' for the butterflies. The climate and richness of the habitat also contribute to a tremendous natural abundance.

The fields along the coast are rich in wildflowers and are a haven for many birds, in particular, the nationally rare Cirl Bunting. This little bird is only found in South Devon and Cornwall, about the size of a sparrow, a small green and brown bird with a yellow and black striped face. It thrives on the arable weed seeds here and feeds its young on the abundant grasshoppers and similar insects in the area.

From the South Devon AONB: February 2017 News, headline: Cirls - the wildlife success of 2016:

This classic bird of West Country fields and natural grasslands had suffered badly from hedge removal, pesticide use and autumn planting doing away with stubble fields for foraging. By 1989, it had dwindled to 118 pairs in Devon. Thanks to wildlife-friendly farming schemes, numbers have risen to 1,078 pairs in Devon and 65 pairs in Cornwall.

Stonechats and Whitethroats are also common sightings, perched on gorse and blackthorn scrub along the cliff edge. Peregrine Falcons can regularly be seen on the crags around the coast line from Lannacombe.

The following notice appeared in the Kingsbridge Gazette of February 13th, 1864, headed Ornithology, from S P Fox:

That very rare bird, the Little Bustard (Otis Tetrax, Linn), was shot at Prawle on Saturday last. The bird is a mere straggler in this country; one was shot in the parish of Stokenham about twenty-five years since; and, a few years before, one at Bigbury. The Little Bustard is a bird of considerable powers of flight; the great deserts of Tartary being its principal stronghold. Large flocks of them have been seen wandering thence in the direction of the Caucasus and the Caspian Sea, also to the south of Russia, Siberia, Turkey, and Greece; and in small numbers in Italy, Spain, and France.

Paperwork

This was written by my mother during the Second World War. How much worse is it now?

There is something peculiarly nasty about form filling. If one could make up one's mind to sit down and fill the beastly thing the moment it arrives it would be really quite simple. But one never does. In consequence it takes its place amongst a bundle of other papers to wait for a rainy day.

Fishing

Oh dear! Yet another topic I know little about. However, the fishing industry played a large role along the South Devon coast and around East Prawle. Although farming was, perhaps, the main occupation, fishing was also important and had a strong connection with the village.

Fishing is very different today from a hundred years ago. Many of the locals fished around East Prawle, but today, competing with the large trawlers, it is no longer viable. Fishing was mainly for crabs and lobsters – any other sort of fishing was for bait. In the old days fishermen caught their own bait, but now they buy it. As Bill Login said, things move on. Crab pots changed from wooden crab pots, to wire ones, to metal ones, and now plastic ones.

Fishing was seasonal. The winter was spent making crab pots (50-60 over the winter) and the fishermen would often also work as rabbit trappers (see page 120 on rabbit trapping).

Much of the local fishing took place at Landing Cove (known as Lanty Cove) below Prawle Point, and Ivy Cove at Lannacombe.

Several fishermen fished at Landing Cove: Albert Rundle, Bill Putt and Bill Hannaford, John Putt, Bob Phillips and Dick Putt. Richard Partridge told me the metal rings on the Landing Cove rocks were to tie store pots, to keep crabs in, before sending to market.

Landing Cove

Metal rings on Landing Cove rocks

Landing Cove is quite sheltered and rocky, but the currents are strong making everything difficult when a south west wind is blowing.

Ivy Cove is also very sheltered, with steep sloping sand ideal for launching fishing boats. It has been used by fishermen from East Prawle and, latterly, Hallsands for over 200 years, well before the coastguard cottages at Lannacombe were built.

A problem arose during high tides because there was nowhere to leave the boats above the high water mark, so Lord Mildmay of Flete, who was Member of Parliament for Totnes from 1885 to 1922, organised for a slipway to be built in the late 19th century.

The slipway at Ivy Cove

The slipway had two winches. The first pulled the boats up from the sea onto the slipway and the second, at the top of the slipway, pulled the boats right up. The boats were 'parked' two abreast.

Steve Mitchelmore at the winch

From Lannacombe the Login family (five brothers) fished down at Ivy Cove, as well as Bill Blank from Prawle (before he joined the Navy in the Second World War). The Logins lived at Hallsands until the disaster in 1917.

To quote Wilf Login:

My father was on leave from the Navy when there was a tremendous storm which battered Old Hallsands and the Login family home was lost to the sea. The few saved possessions had to be carried to the top of the cliff.

Grandfather William was able to rent adjoining farm cottages at Northern Town, South Allington where the family remained until 1922. Each day they walked back to Hallsands to fish and earn a living.

Three Coastguard cottages at Ivy Cove, Lannacombe Bay eventually became available to rent and in 1927 William (snr.) purchased Cottage No 1, John No 2 and Frank No 3. Frank's widow (Gladys) lived there until her death in 2006.

The Login family (with Bill Blank and Mrs Knight) parting the lines and hooks

Bill Login, son of Frank and Gladys Login still lives there today.

In Steve Pedrick's book Gladys Login, (Margaret and Bill's mother), said:

My husband was a Login, whose parents got washed out of Hallsands... you know, when the village was destroyed. His father was also a fisherman. They managed to save their boats and went in and out from the little cove down below here, Ivy Cove, and the family lived in the first cottage here. My father used to go to sea with his father... they had a little boat and used a little cove called 'Lanty Cove', just after you leave Prawle Point, for the fine summer months. In the winter months they used to rent bits off the farmers where you could go trapping: catching rabbits.

The cottages were built in 1900, as an extra Coastguard station to improve coverage between East Prawle and Hallsands. The local farmers and fishermen were often auxiliary coastguards and many manned the LSA teams (Life Saving Apparatus) rescuing people from ships wrecked on the rocks.

Crabbing

I have already mentioned much of the fishing was for bait with which to catch crabs. Crab pots needed to be baited with fish which didn't readily disintegrate while in the water and fall off the skewers by which they were fastened. Such fish were usually taken by long lines (particularly after the First World War) but other fish, 'too soft' to be used for crab bait, were obtained by seining and used as baits on long lines.

Fishing for bait with a seine net: this was a 'shot' from the shore out to sea and returned surrounding a school of fish. These were sighted by a 'hillman' stationed upon a nearby height who then directed the paying out of the net by hand signals. The seine boat was rowed by three men and the fourth 'shot the net.' Wives helped haul the seine and received two-thirds share each. Men

John Login senior and Bill Blank, with Mrs Knight from London, and boat SE20 at Ivy Cove, Lannacombe

Coastguard cottages at Lannacombe

Displaying the skate

1920s Fishermen (Logins and Putts) at Ivy Cove taken by Ceda Ford, of Kellaton stores and post office, with her Box Brownie camera (Cookworthy PS0249)

received one share with three shares going to the owner of the net and boat. Bait was shared equally between boat crews while proceeds of fish sold were divided according to the above share system. Seine netting was used by the Logins at Lannacombe for catching sand eels used to bait long lines. Fish thus caught was in turn used for baiting crab pots. They had a boat where: 'they would start at one end, go around and come back and pull it in by hand and gradually closed in'.

1930s Seine netting at Lannacombe (from Margaret Mitchelmore and Bill Login)

Bill Hannaford making his crab pots

pre 1940 Bill Blank repairing a crab pot, Ivy Cove

Bill Login told me that in the summer they baited the long lines to catch skate, ray, conger eel, anything for bait for the crab pots. Otherwise they had to buy it.

The Login family fished out of Ivy Cove until 1969. Between the wars there were four boats working from Ivy Cove, catching crabs and some lobsters. The number of boats diminished after the Second World War, mainly because the new purpose-built crab boats were too large for shallow water. Bill Login and Steve Mitchelmore went to Dartmouth, while Bob and John Login went to Salcombe. Both their boats were about 40 ft long whereas they used to be about 18 ft long. Also it was much easier to land the crabs straight onto the quay, from where a lorry could load them up for market.

Willows

Because fishing was seasonal the fishermen made their crab pots during the winter months. Crab pots were made from willow.

From *Sisters Against the Sea* by Ruth and Frank Milton:

During autumn and early winter, the willow reeds, known as 'withies', were cut and sorted. They were cultivated in plantations called 'groves' or 'platts' situated alongside streams. Grown in bush form, they were easily propagated by inserting a willow cutting into the moist ground where it quickly developed roots. The established rod was cut off about 2ft above the ground, at the point where it had developed a bulbous head from which the 'withie' grew. Although predominately green in colour there were also red and golden varieties. Some fishermen considered that one colour attracted crabs more than another.

Frank Login mending a crab pot, Ivy Cove, circa 1945

Again Bill Login remembered they would grow willows in wet places, kept free of weeds and protected from rabbits and other animals.

Wilf Login described to Stephen Pedrick:

You had to keep it clean, you had to look out for bindweed in the grove, because that would grow up and catch hold of the willow and pull it right down. It would spoil the willow ... instead of going up straight it would be curved down around. It took us two days to cut the willows, then we had to carry them up to West Prawle, and a lorry would collect them from there.

Withies were also used to make large baskets, locally called mawns', to carry fish from the beach.

Richard remembered Bill Putt used to rent the willow groves at the back of the fields behind Stuggy Lane (at the top of the village), and Derek Wotton remembered Bill Hannaford used the willow grove opposite the National Trust car park down at Prawle Point. Derek also remembered Bill used to make his own pots, and Derek used to take the willows on his trailer up to Channel View – now known as Crab Cottages. Every day when Bill went back to sea he'd carry a pot down on his back - crazy in Derek's view with a heavy load all that way.

Socialising

From *Sisters against the Sea:*

The old Mission Room at Hallsands became a purely social centre where concerts and sing-songs were held. The villagers shared these gatherings with their fishing neighbours from Prawle, Beesands and Torcross. Despite occasional rivalry over the fishing, there was a great spirit of camaraderie between these villages. Many a young man or woman looked no further afield than these gatherings for a marriage partner.

Again, from *Sisters against the Sea* 'to the onlooker their livelihood may have seemed poor and meagre, but it was also rich in comradeship and community spirit.'

Fishing prior to the 20th Century

From Harold Fox:

During the century or so after the Norman Conquest almost all references to fisheries in Devon come in grants to religious houses. For example, in 1088, as part of the foundation endowment of Totnes Priory, Juhel of Totnes gave the Saturday yield of his two fisheries of Ashprington and Cornworthy both … recorded in the Domesday Book.

In the time of Richard II (1367-1400) hake was exported from Exeter (presumably dried). The rich fishing grounds off the south Devon coast were well known and exploited all through medieval times, and also the catching, salting and exporting of pilchards was one of the chief activities of Plymouth up to the late 18th century… The south coast of Devon was one of the most productive English fishing areas in Henry VIII's time (1491-1547).

From the middle of the sixteenth century to the latter part of the eighteenth century, there was an active pilchard fishery in South Devon and fishing for pilchard continued in Start Bay until at least 1863. …This was also the period of the Newfoundland cod fishery.

For many centuries, certainly from the fourteenth-century at the manor of Stokenham:

The lord has the option of taking one-third of the mullet which they [the bondmen] catch … no fish may be sold on a manor without the lord having first choice as a buyer at an agreed price … and no one may sell fish for money when the lord is on the estate without informing him of it. … the lord of Stokenham … not only requisitioned one-third of the mullet but was also 'entitled to buy every porpoise his men take at 1s. apiece' while people selling fish (other than mullet) from their boats must first, if asked, 'provide for the lord at a fixed price.'

Both W A Roberts and Harold Fox wrote that fishermen's homes were never made by the coast, although their boats and workshops were established there early on. The long-standing experience of occasional raiders from the sea forced the fishermen to build their homes a little way back from the coast in settlements such as Bickerton for Hallsands and Widewell for Torcross.

Again from Harold Fox: 'The Devon solution was for farmers living inland to use cellar settlements, collections of storage huts on the beach which served as bases for their fishing.'

We know from W A Roberts that: 'There is documentary evidence that the local fishing industry was already well established at the beginning of the 14th century … The catches then discussed included mullet, salmon, plaice, bream, skate and conger.'

That situation began to change during the reign of the Tudor monarchs – notably Henry VIII and Elizabeth I. These monarchs were striving hard to build up England's naval sea power, to provide a defence against the attack and invasion expected from Spain and from the Netherlands after the seizure of church property and power by the Tudors.

That great English sea power active along the coasts meant that piracy became a risky enterprise. The hanging in chains on Start Point of Henry Muge, a pirate of the high seas, can be said to mark the end of the coastal unease about raiding pirates. Soon afterwards, in the early 1600's, substantial settlements began to appear on the coast where the fishermen operated. Torcross, Hallsands and, much later, Beesands, were Stokenham examples of that date. They were among the last Stokenham villages to come into existence.

There are references in the 'Chivelstone Parish Heritage Appraisal' as to evidence for sea fishing at Woodcombe in the late 15th century and another possible sea fishing reference to Woodcombe in the late 16th century and an early 17th century survey of maritime manpower named 21 sailors and three shipwrights in the parish.

In 1854 an account of a walking tour of the South West described Woodcombe Sand being used as a harbour for 'some half a dozen fishing boats'. In the same account, in July 1854 the Londoner Walter White made a pedestrian tour of the South West; he was a perceptive observer of both the landscape and humanity, and recorded his experiences in a book published the following year.

He entered the parish at Lannacombe Mill, which with one solitary house, stands in a break of the cliff, where a noisy brook rushes to the shore …. A little farther and you come to a port in miniature – a small basin in which some half-dozen fishing boats may float, surrounded by rocks, with no outlet but a narrow groove worn through the reef. The fishermen, however, turn it to account, notwithstanding the contracted entrance, which must necessitate delicate steering, and use it as a harbour; and in the hollows of the big rock close by they find storerooms for their tackle and vaults for their fish.

Harold Fox quoted the same story in his *The Evolution of the Fishing Village.*

By the middle of the 18th century the improved roads enabled flat fish such as turbot and sole to be landed at the Devonshire ports and sent up to Bristol, Bath and other fashionable inland places; Brixham was sending fish to London, Bath and Exeter. Fifty years later it was the most noted wholesale fish market in the West of England. Fish was carried up to fifty miles inland on pack-horses but the fish for London was sent by sea to Portsmouth and thence overland.

The end of the 19th century however, saw a decrease in demand for locally caught fish, as the presence of railways at Dartmouth, Kingsbridge and Plymouth created new centralised markets with which local fishermen could not compete.

Newfoundland Dogs

Although Newfoundland dogs have nothing to do with East Prawle, they did have a lot to do with Hallsands, Beesands and Torcross, and I cannot resist writing about them.

The Newfoundland has a stiff, oily outer coat of moderate length and a fleecy undercoat to adapt to the harsh climate of its home island. The oil repels water. A Newfoundland can swim for hours, yet remain completely dry and warm at the skin. The breed has webbed feet and swims with a breast stroke instead of a dog paddle.

S P Fox wrote in her book *Kingsbridge and its Surroundings* that there were Newfoundland dogs kept by the inhabitants of Hallsands, Beesands and Torcross:

Noble, not so much on account of their appearance, for we have often seen handsomer animals, but for their deeds: they seemed as essential to the fisherman here as the sheep-dog is to the farmer. … On a dark night when the wind is blowing hard … and there is such a surf it would be impossible for boats to approach near enough to the shore for a rope to be thrown to any one there, the word is given to a dog, and immediately away he plunges into the waves. He may be buffeted and knocked back by the surf, perhaps lost to sight for some time. Still the faithful creature will not give up, but perseveres till he gets hold of the rope and returns to the beach, grasping it firmly between his teeth, until he delivers it up to the men (or women) waiting.

Newfoundland dogs were originally bred and used as a working dog for fishermen in the Dominion of Newfoundland, now part of Canada. They are known for their giant size, tremendous strength, calm dispositions, and loyalty. Newfoundland dogs excel at water rescue/lifesaving due to their muscular build, thick double coat, webbed feet, and innate swimming abilities.

Drawing of a Newfoundland dog

Sarah also told the story:

A dog was sitting up on the cliff above the quarry, and all at once he pricks up his ears, and cuts away right into the sea, of his own accord, and brings out a little drowning child. He carefully laid her on the shore, and began licking her face, but there was no sign of life, so he thinks to his self, 'what's to be done next? I can't bring her to? ' So away he goes to the nearest cottage, and pulls the clothes of the people to attract their attention. Guided by the dog, they soon brought in the poor child, and the means used were successful in restoring animation.

But with all their good qualities we are bound to confess they sometimes manifest a propensity towards cheating the revenue ! Here is an instance, related by the dog's master. 'One night I was out with the dog when it was dark, and presently he began snuffing about, and then dashed off into the waves, and soon returned, lugging along something, which he dropped, and began digging a pit in order to bury it in the sand. It proved to be a tub of brandy, which I brought home, and was very glad of, as my missus had been ordered to take brandy.' Another time, a dog, probably the same, brought in two tubs of this much desired liquor, and again, 'he brought in quite a lot of them'– but alas for the smuggling trade, those blue-and-white gentry, the coastguard, have pretty nearly put a stop to these proceedings, both of dog and man.

In *Hallsands A Village Betrayed* Steve Melia wrote that Frank Mildmay MP for Totnes 'had already endeared himself to the fishermen of Hallsands with a solution to one of their most challenging problems – the hazards of landing the boats in high surf – with a gift of several dogs, trained to swim ashore with ropes in their mouths.'

This seems a trifle strange when S P Fox was writing about the dogs many years earlier. However, they are again mentioned in *Sisters Against the Sea*: two Newfoundland dogs were specially trained by the villagers to swim out and bring back the end of the rope, which was tied to a piece of wood for the dog to bite. Combined efforts such as those were a feature of village life in those days.

The two girls 'helped to care for their Newfoundland dog who worked for his keep by helping to get the boats in.'

28 September 1875 James Clarke Hook's drawing at Hallsands on (By permission from Juliet McMaster FRSC)

Eyes along the Coast

Coastguards

I understand that the Coast Guard (later known as Coastguard) was formed in 1822, but was based on the consolidation of the preventative water guard, formed in 1809, the revenue cutters, the sea going anti-smuggling cutters and the riding officers.

Roger Barrett told me that until the 1850s the Coastguard was about suppressing smuggling, and they took on the continuation of the preventative service to combat smuggling. The patrol walked the coast paths, but the stretches were too long for one man to walk all the way from Prawle to Hallsands. They had intermediate watch stations – presumably there was one at Lannacombe before the cottages were built. Two or three men were detailed to spend a few nights at each of the watch stations. They would meet and exchange a letter, or some token, to prove that they had actually carried out the full patrol. They then returned with the token to prove they had met the man from the other station. Watch houses were established at places like Prawle Point away from the main coastguard station.

A typical Napoleonic War Admiralty Signal Station. A naval lieutenant, a midshipman and two seamen lived in the two-room signal house (John Goodwin and Roger Barrett)

Signal Houses or Stations

From the 'Chivelstone Parish Heritage Appraisal':

In the eighteenth century relations with revolutionary France soon descended into actual war. Beginning in 1794, a chain of inter-visible signal stations was established along the channel coastline, connecting in one direction to Devonport and in the other to the Admiralty in London via Portsmouth. Signalhouse Point, shown on current maps at the highest point of the Prawle headland dates from this period, the location seemingly being known officially as either Hunter's or Hurter's Top. It was in sight (assuming clear weather) of the neighbouring stations at Start

Map by C & J Greenwood 1827

Point and on the cliffs west of Soar Mill Cove in Malborough parish. A civilian signal station, later contracted to Lloyd's, was established at Prawle Point in the same period, and a coastguard station was built at East Prawle.

circa 1919 Rickham Station - Gara Rock

The Coastguard Station at Gara Rock, including a Watch House and cottages for those who were to man the station, was built in 1846/7. The 1890 First Edition Ordnance Survey map shows the station as a long rectangular block with a small north wing at the west end. The map labels the site as being a Coastguard Station containing a Lookout House, Watch House and Life Saving Apparatus House.

(Postcard early 1900s) Original Coastguard cottages

The Coastguard cottages down New Houses in East Prawle were on land leased from Richard Tucker and built in about 1823 (see the Original Coastguard Cottages on page 25). The cottages at Lannacombe were built in 1900. The Prawle Point Coastguard cottages were built in 1905.

Coastguard cottages at Lannacombe

In *Myrtles and Aloes*, in 1861, Ellen Luscombe described Rickham Station (Gara Rock):

as one of the loneliest spots imaginable, and tolerable only on account of being composed of several cottages, the abodes of the men, under the same line of roof with their chief.'

Later:

for Prawle is the most dreary and treeless place imaginable. There is a station subordinate to that of Rickham, where we rested ourselves for a while at Mr Pengelly, the chief boatman's house, … in spite of his hearty welcome and reiterated invitations to repeat our visit, we never had the courage to return to Prawle, though after a long absence from wild scenery even that dreary place would have charms in our eyes.'

Coastguard cottages at Prawle Point

In 1868 Sir William Mitchell (owner of the Shipping Gazette) got permission to erect a signalling flag as a rival to Lloyd's, in what is now known as Molly Tucker's field, above the East Prawle Coastguard cottages. This was manned by the Coastguards on his behalf. In 1882 Lloyd's took over the old admiralty watch station at

Prawle Point and it became a Lloyd's Signal Station. From here signalmen telegraphed details of passing ships to Lloyd's of London for the benefit of anxious owners and underwriters.

It was very quiet up at the lookout between the wars. The main occupation for the signalmen was earning two and sixpence every time they reported a ship to Lloyd's of London.

From the NCI Prawle Point website:

Between 1903 and 1951 the Lookout served as a Royal Naval Shore Signal Station, with both Lloyd's and Admiralty signalling, undertaken by Naval personnel who also carried out coastguard functions. Lloyd's signalling continued until 1956.

In 1951 the Admiralty handed the Station over to HM Coastguard and by the early 1970s constant 24 hour watch was being maintained by a team of five regular officers and six auxiliaries. However, the growing use of VHF radio for distress signalling led to a steady reduction in visual watchkeeping and, from 1982, the Lookout was manned only during bad weather by the local Auxiliary Coastguard company. Closure finally came in 1994, although the Prawle Point Coastguard Rescue Team continue to operate from their Station in East Prawle village.

(Built in the 1980s) Coastguard Station at East Prawle

National Coastwatch Institution

The Prawle Point station stands 200 feet above sea level at the most southerly point in Devon.

Quoting again from the NCI Prawle Point website:

The National Coast Watch Institution is an entirely voluntary organisation keeping a visual watch along the UK shores.

In May 1997 retired sea Captains John Chapple and Christopher Trinick saw the potential in restoring the abandoned Lookout to form Devon's first National Coastwatch Institution (NCI) station.

Whilst it was closed the familiar landmark above the Point had become semi-derelict and open to the elements. However, with the help of generous funding from local people, companies and organisations, it was transformed into a well equipped and efficient working station.

Rebuilding of the Prawle Point Lookout

Regular watchkeeping was resumed in August 1997 and in April 1998 the NCI Prawle Point Station was formally opened. In 2001, following a successful appeal that raised £50,000, the Lookout was partially rebuilt and completely refurbished.

The NCI Prawle Point Station has grown in strength and now a fully trained team of over 60 volunteers turn out in all conditions to keep the station open 365 days a year. Between them they keep morning and afternoon watches between 9am and 5pm, with an additional evening watch between 5pm and 8pm during the summer months.

Visit from Sarah Woolaston MP in 2011

NCI Prawle Point is a recipient of the Queen's Award for Voluntary Service.

Snippets in the NCI Newsletter (2005) by Joan Gross about Winnie Easterbrook aged 93:

Is 'Auntie Winnie' our Oldest Supporter? She has been a loyal supporter of NCI Prawle Point right from the start. She is 93 and has lived almost all her adult life in a cottage overlooking the sea in East Prawle.

She can see the lookout from her kitchen window and, with a pair of binoculars at the ready, takes a keen interest in what passes by at sea. Auntie Winnie would make an excellent watchkeeper. She has, in fact, been up to the lookout. About five years ago she managed the steep climb up from the Coastguard Cottages at Prawle Point to be greeted by Alan Shearer who was the duty watchkeeper at the time. She took a look through the binoculars while Alan explained the various duties of the watch.

Winnie Easterbrook with Alan Shearer

When I called on her recently, she was so intrigued by the antics of a large warship opposite her window, I had to call the lookout to find out what was going on. She was thrilled to learn that HMS Illustrious, a 22,000 ton Aircraft Carrier was on manoeuvres just a mile or two from her window.

Friends of Prawle Point

I mention it because I was on the Committee of the Friends of Prawle Point (FOPP), although their activities are currently in abeyance. Because the NCI at Prawle Point is entirely voluntary and receives no government funding, the support group Friends of Prawle Point was set up to raise funds and awareness of the work of watchkeepers. Jane Shadbolt (many of the drawings in this book are by Jane) was a founder member and became Chair, Secretary and Treasurer initially until a committee became established.

The Friends have provided valuable equipment for NCI Prawle Point, such as telescopes and weather stations, by rasing funds with coffee mornings, quizzes and musical evenings. 2014's evening event of the Carrivick Sisters raised almost £1000 in one evening, followed by Becky Brine and the Gazunder Band in April 2016 with just over £1000. A favourite annual event in August is the cream teas afternoon in the Community Hall in East Prawle village.

Smuggling

There are many stories of smuggling in England and the South West. Sunken lanes are a common feature, particularly on routes leading down to the sea. High hedges on either side concealed the way and all along the South Devon coastline there are secluded beaches with caves and easy access up to the villages above, from Start Point to Prawle Point, Great Mattiscombe Sands (an obvious choice), Lannacombe and Ivy Cove and Horsley beach below East Prawle. Beyond the point is Maceley and Moor Sand, and below Gara Rock, Seacombe and Rickham Sands, to name a few – surely any one of these a smuggler's paradise. The whole area was renowned for the practice.

Maceley Cove

Sharpers Cove

If I don't include the current issues of migration in the world today, smuggling was about barrels of brandy and other goods secretly being smuggled into the country under cover of dark. All trade into and out of England was free until the beginning of the 14th century. Smuggling started when King Edward I (1239 – 1307) brought in a customs duty on the export of wool to fund the many wars in which he was involved.

Quoting Mary Waugh's *Smuggling in Devon and Cornwall 1700-1850*:

In 1783 George Bishop estimated that the numbers employed in smuggling were as many as 60,000 of the youngest and ablest men, and 100,000 women and children acting as hawkers distributing the contraband about the country. Also a fifth of all the horses in the country were kept for smuggling. In what can have been little more than an inspired guess he wrote that 4 million gallons of gin and almost 11 million pounds of tea were among items brought in illegally in a single year, causing the Revenue to lose £3 million ...According to estimates made by Excisemen in 1783, half of all the brandy being smuggled into England and Wales came in along the coasts of Devon and Cornwall.

Also from Mary Waugh:

It was confidently expected that they would soon hear all about the 'Prawl People'. The villagers of East Prawle, close to Start Point and above Lannacombe Beach, were clearly up to no good. The best account came from

Richard Valentine, the Customs officer at Salcombe who reported in 1783: '…the practice of smuggling has been carried on by people who live in little villages along the coast, who are in general poor, and assist in unloading the smuggling vessels and bringing the same to the shore where the horses are in readiness to carry off the same.' The ships are chiefly fishing craft and generally land their cargoes on or near the Start or Prawle. He goes on to say … 'myself and the rest of the officers under my direction have kept a constant look-out at nights when the wind is fair, and in times past have made considerable seizures, but the smugglers have altered their proceedings which is that they never land any goods before the horses are in readiness on the spot to take the same away, which are seldom less in number than fifty and often times a hundred at a time and every horse has his rider armed with a loaded whip or a brace of pistols in order to despatch the officers if they attempted to make seizure of the goods…'

Possible remains of a watch house on Sharpers Head

In South Devon officers were based at Plymouth, Salcombe and Dartmouth with a detachment of Dragoons at Kingsbridge. Even then the smugglers still had the upper hand. Many of the officers were on horseback to help them cover the large distances between postings. However, much of the coastal path was unsuitable for horses, so many patrols were made on foot and it could take up to three hours for a message to get from Prawle Point to the Dragoons in Kingsbridge, by which time the smugglers would be long gone! In 1809 the Preventive Water Guard was formed and things looked up for the customs men. Watch houses were built around the coast, one about a mile east of Prawle Point. Boats also patrolled stretches of the coast.

Anne Born in the *History of Kingsbridge and Salcombe* wrote:

Geographically South Devon was and still is the perfect resort for 'the gentlemen'; sheltered estuaries, secret inlets, a plethora of caves and hidden lanes winding between the high hedge-banks leading inland to safe caches in cellars, barns, church towers and storage places unlimited … and other places accessible in calm weather between Salcombe and Prawle ... Business was brisk, for although it was an offence to evade customs, until the 19th century it was not an offence to sell smuggled goods. Hence the regular deliveries of 'brandy for the parson, baccy for the clerk.'

Stone & 'creeper' from Horsley Beach

Richard Partridge let me take a photograph of the stone below. It was found on Horsley Beach, East Prawle. The stones were used by smugglers to weight down their contraband barrels below the surface of the sea, to be collected later when the Revenue men were not about.

The stones were called 'sinking stones'. This 'sowing of a crop' and its subsequent recovery by 'creeping' with grapnels became increasingly common once the smugglers faced determined opposition. If the brandy remained too long in the sea it became undrinkable.

There were many schemes to warn or encourage the smugglers: beacons on the cliff tops; special spout lanterns to direct a beam of light to an incoming ship. By day all sorts of techniques were used: whistling a popular song, red shirts on the washing line.

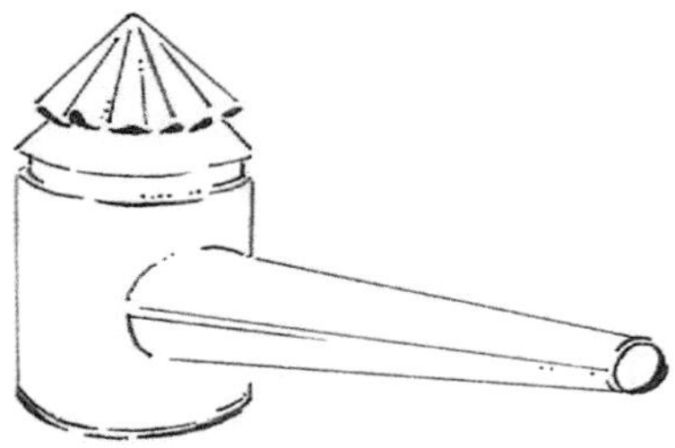

Spout lantern

Smugglers' wives frequently feigned pregnancy, hiding dutiable goods under their clothing.
Jane Shadbolt's drawing of a pregnant lady

An appropriate story from the Woodleigh Deanery Magazine in September 1901 (Thurlestone):

A woman was bringing home a long block of smuggled salt from Lea Foot. In order to disguise it she had dressed it in long clothes like a baby, and kept its blank and expressionless face tenderly clasped to her bosom. She was overtaken by the Revenue Officer, who wished her good-day and rode by her side up the road towards Thurlestone. After a time he remarked 'that is a very quiet baby of yours.' 'Yes indeed he is' she replied all of a flutter, ' he never cries and gives no trouble at all.' If he suspected something he said nothing more, and the baby stripped of his clothes was soon safely stowed away in a secret place near the hearth.

Bill Hurrell in Stephen Pedrick's book *A Century of Memories* said:

the coastguards … on the look out for smuggling, but the smugglers had their own ideas of what to do. They were notified not to come in by a keg of tar, set on fire in a cave somewhere. Smuggling was a way of life, and the brandy was brought in for the parson and the farmers, people of notoriety.

A story from Mary Waugh: 'The Rev S Baring-Gould wrote about "Sir Thomas … in his stately home near Dartmouth" whose house was carefully but respectfully searched. The spirits were in the family coach and escaped detection!'

Roger about his great grandfather, William Eales Tucker who was born at Chivelstone in 1831:

He worked in the Slate Quarry at Winslade, Frogmore, five miles from Chivelstone, but his sideline was collecting contraband from the many coves between Start and Prawle Point. At night they would collect the booty and transport it to Winslade Quarry, hide it in the tunnels in the quarry to be collected at a later date by stage coach.

Roger also told the story of the donkey with tin cans on his saddle going one way to distract the coastguards, and the smugglers going in the opposite direction!

A well known story told of East Portlemouth: the vicar was in the middle of his rather dry sermon. A man entered and passed a message up to the pulpit. The vicar immediately stopped and called out. 'There's a ship ashore between Prawle and Pear Tree Point! Let us all start fair'. The congregation rose and charged headlong to the beach, with the vicar in the lead.

From Anne Born:

Frank Coope [vicar of Thurlestone] heard elderly parishioners say that the mid-19th century times were good for the working classes: 'Many and many a time' said one, 'I have carried up a ladder as many as 50 barrels of spirits on a dark night, and hid them on the top of the roof of the church porch behind the battlements. Us always kept the door locked them times…' The tower roof of Portlemouth church was doubtless put to the same use. When the Duke and Duchess of Cleveland demolished much of the village in 1879, one of the reasons for the wholesale evictions was that the two inns were hotbeds of smuggling. The profits from contraband and from fishing made the villagers reluctant to work the Cleveland lands for a pittance.

Today most of the houses in East Portlemouth were built in the late 19th and early 20th centuries.

Derek Wotton said his grandfather was caught and had to go to Salcombe to pay his fines. He was always around the shore every day, picking bits up, brandy or timber.

The Pigs Nose Inn (originally the Union Hotel) was well known as a place for smugglers. Coming up from Horsley Beach, or from Maceley up through Merrymore Lane, it was a perfect place to hide their goods. Farnicombe Lane leading from Waterhead up to South Pool must also have been ideal for smuggling, a long steep lane, barely visible.

A Smuggler's Song by Rudyard Kipling:

If you wake at midnight, and hear a horse's feet,
Don't go drawing back the blind, or looking in the street,
Them that ask no questions isn't told a lie.
Watch the wall my darling while the Gentlemen go by.

Five and twenty ponies, Trotting through the dark -
Brandy for the Parson, 'Baccy for the Clerk.
Laces for a lady; letters for a spy,
Watch the wall my darling while the Gentlemen go by!

Wrecking

W A Roberts described how a lord of the manor of Stokenham, Edward Ameredith, wrote to Queen Elizabeth in 1588, complaining when a treasure ship, probably from the Spanish Armada, was wrecked on Slapton Sands, certain named men of Stokenham raided it and carried away bullion which they refused to yield up to him.

People were poor and often the source of the next meal was uncertain, so it's not surprising that when news of a shipwreck was heard, they would flock to the clifftops in all weathers. For the men at sea however, shipwreck meant only one thing, death and a gruesome one at that.

Anne Born's description:

A crime allied to piracy, with even more unsavoury connotations, was wrecking, the deliberate luring of ships to their doom on the rocks so that their cargoes could be seized. …The boundary between deliberate and accidental wrecking is another blurred area. The region was a poor one, and people were used to treating every kind of bounty provided by the sea, whether fish or ship's cargo, as fair game.

From Roger Barrett:

Whilst it is unlikely that ships were deliberately lured by guiding lights onto the rocks along the coast by wreckers, the looting of shipwrecks was common practice. Between 1236 and 1771 the law sanctioned the pillage of wrecks provided no man or beast survived. It was a law that invited murder.

Lannacombe was described by Brian Wigley as being:

Relatively secluded with a safe approach and good access to the interior. ... More directly north is the village of Kellaton (SX802394). Again there is no evidence of 'free trading' but it would have been a convenient stopping off place and a visit to the village is enough to convince that much has happened there in its ancient past.

Wrecks and Rocket Apparatus

Wrecks

Further reference can be made to Kendall McDonald in his *Shipwrecks of the South Hams* and Roger Barrett in *A History of Prawle Point and the Coast between Start Point and Salcombe Bar*, who have written extensively about the wrecks around East Prawle; and I have written about burials in the sand on page 10, which are likely to have been as a result of wrecks and/or wrecking.

Kendall McDonald wrote: 'Wreck followed wreck, sometimes with only hours between them. At Prawle Point, Devon's most southerly tip, there are at least seven wrecks close together. One is right on top of another and three are lying side by side with a fourth across the top of them!'

Peter Mitchell in *Wrecker's Guide to South-West Devon* described Prawle Point as: … 'one area along this coast that seems to have outstanding ability to act as a ship trap, and that is Prawle Point. On a sunny day this is the perfect spot for a picnic. …. But come the storms all this calm is swept away …'

Below are descriptions of some of the wrecks in and around the local area.

Moor Sand – Bronze Age Wreck

In an earlier chapter 'The Area in Early History', I mentioned the possibility of a Bronze Age occupation, and reports of 16th or 17th century gold and silver coins being found all along the coast from Gara Rock to Prawle Point. Any ship caught around here stood little chance of escape.

In July 1977, Phil Baker, a diving instructor, discovered a bronze age sword and two other bronze age weapons, whilst diving off Moor Sand – now a protected site. The sword was subsequently dated as 3000 years old and Moor Sand became the first prehistoric wreck to be discovered in Britain. In 1978 an archaeological survey was carried out under the direction of the late Keith Muckelroy and 3,000 year old bronze weapons including two axe heads were also

Moor Sand

discovered. No traces of boat structure have ever been found on the site so its history is largely unknown. This wreck is near the well known Bronze Age field system close to Gara Rock. However, the apparent Northern French origin of the finds may be evidence of cross-channel trade.

Andrew Elliott with the bronze age sword he found next to the Moor Sand site along with copper and tin ingots dated 1250 BC

In April 1995 a dive planned in the Erme Estuary had been aborted by the South-West Maritime Archaeological Group due to bad weather and, rather than abandon the weekend, the team decided to measure the cannon on the Salcombe Cannon Site at Moor Sand. Little did anyone know what would be discovered on this dive or where it would lead. On returning from his first dive Ron Howell told the guys in the boat 'Get hold of my glove, I've got a flaming[sic] fortune in it!'. He had found 3 gold coins, a finger ingot and pieces of jewellery.

©2011 South West Maritime Archaeological Group

That was the start of a huge treasure find. It took over two years, 3,800 dives and almost as many hours underwater for 13 divers to tease the coins from the cracks in the rocks. The hoard is now in the British Museum and only licensed divers are allowed onto the site. One of the tasks of the NCI Look Out at Prawle Point is to help protect the site from illegal diving.

South West Maritime Archaelogical Group have since discovered two further possible Bronze Age sites on the sea bed, in a protected area off Gara Rock and Moor Sand, where they recovered the largest load of tin and coper ingots found outside the Mediterannean. The tin ingots are similar to those found in the Erme.

Maria Teresa

Mention has to be made of the *Maria Theresa* wreck on 4 December 1872 because the murder is still talked about today in East Prawle. At the time there were articles in both the Exeter Flying Post on 11 December 1872 and the Kingsbridge Gazette on 14 December 1872. Roger Barrett has written in detail about it in *Prawle Point and the Coast between Start Point and Salcombe Bar.*

On 14 November 2011, Michael Partridge led a walk for the Kingsbridge and East Prawle History Societies through East Prawle village to the old coastguard station and told the story. With a few additions from me his version is succinct and brief.

Suffice it to say, Salvatori Hari, a Sicilian, the villain of the story, was of an extremely quarrelsome disposition and the crew were afraid of him. He was known to say 'Ninety-nine are mine, and I am the hundredth', meaning that he would kill a great many and then take his own life.

The Italian brig *Maria Teresa* collided with a large schooner off Start Point on the Wednesday night at 9.30, and was then run ashore near Prawle Point, on the Brimpool Rocks. The captain and crew managed to get ashore and up to the Union Inn (now the Pigs Nose). A telegram was transmitted to Messrs Hingston and Sons, the Italian consuls at Dartmouth, and George Browne was sent to act as interpreter. John Ambrose Patey, the innkeeper, gave the eleven Italians a meal and lodging and soon after seven o'clock they all went to bed.

Later that evening Mr Browne sent one of the villagers down to see the state of the brig, who reported that the vessel was breaking up. The captain called the crew out of bed to go and try to save what they could. It was impossible to do anything and several of the crew returned to their beds, including Salvatori Hari. The captain and five of the crew remained near the wreck.

Soon after two o'clock on the Friday morning a hideous noise was heard from the bedroom occupied by six of the crew, several of whom had been attacked and stabbed by Salvatori Hari. Michael Partridge now carries on the story:

Now he (Salvatori Hari) was a troublesome shipmate, and got fightable (drunk too much cider I reckon) and stabbed different people. There weren't any police and so the coastguards were called and came up, but he had disappeared out of the pub. He went down New Houses and stabbed the coastguard's wife and left her for dead, (she survived although her hand was so badly hurt she was never able to use it again). He continued on down to the coastguard station and attacked the Brown family at their cottage before rushing back up the hill again.

When the coastguard (John Segrue) and his understudy (Willcocks) with his sword stick came to help and apprehend him, they couldn't find him and so they made their way out here (by Sture's Court), and where was he? He was hid away down here. It was dark in that corner: he was crouched down by this walled garden and he rushed up to stab the coastguard officer, but the coastguard's man with the sword stick stabbed him in the back and he died. He's buried down Chivelstone church. And the tale is that it thundered and lightened and rained like anything when he was buried and it washed out the wall of the churchyard.

The body of the dead man was conveyed to the Union Inn to await the Coroner's inquest, which was held the following Saturday. The jury found that 'the deceased died from a wound given by Willcocks accidentally whilst attempting to disarm the man'. The Coroner remarked that if the deceased had been an Englishman he probably would have been an inmate of a lunatic asylum.

Derek Wotton remembered that as a boy he used to walk down New Houses Hill with Bob Login to No 2 Sea View Cottages and Maurice Putt who lived at Allington Cottage. 'They were always scared going past the spot. They said all he had around him was a white sheet, that shines up in the moonlight!'

The Betsy Anna and The Olivine

On 17 August 1926 at 9.15 am in dense fog the *Betsy Anna*, built in 1892, ran onto the rocks at Prawle Point between Prawle Island and Gull Rock under the coastguard station. She was there for several days and was refloated and beached at Mill Bay for temporary repairs. She was towed out again on the way to Cowes for full repair. As she was being towed she met bad weather and gale force winds and sank off Portland Bill for the second time.

The Betsy Anna and the Olivine, photographed by Winnie Easterbrook with her Box Brownie camera

The *Olivine* went ashore on 24 March 1929 at Lannacombe Point, half a mile east of Prawle Point, wedged in the rocks. The propeller was completely smashed. She got off but was beached at Horsley with 10 feet of water in the hold. Her cargo was cement in hessian bags and everything had to be jettisoned. After patching her up she was refloated on 12 June and renamed several times before breaking up in 1959.

Horsley Beach at low tide showing the remains of the Olivine cement bags

When it's very low tide you can still see the oval shapes, all covered with sea weed. The bags of cement hardened and became solid. As a child Elaine Trant remembered they used to hunt for the bits of sack.

Fred Login's daughter was born at the time of the Olivine incident and was name Olive as a result, and a second daughter was called Betsy Ann.

The Demetrios

The most recent wreck at Prawle Point on 18 December 1992 in a force 10 gale, is the *Demetrios* which was being towed from Dunkirk by a Russian tug, *Nastoroh*, to a Turkish breaker's yard. No one was aboard and it crashed into Prawle Point, just before Gull Island. Thousands came to see the wreck, East Prawle became jammed with traffic and police had to close the road down to Prawle Point.

More wrecks are described below as part of the Rocket Apparatus.

The Rocket Apparatus

Over the years Prawle Point has gained a fearsome reputation as a 'shiptrap'. In the last century, for example, no less than seven merchant ships were wrecked on the west side of the Point. With the help of the Prawle Rescue Team, a volunteer Life Saving Apparatus Company formed in 1872, the men at the Prawle Point Station brought many survivors of these and other wrecks safely ashore using rocket lines and breeches buoy.

Kendall McDonald in his work on the *Lalla Rookh* wreck at Elender Cove in 1873 wrote:

... this was one of the first ships to have her crew rescued by the newfangled rocket apparatus.

Mr Segrue (the Chief Boatman) and his men speedily got it, brought it to the scene of the disaster, where it was worked with a will. The first line fell across the ship and was secured. The basket soon followed. One man and a boy went across singly, but the rest of the crew, who clustered on the mizzen top-mast, most of them nearly naked, hesitated to trust themselves to the basket two at a time until Captain Fullerton, the master, said that he would set an example and got in with a sailor. When they were drawn ashore there was no longer any hesitation and the men followed, the coastguards working the apparatus with such hearty good will that in 25 minutes the fifteen were rescued....

In *Kingsbridge and its Surroundings* (1874), S P Fox wrote of the *Gossamer*:

A China tea clipper ship, of 735 tons register, was wrecked in December, 1868, (near Prawle Point) and thirteen lives were lost. There was a strong south-west breeze, and a heavy sea. ... Watched by the coastguards, who, under the orders of their chief officer (Mr Pengelly) had got out a rocket apparatus, and conveyed it to the point nearest to the wreck. The crew were so terrified that they were unable to perceive the preparations being made for their rescue, and several of them jumped overboard to swim ashore. Most of these, however, perished in the attempt; but all who maintained their position were ultimately brought ashore by the rocket apparatus. The captain and his wife were both drowned and are buried in Chivelstone Church. Had there *then* been a rocket apparatus at Prawle, as there now is, most probably all would have been saved; but Mr Pengelly had to send to the next station, Rickham, about two and a half miles off, which, of course, took a considerable time. The survivors were unable to save anything more than the wearing apparel they had on.

Tombstone of
Captain John Thomson
and his wife Barbara Kerr

The Captain was seen to lash his bride of just two weeks to a spar in the hope that she would stay afloat. For a time the two of them clung to the storm tossed bit of wood until the sea took them. Apparently their bodies were washed ashore shortly after.

Again from Kendall McDonald regarding the *Theckla* in 1891, which eventually beached reasonably gently in Horsley Cove when the tide had been rising for an hour. The coastguards got the rocket apparatus ready, but the first two rockets missed the ship completely. The third was a perfect shot. However, the crew didn't know how to work the rocket lines, got in a terrible muddle, and made fast the gear to the ship so that the ropes couldn't move and then launched their boat and landed safely.

Below is a shortened version of the *Marana* story from: *Eye-witness accounts of the Great Blizzard of March 9th and 10th 1891 in the South Hams of Devon*, reprinted by the Kingsbridge History Society:

The blizzard and great storm of March 9th and 10th, 1891, was extremely severe. A 36-hour blinding snowstorm, drifts up to 26 feet deep, roads blocked for over a fortnight, coaches stuck, mail abandoned, food shortages and much in similar vein.

During the snowstorm of Monday evening, at about half past five, the steamship *Marana*, ran on the Blackstone Rocks just off the Start Lighthouse. At the time she was steaming full speed. (Mrs Briggs, wife of one of the lighthouse keepers at Start, gave the alert.) Orders were given to get out the starboard lifeboat, and 22 of the crew got into her, with a warning from the captain to be careful and keep off the shore else they might be drowned. The only persons left on board were the captain, the three mates, the chief engineer and the messroom steward. The crew saw them get into the smaller lifeboat and leave the ship, but there is no doubt all her occupants drowned.

The crew in the first lifeboat attempted to make a landing at Lannacombe Bay, a little to the westward of the Start, but it being very dark they again pulled off. A landing was again attempted at Horsley Cove, which is slightly to the eastward of Prawle Coastguard Station, but as there was heavy surf breaking on the shore, the boat was once more headed for the sea. Unfortunately in turning the boat round, she capsized, and all the twenty-two were thrown out. Most of them got on to the keel of the boat, and after a time she righted, but of course was full of water, and only some eight or nine then remained, the rest having lost their hold and were either drowned or killed by being dashed against the rocks. ...

Mr Crickett, chief officer of coastguards at Hallsands, received intelligence of the casualty at 6.45 pm, and he immediately despatched a messenger to Prawle, a distance of nearly five miles, for the live-saving apparatus. This message was received at Prawle Coastguard Station at 7.30 pm, and about eight o'clock the apparatus left for the Start in the charge of Mr Hewett, the station officer, accompanied by six coastguards and eleven men belonging to the Volunteer Life Company. The journey was long and very trying and greatly impeded by the snow and fallen telegraph wires. However on arrival, as nothing was known of the crew, but that they were supposed to be all drowned, Mr Hewett proceeded to Beesands, to the assistance of the schooner, *Lunesdale* that had gone on shore there. He also sent two coastguards to the Start Lighthouse, with instructions that they were to examine the coast to Prawle, to try and find anything of the crew of the wrecked vessel. They eventually found Perry, Lloyd's signalman, and Rich, coastguard, who were searching for the three men who had drifted ashore. The search party soon found two survivors and a dead comrade in Mr Foss's Brake.

Seven bodies of the crew were washed on shore at Prawle, very near to where the boat capsized, on the following Wednesday, and these, together with the body of the fireman that died in the field (Mr Foss's Brake), were brought to the village and placed in a loft.

In August 2013 members of the East Prawle History Society carried out an exercise to plot the graveyard of St Sylvester, the church at Chivelstone. To their amazement they discovered buried under ivy and bushes a single grave and a further grave containing eight bodies belonging to those who died on the *Marana*. Photographs and the inscriptions are below:

In loving memory of my dear brother James Watson of Waterloo Liverpool. By the loss of the S S Marana off Start Point in the blizzard of March 9th 1891. Second son of the late James Watson. *My best beloved I miss thy greeting, Thy pleasant smile at every meeting, Thy loving kindness now I miss, And wish thee wrapt in endless bliss.*

[Against the wall] To the memory of John Monk boatswain, J Mitchell AB, C Stenborn donkeyman, A Nielsen fireman, E Rassmussen do, also three other unidentified who lost their lives in the wreck of the S S Marana off Start Point in the great gale and snowstorm on 9th March 1891.

James Watson on the left and the tombstone on the right has the inscription for the eight further bodies

The late 1920s and early 1930s was a busy time for the Prawle Life Saving Apparatus Company (LSA) with at least four shipwrecks around the Prawle area. In September 1930 the *Ida* ran aground at Prawle Point. Despite thick fog, the men at Prawle Point signal station saw her flares and heard the crew's shouts and alerted the coastguards. Both Plymouth and Torbay lifeboats were called out as well as the Prawle rocket rescue team.

One man swam ashore but the remaining eleven were rescued and hoisted to the top of the cliffs using the rocket apparatus and the breeches buoy.

British Pathe informed that in 'February 1931 at Prawle Point the 6,000 ton steamer *Benmohr* ran aground to be pounded to pieces, as were 2 other ships within the last two years. Crew were all saved by breeches buoy!' In fact the LSA took off 43 of the crew of 49.

The Rocket Apparatus team including Roger Tucker rescuing the crew of Friars Craig, 1972

There was the double wreck on 12 March 1978: a Brixham trawler *Yvette* on the eastern side of Langerstone Point. Prawle LSA took off 3 of the crew by breeches buoy, skipper taken off by helicopter; and on 8 September 1978 the yacht *Mindy*, ran aground on Meg Rock.

The Yvette on the right and The Mindy on the left.

Richard told me what happened:

We didn't know where the boat was. Initially, we searched around the Start Point area and then a message came through from the Salcombe lifeboat to say they thought they had located it in Horsley Bay. We came rushing back, straight down to Horsley. This is one or two o'clock in the morning and two ladies had come ashore in a dinghy, in a rubber dinghy, so the ladies were safe.

However, there were two men left on the yacht, but we were frightened to fire the rocket because the yacht was smelling of petrol, and we didn't want to fire the rocket to put the line over in case the boat caught on fire. So we donned the ladies' life jackets, jumped into this little rubber dinghy, tied the rope to the back – the people on the shore had the rope – we were going to flash our torch to send a message but the torch dropped in the water and the light went out! Anyway we managed to shout and make a noise and then they pulled us back with the rope.

The LSA were mentioned in despatches. The Prawle Coastguards also received a letter from the Chief Coastguard, J T Fetherston Dike on 4 January 1979 thanking them for the good work of the Regular and Auxilliary Coastguards.

The *Heye-P*: It was the last time the rocket apparatus was used by the Prawle Coastguards. On 16 December 1979 she ran aground near Prawle Point in near-hurricane winds after engine trouble. The rocket section put a line aboard the ship but the crew signalled they wanted a helicopter and would not get in the breeches buoy

A comment from Michael Partridge on his walking talk around East Prawle for the Kingsbridge and East Prawle History Societies on 14 November 2011, when he was wearing a hat taken from the ship:

Anyway this hat came off the *Heye-P* – this is what you call it when you go aboard a ship and pinch stuff. Wreckers! So the wreckers were still about when I was a boy. Look that's the one from the *Heye-P*!

How the Rocket Worked

In the field on the left below the old coastguard cottages a tall standing post can be seen. It is a rare example of an old coastguard rocket post, used to simulate the mast of a ship for training exercises in the use of the rocket apparatus. This system of rescue from sea to land has since been superseded, most notably by the helicopter.

The Rocket Post on Sharper's Hill

A description by Richard Partridge:

The rocket took a light line over to the ship, then the rocket crew on shore connected a pulley block to that light line, and through that pulley block went the whips - a slightly heavier rope which was endless. The men on the ship pulled the whips out to the ship and connected the pulley to the mast. Then the men on the shore connected the hawser to one of the whips, and pulled it out to the ship, and the men on the ship connected that to the mast. On shore a block with the breeches buoy attached was connected to the hawser, with a pulley block. The whip was then connected to the breeches buoy, and pulled out to the wreck with the endless rope, which could be pulled out to the ship. By this method the men from the ship could be brought to shore. The shore end of the hawser went through a tripod, and was tied to stakes driven into the ground (the hawser was a rope roughly two inches in diameter and the whip was a rope about 3/4" in diameter).

Christopher Wotton summer practice in the Breeches Buoy 1970

In the early days, the apparatus was kept in the building just below the old coastguard cottages. They stored a wagon there with all the necessary gear.

The Rocket House, East Prawle, down New Houses

Richard told me Harry Foss was the main man who fired the rocket; he was the best shot. After Harry, there was John Henry Putt followed by Bill Sanders. However, if it was a tricky situation, Harry would be called on to fire the rocket even after he'd retired.

Richard also told me that, as it is very steep going down New Houses Hill, the horses would run away. To stop the wagon going too fast downhill a 'drogue' was fitted under one of the back wheels. There was a chain fixed to the side of the cart just long enough to let it go underneath the wheel, and this way the wheel would gradually slide down the hill.

The drogue

Prawle LSA Company & Coastguards, taken in the late 1920s
Age of men in 1930 taken from Census details (courtesy of Richard Partridge)

Back Row: Harry Foss(60) Farmer at Lower House, Bill Hannaford(49) Fisherman/Rabbit Trapper, Phil Putt(61) Carpenter/Undertaker, Jack Partridge(29) Farmer/Carrier, William Putt(67) Farm worker, John Putt(43) Fisherman, Bill Putt(40) Farmworker, James Holland(?)
Middle Row: George Jarvis(54) When retired built Welle House, Ern Tucker(43) Farmer at Locks Farm, Sid Pepperell(43) Farm worker, John Henry Putt(38) Carpenter & Carrier, Bill Beer(?) Farm worker, Harry Putt(54) Carpenter
Front Row: unknown, unknown, Mr Gordon (Station Officer), unkown, unknown

Richard was told by Bill Blank that Harry Foss was a bit of a shooting man and he would go out shooting with the youngsters and say 'Chuck your hat up there boy.' They'd chuck their hat up in the air and he'd blow their hat to pieces. He then gave them half a crown to buy a new one!

LSA Sunday 16 February 1964 with Webber cup won in 1963 competitions with 25 LSA teams

Back Row: Roger Tucker, Frank Green, Michael Partridge, M Cawse (Coastguard), Richard Partridge, George Rundle, William Tucker, Bobby Logan, J Currie, Derek Wotton, Harry Curry, Mr Sly (Coastguard), Ernie Green, Dick Putt, Bill Blank
Middle Row: Ron Sly, Bill Sanders, J Currie (Stations Officer), Commander H D Smallwood (District Officer), Jack Rendle, R G Rowlands
Front Row: Basil Perry, John Tucker, Bill Tucker, Steve Mitchelmore, John Logan, Ernie Green

Sunday 14 June 1970 receiving the local breeches buoy cup for being the best company in the Brixham area. Jack Partridge received his belated long service medal, then presented the cup to Station Officer, John Curry. Jack Partridge – the man with the Trilby hat – was about six inches taller than anyone else.

Memories from Derek Wotton

Derek was a member of the team for 31 years and recalled that the maroon would go off – a big rocket, at the coastguards down at Prawle Point:

If the maroon went off you'd always run to the station. And they'd say 'out cart', and everybody would load up all their stuff. The cart started when they were down New Houses with horses and the wagon. You'd load all the stuff up on the wagon and you'd sit on the wagon, or if the poor old horses couldn't pull it, you had to run beside them – that was before I started. When I started they had a tractor.

The rocket cart was moved up to the green just before the road going down to Prawle Point. The horses were housed at Lower House Farm.

Memories from Roger Tucker

Roger remembered the pulley with a rope had a large label with all the different languages on it, saying to attach it to a higher part of the ship:

There was Bill Sanders - he was number one. He fired the rocket. And then in the team was myself, William and John Curry, the four of us. We would go up and set up the tripod, aim it in the right direction, and then my job was to thread the rope up through the launching thing, attach it onto the rocket and then trial the rope back.

After you'd fired it, you wound the rope up roughly by hand and then you had to go back in the shed where there was a square box with all metal pins up through. You had to loop the rope all around these pins. Ready for the next time.

Memories from John Tucker

In the 1950s I would play with John Currie, whose grandfather Jack Putt was in the Coastguard Team. They had four drills a year, so we would go to the Coastguard hut on the village green, catch a ride on the tractor and trailer up to Aerodrome Field, which was used in the First World War by the RNAS. The highlight was to ride in the breeches buoy. Sometimes if it got too close to the ground, we would have to run through thistles and cowpats etc.

There were 20 men in the team, plus full time Coastguards from Prawle Point. The team would set up the equipment. Bill Sanders Number 1 would say 'Ready to fire'. Everyone moved to behind the rocket launcher.

The coastguard in charge would say 'Fire'. All the equipment was set up to bring casualties back from the pretend mast in the field. This is when one of the youngsters would cadge a lift in the Breeches Buoy.

Sometimes, after the Rocket Drill, we would practise the Holger-Nielsen method of artificial respiration, using a plastic dummy.

The last time the breeches buoy was used was in 1978, when we took off 3 of the 4 crew of the *Yvette* at Langerstone Point. (The skipper was rescued by helicopter, as conditions worsened.)

Times of War

Until the twentieth century East Prawle has been largely unaffected by war. Below are perhaps the most interesting incidents.

The Spanish Armada (1588)

The battle raged along the Channel, and the coastline of Stokenham is reported as having been littered with wreckage. Beacons were lit and legend is that locals watched the defeat of the Armada from Start Point in 1588.

The English set alight eight fireships, sacrificing regular warships by filling them with pitch, brimstone, some gunpowder and tar, and cast them downwind among the closely anchored vessels of the Armada.

Roger Barrett wrote a moving picture:

Whether or not Prawle Point played its part as a beacon site is not known but in the fading light of Sunday evening, 31 July 1588, local people would have gathered there, as well as above Start Point, to witness a spectacle of unsurpassed magnitude as 'the greatest navy that ever swam the sea' sailed by in slow procession. Spread over seven miles of water, in crescent formation, were 125 Spanish ships. Two miles astern, the English fleet – 105 vessels commanded by Lord Howard of Effingham – passed by as darkness fell. The Great Armada sailed on towards Portland Bill but, with much of it later driven onshore by English fireships and a 'Protestant wind', only a shattered remnant would return to Spain.

The Civil War (1642-1651)

In 1642 the Protestation Oath was taken by 116 adult males, none of them designated as gentry, which suggests a total population of somewhere around 385. The ensuing Civil War seems to have passed Chivelstone by, perhaps due to its remoteness and absence of high-status residents.

I haven't been able to find anything else about the Civil War in and around East Prawle, except that in January 1646, Salcombe was the last Royalist stronghold to be defeated in Devon by the Parliamentarians. Both Anne Born and Robert Waterhouse suggested a battery was built at Rickham Common on the east side of the estuary.

The Battle of Prawle Point (1793)

Roger Barrett introduced me to this topic, otherwise I doubt I would have discovered it. This was the first sea fight in the war between France and England. Roger quoted from Ellen Luscombe in her delightful book *Myrtles and Aloes* and I also quote from it below:

Nymphe and Cléopâtre
sketch Nicholas Pocock, c. 1793

… Mr Edwards saw this battle from Prawle Point; and doubtless as his eye kindled, and his blood swept through his veins in quickened rout, he longed, as any Englishman would long, to be in the midst of the fury of the fray. He saw the *Nymphe* of 36 guns, commanded by Captain Edward Pellew (afterwards Viscount Exmouth), slowly beating up channel on the morning of June 18th 1793, a few miles to the south-west of the Start. He saw the English frigate at six am fall in with a French ship of war … the *Cléopâtre*, and, a little later, a burst of white smoke from the portholes of the latter, which announced that the action had commenced. A furious cannonade followed, which was kept up until seven o'clock by both vessels, when the *Nymphe* was skilfully laid alongside her opponent; and in ten minutes from that time every Frenchman was driven from the decks of the *Cléopâtre* by the irresistible rush of Pellew's sailors, who had thus gallantly won the first-fruits of the long series of naval engagements which immediately followed.

The *Cléopâtre* crew lost 63 casualties compared to 50 on board *Nymphe*.

Napoleon Bonaparte: An English Prisoner?

After the battle of Waterloo in 1815 Napoleon requested passports for the United States of America and tried to escape many times. However, with British ships blocking every port to prevent his escape, he decided to put his trust in the British. He wrote to the Prince Regent (Britain's acting head of state during his father's illness), and threw himself on British hospitality. He formally demanded political asylum from the British Captain Frederick Maitland on *HMS Bellerophon* on 15 July 1815.

Napoleon's arrival aboard *HMS Bellerophon*, and his surrender to
Captain Frederick Lewis Maitland
(The National Maritime Museum, G M Brighty)

Napoleon Bonaparte never actually set foot on English soil, although he was held aboard the *Bellerophon* warship off the coast of Devon, and certainly sailed past Start Point on the way to Plymouth. He became the object of massive English public interest and usually appeared at about 6 pm for the benefit of the numerous boats loaded with sightseers.

Frank Giles, a former Editor of *The Sunday Times* wrote:

If respect and admiration for the would-be conqueror of Europe characterised the attitude of the Royal Navy, the popular reaction once *Bellerophon* (known to British soldiers as Billy Ruffian) dropped anchor at Torbay was one of burning curiosity. The warship was immediately surrounded by a number of small boats crammed with people intent on seeing 'this extraordinary man'. Napoleon's response was that of a man never averse to adulation: he showed himself on deck, at the gangway and at the stern windows of the main cabin, taking off his hat and bowing.

In due course it was decided *Bellerophon* was too old and the 74 gun ship *Northumberland* should take her place. The Admiralty were also worried about the crowds besieging the *Bellerophon*, and the possibility of Napoleon escaping. On 3 August the Admiralty sent an order marked 'secret and confidential'. *Bellerophon* and escorting frigates must put to sea at once and take up a position off Start Point. They must remain there until *Northumberland* arrived and the transfer of Napoleon and his suit could take place ... for two days the ships waited in a loose formation off the coast between Start Point and Bolt Head until the *Northumberland* appeared on the eastern horizon. On 7 August Napoleon was transferred from *Bellerophon* to *Northumberland* which set sail down the channel on the way to exile on St Helena. Apparently by the time they sailed past Start Point Napoleon had become very depressed and no longer appeared on deck.

The Twentieth Century

Life in East Prawle wasn't too bad as people were fairly self sufficient. Most people had home-grown vegetables, perhaps a few chickens, with fresh milk from the farms and plenty of rabbits to catch. However, there were more casualties from the First World War than the Second (see page 170 regarding the Chivelstone War Memorial.)

Derek Wotton's father got caught out because, under age, he joined up in the First World War – he was fairly tall and they never asked his age. He lost a brother and so walked to Plymouth to join up. After the war he went on to do 21 years service in the Navy before coming out. However, because he was so young he was called up again for the Second World War!

Derek was told two of their horses were commandeered during the First World War. They returned after the war, frightened of very little:

The one I'm on was an ex war horse. They took every horse from every farm to help with the war, the First World War. Then you had the horse back. If the horse was killed you'd get another one. In the Second World War Bill never took any notice of gun fire; he was a young horse in the First World War but about 30 in the second.

Derek told another story about the Second World War, at harvest time when aeroplanes came over from Start Point right into Salcombe on the shore level. They came zooming past the horses and bombs were dropping as they tried to hit Gara Rock - they failed. We were cutting corn. The horses were still in the binder and they were trying to unhook the horses, to free them from the binder. Captain ran away and was found back in his stable. Back to the safest place he knew!

The First World War

Around the time of the First World War, farming became a primary industry and sale prices rose considerably which was an incentive to produce and market more of everything. However, there were no ration books and no shortages of food, and no black-out during the First World War.

Many horses were commandeered by the army for use in France and the slaughter of them at the Front was terrible.

Ken Williams and Dermot Reynolds wrote:

With the outbreak of the 1914/18 war, troops came to the South Hams for training and brought additional traffic to the Branch. As a result of the carnage in France, horses were required to make good the casualties suffered by the Transport Regiments. A decree was issued and all farmers were required to bring their horses to the Quay for inspection. Eventually several hundred horses were selected and were led to the Station for despatch to the army for training. About 1917 a similar happening took place when beef cattle were required to provide food for the army.

In the weighbridge area, with Quay Garage - now Wills Marine (Cookworthy Museum P0070)

From the Woodleigh Deanery Magazine of September 1914: 'From Thursday to Saturday a sale of horses for war purposes was in progress on the Quay and Mr Bailey took some good photographic records of the scene, which for those who saw it will not soon forget.'

The RNAS and the RAF

There was much German U-boat activity around Prawle Point during the First World War and many ships were sunk. As a result Chivelstone Parish provided the first airfield for land-based aircraft in South West England. Royal Naval Air Station Prawle opened in April 1917 on a 50-acre site west of the village with four canvas-covered hangars in the fields known as the 'Aerodrome'.

Sopwith 1½-Strutters of 54 Squadron were flown on anti-submarine patrols, but they proved to be accident-prone and not very effective. They were unpopular with the pilots as they were difficult to land and, with the pilot between the engine and the fuel tank, very dangerous. The station was closed during the following winter. The Royal Air Force was formed on 1 April 1918. Later that month the station was re-opened and enlarged as RAF Prawle with 254 Squadron flying DH6 and DH9 biplanes.

World War I biplane with A J Edlin - engineer on the planes at Prawle (ex butcher) - holding the propeller

World War I Airfield hanger in the Aerodrome field

Obviously such an installation in a deeply rural area was not free of problems and the extension led to the closure of the road to East Portlemouth. This caused the Parish Council to appeal to Kingsbridge Rural District Council to 'put a stop to this outrageous encroachment of parish and public rights'. The station closed in February 1919, after which the Rural District Council claimed damages from the Air Ministry of £1434 10s.

Ralph Pepperell, as a young boy, remembered:

The bi-planes... we used to go over to Prawle on Sunday afternoon and evening watching them training... taking off and landing, and on one Sunday one pilot was too low, his wheel caught the hedge and he landed with his nose on the ground and his tail up in the air.

William Stone (whose father was farm manager of Higher Farm during the Sawtells' time there) talking to Stephen Pedrick about the First World War:

...We had the Air Station out at Prawle, and weekends I used to go up with William Tucker and pick up the swill with a pony and a little trolley. They wouldn't allow just anybody in to fetch something – unless they was with somebody. I could go in, I seen the aeroplanes upside-down up there... I heard the bangs, us would run out top of the cliffs at Start Point... there's a ship going down ...yes, blowed up... us used to run out and see the ship going down... Yes, I can mind that!

Winnie Easterbrook also talking to Stephen Pedrick:

I remember the First World War... the planes, 'cause the farmers gave up a couple of fields to become an 'aerodrome', and it's still called 'aerodrome' now. There were several men from the village who were in the War and came home maimed. My cousin Bert, whose father was the shoemaker here, he went to War and was shot right through the face. He was missing, presumed killed, and then a message came through to say he was found, but wounded. He survived and lived for many years.

Winnie also remembered they had a great marquee up there in the field, where they had a concert. She didn't remember the concert but remembered the marquee, going for a walk with her father and seeing a plane come down into the field. She was only about four or five.

The aerodrome fields ran from Vinivers Cross (on the way to East Portlemouth) down across the road and over the next fields down towards the coast. As there were no permanent buildings, virtually no trace remains of the site. Some of the airmen's huts were purchased by locals: one is now the Pigs Nose Hall, and another was Bonaventura, since rebuilt by Christopher Trinick.

Bonaventura, a hut from World War I

The Second World War

During the Second World War at least 800 servicemen were billeted in and around East and West Prawle: The RAF, the Royal Artillery, the Devonshire Regiment and the American Marines.

The RAF

June 1940 saw the formation of RAF West Prawle. The RAF website reported that the CHL (Chain Home Low) established at West Prawle, was to provide low-level raid cover for the approaches to Exeter and Plymouth and confirmed the station was in operation during the Battle of Britain (July-October 1940). A further report dated 5 October 1940 stated that West Prawle 'has been operating on advanced CH (Chain Home) equipment since 23 September 1940.' The file also included a report (December 1940) praising the 'efficiency and enthusiasm of WAAF operators during a raid.'

In view of the secrecy attaching to the technology they were referred to as Air Ministry Experimental Stations (AMES). RAF West Prawle was also a GEE station. GEE was a new top secret direction finding system for guiding bombers onto targets on the continent. Other GEE sites were mainly in the South East of England where they were used for guiding bombers on raids into Germany. West Prawle GEE was one of three sites in the South West giving coverage for raids over Northern France.

For further information on radar please visit the website www.katejenningsprawle.co.uk.

When invasion threatened, defensive measures against the landing of enemy aircraft took the form of poles being driven into likely fields, among them the old aerodrome at Prawle. The radar installation was expanded with a remote reserve being established above the low cliffs just east of Prawle Point in 1941. At the main site two masts were present but all that remains today are transmitter, receiver and generator buildings. It's closure took effect in November 1944. Richard remembered Prawle people telling him that the Americans were in charge at Prawle Point in the D-Day period.

RAF West Prawle

The lower site towards Prawle Point

The remains of the reserve station on the coast at Western Cove, East Prawle

Station personnel were accommodated in a hutted complex in the village of East Prawle. Officers were accommodated in part of the Gara Rock Hotel. Little is documented on staffing but in January 1945 the station strength was 180 personnel – two RAF officers, one WAAF officer and one hundred and seventy-seven other ranks, of whom sixty-four were WAAFs.

Two photographs of the RAF Domestic Site: top from Phil Haynes, bottom from Dave Pike

Joan Delamere, née Selwood, came back to visit East Prawle in 2010:

I remember we WAAF were all together in the same hut on B site because our work was so secret, but we were allowed off camp! Apparently in the hut we might have divulged secret information - even in our sleep. I think we had the reputation of being 'snooty' because of the secrecy but we weren't really.

The proximity of the main site to the school led to an air raid shelter being provided at the north-east corner of the school yard.

Cinema and Pantomimes

The RAF cinema (situated at the domestic site) was available to the local people of East Prawle as well as RAF staff. Many locals remembered going to the cinema. For several years dances and pantomimes were also held.

Roger remembered going to the cinema and paying nine pence. 'Nine pence to go and watch a film, so we always paid nine pence and got in the front row of hard chairs. As soon as the lights went out we jumped over into the armchairs for one and six'

Cinderella 1955

Back left: (maiden names in brackets): Shirley Rendle (Login), Doreen Stone (Maurice), Christine Weymouth, 4 unknown RAF, Daisy Brockington, Sally Tucker (O'Connell), Pat Green, Brenda Blank (Jeffery), Joan Rendle (Bailey), Peggy Green (Bowles), unknown, Janet Foal, Angela Sullock (Lynne), Cheryl Presley (Hallam), unknown RAF, Marilyn Robson (Rose).

Elaine recalled playing up there - they'd been empty since 1958 - 'running in and out the buildings. Also going to a pantomime, I must have been 6, 7 or 8 to remember it'.

There was a huge pool, not actually a swimming pool, but a water butt in case of damage – much enjoyed by the children of the village.

Michael Partridge told the story:

The water tower was built of cast iron squares bolted together inside and rounded corners. When the camp was vacated and being knocked to pieces the gypsies came to get scrap iron from the owners. They saw Uncle Johnnie, and they said 'I shall buy that one off you', but he said 'no I don't want to sell. I want to put it out on the edge, where the Fairfield windmill is to water the fields, and put in a drinking trough'. 'Oh we will take him down for you'. So they came with their gas and cutting and smashed it all to pieces and got the scrap anyway.

RAF West Prawle Closure: The final years of RAF West Prawle are documented by the AHB and No 390 SU's ORB. No 620 SU was disbanded in 1956 and a closing-down party established on 1 July 1956, this being disbanded some two months later on 14 September. The GEE commitment (No 380 SU) ceased on 1 December 1957 and the SU was disbanded on 20 January 1958. The inactive site was parented by RAF Hope Cove, eventually passing to HQ(U) No 19 Group (Coastal Command) at RAF Mount Batten in November 1958, until that station was relieved of its parenting duties with effect from 22 June 1964 when West Prawle's assets were disposed of.

The War Agricultural Committee

Agriculture was in poor shape by the mid-1930s and much arable land had reverted to pasture. Although some politicians continued to argue against government intervention, a Food and Supply Sub-Committee was established in April 1936, which proved to be not just necessary but also successful. Food, and in particular the lack of it, was central to the experience of the Second World War.

From September 1939 the Minister of Agriculture and Fisheries appointed a War Agricultural Executive Committee for each county in England and Wales to increase home food production in time of war. Their immediate task was to see that additional land was brought under the plough with all speed. The aim was to obtain for next year's harvest an increase of about 1½ million acres in the tillage area in England and Wales compared with the previous year.

Farmers were very closely supervised as the war progressed because every square yard of land was needed. Farmers who didn't come up to expectations were classed as 'C' farmers and if they didn't do as they were told their land could be taken over. … If the farmers were told to plough up a field and put grass to crops they didn't have any option.

Roger Tucker told the story of his grandfather:

The War Ag compelled farmers to grow potatoes and plough grassland for crops. Granfer said it wasn't possible to plough the land at the top of Langlers (Signal House Point) but the War Ag Inspector (Percy Luscombe who farmed at Scoble) insisted and delivered a single furrow prairie buster plough so Grandfather could plough it.

My mother writing in 1940 about buying stores (cattle 15 to 18 months old) to fatten on her grass during the summer:

The War Ag took no account of the possibilities of both a spring and summer drought, nor was it formulated in the light of the knowledge that the might of the German army, while forcing the French to capitulate, would also force the farmers of Britain to a ploughing programme of dimensions not as yet imagined or foreseen. I doubt if ever in history there has been a worse moment at which to buy store cattle.

The Army

The army also played a part in the Second World War in East Prawle. Anti-aircraft guns were placed up by Vinivers Cross, where the Nissen hut is, on the Portlemouth Road. Derek told me:

There's still the foundations and ammunition hut. There was an army camp on High House Farm, on the way to East Portlemouth. Unlike the RAF camp it was dismantled fairly soon after the war.

Several people have told the story that during the war an army truck was parked outside the Pigs Nose to pick up the crowds from the pub and when they came out the truck was gone! The brake wasn't on properly and it just kept on going down the hill into Penny Hill cottage, knocking the wall out. Rab Mitchelmore lived there, Steve Mitchelmore's father. He said 'they've made a bloody mess of my table!' He wasn't worried about the house. It was built up again within 48 hours. The Ministry had to put it back.

Bill Login talked of his father and uncles keeping watch in the coast watch building at Ivy Cove day and night all through the war. He also said there was a lookout above Mattiscombe

Beach which was also manned – it no longer exists – and an army camp at Lannacombe.

World War II Nissan Hut

The Home Guard

The Home Guard were volunteers who defended the five thousand miles of Britain coastline in the event of an invasion by Germany. They were originally called the Local Defence Volunteers.

On the evening of Tuesday 14 May 1940, the Government made an urgent appeal on the radio to all men aged between 17 and 65. They wanted all men not already serving in the armed forces to become part-time soldiers. Within 24 hours of the radio broadcast a quarter of a million men had volunteered. By the end of July this number had risen to over a million.

When the Home Guard started they had no uniforms, guns or anything. They just had sticks. Their drill ground was the road between the top of Provi Hill and Higher Farm Corner. Back and forth on that road. Derek, as a child, would run with them.

Some members of East Prawle Homeguard, 1940s

Front row: left to right: Tommy Tucker, George Jarvis, Mr Hockridge, Douglas Trinick
Second row: Harold Rogers, Charlie Partridge, Fred Evans, Freddie Gaines, George Tabb, George Rundle
Third row: Harry Ford, Sid Baskerville, Norman Partridge, Arthur Jarvis, Bill Sanders
Back row: Mr Hoskin, Dick Tabb, Unknown, Ern Rogers or Sid Cudd

Richard said:

I think there were a couple of officers from the First World War in Prawle and they were in charge of the Home Guard. A bit later in the war, they were supplied with uniforms and guns. They had a machine gun fitted in the loft of one of Higher House Farm barns opposite the school, trained over Moorwell Pond and down the road. If there had been anybody coming up that way... They also had a purpose built shed, past Welle House on the right hand side (the last of Geoffrey's fields before you get to the Tucker's big aerodrome field. There's the ruins of it still there, and it's where they used to keep their guns and ammunition. It's now called Ammunition field. On the aerodrome field they had heavy posts put in to stop any planes or gliders landing there. They also had a Bofors gun (an anti-aircraft gun) on the field near Vinivers, to fire at any aeroplanes.

The remains of the ammunition hut in what is now known as the Ammunition Field

War Memorial, St Sylvester's Church

Several young men from the Chivelstone Parish were killed in the First World War, but fortunately not so many in the Second World War.

In the Woodleigh Deanery Magazine of April 1919: it was decided to 'place a Parish Memorial in the Churchyard to our men who have fallen in the War,' and in February 1920:

We had a goodly muster of people from all directions at the Dedication of our War Memorial. After Evensong in Church, at three o'clock we passed into the Churchyard, where the Rural Dean offered appropriate prayers. A wreath was placed at the foot of the monument which is surmounted by a Celtic Cross, with the names of the men in letters of gold. They gave their best for us and we should give our best for them. The muffled peal added a note of solemnity suitable to the occasion.

[War Memorial][South side] *In memory of those of this parish who gave their lives for King and Country in the Great War 1914-1918.*

2nd Lt J A Helby Royal Dub. Fus.
C P O A Shimmield R.N.
Tr E J Baker 6th Regt. Aus.
L H - Pt F E Baker 1st Coldstream Guards
Pt W T Hutchings — 5th Devons
Pt R H Putt 11th Hampshires
Pt F H Sullock 8th Devons
Gr W H Sullock R.F.A
Pt J S Thornton 11th Devons
Pt F A Weymouth 6th Dorsets.
[North side] These gave their lives in the World War 1939-1945
ACW2 M A Cudel WAAF
CPO G H Jarvis R.N.
CPO W T Tabb R.N.
CPO E G Wood R.N.
D W J Standfast boy, aged 11 years. Fell in air raid.
Their name liveth for ever.

From the Woodleigh Deanery Magazine of November 1919: 'Mr and Mrs Baker are erecting a Tablet in Church to the memory of their two sons who fell in the War, and the necessary Faculty is being obtained through the Consistory Court at Exeter. The public War Memorial

is in course of erection on a suitable spot in the Churchyard.' In the July 1920's magazine 'The Baker Memorial Tablet was dedicated during Divine service by the Vicar on Sunday morning June 20th, the unveiling being performed by Miss Cornish, who had known the two brothers Ernest and Fernley Baker from childhood.'

Some of those killed in the First World War were also mentioned in the Woodleigh Deanery Magazines of the time. The Roll of Honour is still read out during the Remembrance Sunday service.

Remembrance Sunday

I have little information regarding Remembrance Sunday in Prawle, except it was first observed on Armistice Day 1919. However, John Tucker's first memory of Remembrance Day was at East Prawle with the RAF camp and all the soldiers. 'My brothers and sisters and those that went to Sunday School had to walk to Chivelstone Church. The RAF I think parked in the Chippen Heap and marched to church and back again, about 50 of them, very smart'.

Spitfire VB Fighters

Richard told the story that on 15 March 1942 when Bill Hannaford and his son-in-law, Curly Robson, were ferreting on a foggy day, a Spitfire crashed down in Higher Shallowpool field. Bill and Curly rushed over, helped the pilot out and as they were doing so another Spitfire came in and landed almost on top of the first one. They were Polish airmen, part of No 317 Polish Squadron based in Exeter, heading for RAF Bolt Head.

Spitfire crash remains on East Prawle village green: Delving into the Past page in South Hams Newspapers on February 6, 2015; the image came to Graham Collyer from Dan Simpson of Dartmouth who found it in a house clearance in Kingsbridge

The two Miss Fosses, living at Foss Cottage, New Houses, saw the crash and telephoned Jack Partridge who was a special constable. He and his nephew, Bob Partridge, rushed to the area to find both pilots smoking cigarettes, smiling broadly and chatting to the two men who had helped them out of the planes. A few days later Bob went to the field with a tractor and slide to help bring the crashed planes onto the village green, so that the RAF could take them. The photograph on the previous page shows the remains of the planes on the green.

American & Prisoner of War Camp

Between Cousins Cross and Chivelstone Cross, in the field now familiarly known as The Camp, but more usually named Pucka Pitts, there was an American camp, which subsequently became a prisoner of war camp. It is in the dip just after the Wakehams' new barn on the left leaving Prawle.

Reg Hannaford, evacuated from Torcross to Chivelstone, remembered:

We had been at Chivelstone for around six weeks when one of the fields on the farm was taken over by the US Army. A large camp was soon built by black soldiers, which was the first time most of us had seen a black man. As soon as the camp was completed, the white soldiers moved in. Unknown to us at the time, the blacks and whites could not agree and fights were always taking place. From the middle of March 1944, the whole area was awash with American troops, complete with sweets and cigarettes which they supplied to all and sundry (this was the first time I knew you could smoke a camel!).

More than one person has mentioned there were a few problems between the white and black servicemen, and some fights in and outside the Union Inn/Pigs Nose.

Quoting Nancy Richards in Stephen Pedrick's book *Daishels and Figgy Duff*:

There were Germans and Italians there, and American soldiers there. Father used to take us for a walk out on the road and we could stand up on the hedge and the cookhouse was just there so they'd give sweets and all sorts of things. It was just in a field with Nissen huts and that in there, there wad'n no fence around it.

Later on it became a German prisoner of war camp and some of the prisoners helped work on the farms. Elaine Trant remembered her father-in-law at South Allington having Fritz work for him during the war and they kept in touch for some time after. Sarah Trinick remembered Grandpa Tripp was happy to keep one on, but as he wasn't allowed to bring his family to England, he didn't stay.

Evacuation to East Prawle

The War Office had chosen the Slapton Sands area of the South Hams for training the United States Forces because it resembled the beaches in Normandy where they were to land on D-Day. The area of evacuation included the villages of Blackawton, Chillington, East Allington, Slapton, Stokenham, Strete, together with Torcross and many outlying farms and houses. In all, this totalled about 3,000 people, 30,000 acres of land, their possessions, farm stock and equipment.

However, my interest in the evacuation is what happened in East Prawle. Hannafords of Torcross had been in business since 1885 and Reg Hannaford remembered:

On arriving home from school on 12 November 1943, my two brothers, two sisters and myself were told by our parents that we were to be evacuated from our home. ... We all went to share a large farmhouse at a hamlet called Chivelstone with an aunt and uncle.'

John Hannaford remembered they went to Chivelstone during the evacuation because the biggest area of their business was not part of the evacuation: Beeson, Beesands, Hallsands, Kellaton, East Prawle and Frogmore.

They dismantled their refrigerator to take it to East Prawle but discovered there was no electricity there. Harry Putt, the local carpenter in the village, built a lockup in the corner of the garage at Welle House as a cold room where they were able to store the meat.

We know Steve Mitchelmore and his family were evacuated from Chillington and lived in Penny Hill cottage for a time.

Richard remembered they had an evacuee staying with them at Coolings Farm, Johnnie Bridgeman and his sister stayed with Jack Hannaford and Harold.

Derek Wotton in the middle with two brothers evacuees, Bill and Bob Mcloughlin

Rationing

Reg Hannaford remembered farmers were able to forego their bacon rationing for one or two pigs killed a year, which they happily did as the ration for bacon was so measly. They would fatten up their pigs to an enormous size and fare much better than with the rationed bacon. People had to use their rations when the meat was there – Reg remembered they were issued with New Zealand lamb and by the time the meat arrived it had thawed out, so they couldn't keep it very long.

Animals were taken to the Dartmouth abattoir for slaughter, although frozen meat was also available: Argentinean ewes and New Zealand lamb. The allocation of meat took place in Kingsbridge and the ration for the Hannafords at East Prawle's went to butcher Hannafords at

Salcombe, their cousins. They would go down to East Portlemouth with their van and bring it across on the old passenger ferry. Petrol was also rationed but, if they ran out of petrol, which they often did, they used to go to Beesands fishermen who had a good allowance and couldn't always use it when the weather was bad.

Food rationing began in 1940, which meant each person could buy only a fixed amount of certain foods each week. Reg remembered that at one time meat rationing was a shilling's worth of fresh meat and two pennyworth of corn beef per person per week and school age children half ration and expectant mothers had another half ration.

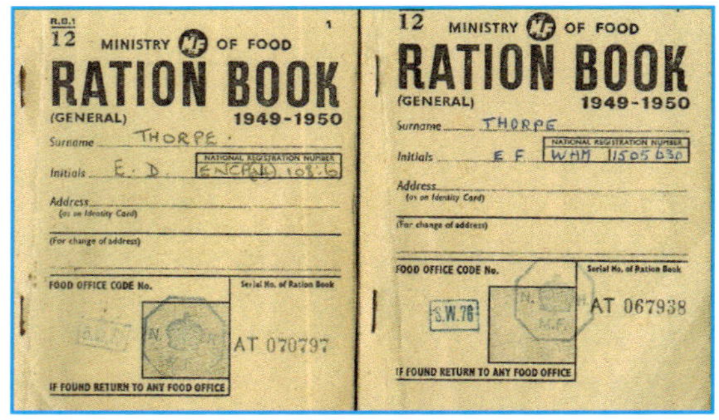

Ration Book 1949-50 but similar to wartime ones

Marriages

We have managed to find a few people who met and married either in the First World War or in the Second World War.

Husband	Wife	Place and Date
Edward Frederick Thorpe	Edith Sawtell	
Harry Ford	Ella Putt	
Frederick Robson	Vera Hannaford	Chivelstone Church 1943
Peter Mann	Cora Trout	Kingsbridge Register Office 1952
James Bailey	Joan Rendle	Chivelstone Church 1958
Jock Berretti	Pauline Stone	Catholic Church Kingsbridge 1960
John Muirhead	Sheila Baskerville	
George Pharoah	Kathleen Weymouth	
Brian Hutton	Mary Toms	
Brian Butler	Ruth Mabin	Bristol St John's Church 1954
? Philbrick	Sylvia Rendle	(Joan Rendle's mother's cousin
Bert Moss	Nancy Hannaford	
Bill Cross	Olga Hopkirk	
Bert Moss	Nancy Login	

Fred Robson (known as Curley or Robbie) was posted here in the war and married Vera Hannaford. Marilyn Rose, their daughter, told me that they met up at the Pigs Nose, during a hands, knees and boomps a daisy.

Royal Events

Queen Victoria's Golden Jubilee

South Hams Celebrations 21 June 1987

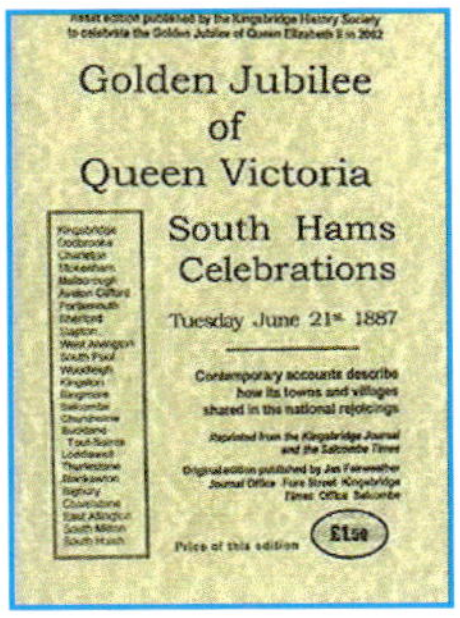

A reset edition of Queen Victoria's Golden Jubilee (originally published by Fairweather of Salcombe) was published by the Kingsbridge History Society to celebrate the Golden Jubilee of Queen Elizabeth in 2002. Contemporary accounts describe how its towns and villages shared in the national rejoicing. A shortened version for Chivelstone is below:

The Jubilee Festival was carried out in this parish under the management of a Committee consisting of the following persons:- Messrs T H Harris Pitts (Chairman), Langworthy (Secretary), Oldrieve, G Foss, Thomas Foss and J Hewitt. The village was prettily decorated with arches, evergreens and bunting. The proceedings commenced with a service at the Church at 12 noon, conducted by the Revs H Haden and J W Dickenson, in the absence of the Vicar (Rev C W Stubbs) through ill health. The service was largely attended, and the National Anthem was sung. After the service, dinner was provided in Mr Langworthy's corn loft, and consisted of roast and boiled beef, bread, plum pudding, cider and beer. Grace was said by the Rev H Haden. The tables were laid in two long rows of 140 feet each, and 386 persons sat down to dinner. After dinner the Chairman (Mr T Harris Pitts), proposed the health of the Queen. The company then sang the first verse of the National Anthem, after which they gave round after round of hearty cheers for Her Majesty.

... A number of sports were held in the afternoon, such as racing for youths, boys, and girls, a three-leg race, jumping in sacks, tug of war, wheelbarrow race, donkey race in heats, and finished with a pig chase to be caught by the tail first, then held by the ear. At 5.30 a tea was provided in the loft, the tables being presided over by Mesdames Harris Pitts, H Foss, W Foss, Pile, Yalland, Weymouth, Langworthy, Hewitt, E Tucker, W Tucker, Sture, Hutchings, Harradon, Moor, Giles and Misses Oldrieve, Foss and Ellen Tucker. Rockets and blue lights were fired in the evening, and at 10 o'clock a bonfire 25 feet high and 15 feet at the base, with tar and oil at the top, was lit in Mr Yalland's field at Borough. At 9.15 dancing commenced, and was kept up until midnight, when the National Anthem was sung and the rejoicings came to an end.

Edward VII's Coronation 9 August 1902

The extract on the right is from the Woodleigh Deanery Magazine of September 1902.

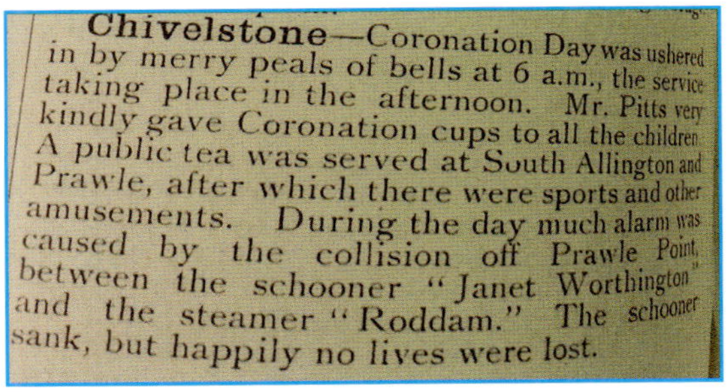

Chivelstone—Coronation Day was ushered in by merry peals of bells at 6 a.m., the service taking place in the afternoon. Mr. Pitts very kindly gave Coronation cups to all the children. A public tea was served at South Allington and Prawle, after which there were sports and other amusements. During the day much alarm was caused by the collision off Prawle Point, between the schooner "Janet Worthington" and the steamer "Roddam." The schooner sank, but happily no lives were lost.

George VI's Coronation 12 May 1937

I have been unable to find any information regarding this Coronation except for the photograph below (from Elwin Ford) and the Coronation souvenir on the right (from Brenda Jeffery).

East Prawle George VI Coronation celebration

Their Majesties King George VI & Queen Elizabeth

Queen Elizabeth II's Coronation 2 June 1953

In 1952 John Tucker remembered when the King died because his mother said 'look there's something up, the flag is half mast at the RAF camp.' There were no telephones or radios in the house but that was soon to change for the Queen's Coronation. The build up to it was fundraising dances in the Pigs Nose Hall every week.

Brenda remembered that at the Coronation they had a big do. They were eating the food nearly all week – there was so much! On the cake was a Coronation carriage which was later given to the youngest child in the village.

Coronation 1953

Richard Partridge as Dick Turpin, Roger Tucker in foreground as King Farouk

Queen Elizabeth II's Silver Jubilee 1977

Very little is reported about it except for a few photographs. There was a celebration party in Higher Farm's new barn. The Queen came to Torcross and the girl guides and brownies attended and Sarah Trinick remembered that the Queen came over to say hello.

Queen Elizabeth II's Golden Jubilee 2002

Following the reprint of Queen Victoria's Golden Jubilee booklet, the Kingsbridge History Society created a similar booklet for the Golden Jubilee in 2002. The Chivelstone report is too long for a book of this nature and so the following again is a abridged version:

The officers for the Chivelstone Parish Queen's Golden Jubilee committee were Roger Tucker (chairman), Cindy Higgins (vice-chairman), Marilyn Tucker (secretary) and Josephine Trinick (treasurer). They were supported by Martin Catt, Josie Sanders, Sarah Trinick-Daglish, Geoff Brotherton, Betty Allen, Jane Bickle, Dawn Kelland, Hathor Hamilton, Vicky Tucker and Norah Kingston.

A four-day programme was devised to celebrate the occasion. Celebrations started on the Saturday with a talk by Robert Waterhouse on Local Parish History, followed by Martin Catt talking about Wildlife in Chivelstone. A Jubilee Fayre was held at 3.30 pm, commencing with a fancy dress parade of queens and consorts. In the late afternoon hot beef sandwiches were available, followed by a barn dance in the marquee. The Fayre was a great success, raising £1,182 towards the commemorative projects.

Brenda's programme

On Sunday there were two services, the morning one in the church and Songs of Praise service in the marquee in the evening. Various exhibitions and demonstrations were displayed through the day,

On the Monday in the afternoon the marquee had been set up with a long line of tables laden with an amazing variety of food set up for the royal garden party at which red, white, blue or gold headwear had to be worn.

At 10 pm a procession of lanterns, handmade by Lesley Webber, of the Pigs Nose Inn, made its way to Stephen's Field where some 600 people gathered to watch the lighting of a beacon, built by Robin Tucker and set up by Richard Tucker. It provided a link in the nationwide chain of beacons. Later there was a fireworks display.

Tuesday was the day for the Exhibition of the Sea in the marquee. Neville Oldham, an archaeological diver, gave a talk on shipwrecks and in particular about the Salcombe cannon site situated off Prawle Point. Displays featuring the work of the Coastguards, National Coastwatch and Trinity House kept people entertained throughout the morning. Walkers joined Martin Catt for a Westward Parish Walk. The chairman of the Parish Council, Roger Tucker, and the vice-chairman, Josephine Trinick, presented each child up to the age of 16 with a Jubilee £5 crown in a presentation mount, made by Neville Higgins.

The four days were brought to a close when the balloons, which had been sold throughout the festival, were released from the Green on a stiffish northeast breeze at the end of Tuesday afternoon.

Queen Elizabeth II's Diamond Jubilee 2012

Three days of celebration were planned for the Queen's Diamond Jubilee. Saturday 2 June was Sports Day, Sunday morning started with bell ringing at the church, a service on the green before the Big Lunch. The band Hogwash played during the afternoon and, in the evening in the Pigs Nose Hall, the Red Bullets. Monday was Jubilee Prawle Fair Day – the weather held off and there appeared to be more people than usual. A barbecue was held in the evening followed by the lighting of the beacon and a really splendid display of fireworks.

Appendices

Appendix I - Chivelstone Parish Population

Below is an assortment of population information, mostly taken from the 'Chivelstone Parish Heritage Appraisal', where greater detail can be found concerning the overall parish population.

The 1086 Survey recorded three manors in what was to become Chivelstone Parish, all assessed at one hide and all owned by Iudhael of Totnes.

In 1524 a tax was imposed to finance war with France and was paid by 77 males, which suggests a total population of somewhere around 350. Highest taxed were Robert Perott, assessed on goods valued at £30, William Wadlond at £20 and John Perott and William Partrigge, both at £16. No one was taxed on income from land, suggesting that all the landowners were absentees.

In the 'Elizabethan Court Roles of Stokenham Manor 1560-1602', translated by W A Roberts, of which Chivelstone was a part, there were lots of tenants renting ground from the Lord of the Manor until about 1580, when parts of the Manor were sold off on 3,000 year leases. Some documents referring to 3,000 leases still turn up nowadays (for an example, see page 12).

In 1642 the Protestation Oath was taken by 116 adult males, none of them designated as gentry which suggests a total population of somewhere around 385. Various documents suggest a variation of about 10.

Quoting from the 'Chivelstone Parish Heritage Appraisal':

The accession of Queen Elizabeth in 1558 led to a threat of invasion by Catholic Spain, in which coastal parishes could be in the front line. Throughout the land all able-bodied men between 16 and 60 were deemed liable to serve with formal inspections known as musters required every three or four years. That for 1569 has been published, with listings of the better-off citizens required to pay for equipment, seven in this case, none of them designated as gentlemen. Also named were the archers (by then obsolescent), harquebusiers (who operated this primitive type of firearm which required to be supported on a rest), pikemen and billmen. In all there were 43 bearing arms in the parish, although given the uncertainty as to the proportion of non-able bodied males nothing can be said with confidence about the total population.

In the 1750s the vicar of Stokenham responded to the questionnaire sent by Dean Jeremiah Milles of Exeter. In so far as his handwriting can be deciphered, there were then nine houses at Chivelstone 'Town', 34 at East Prawle, about 13 at Ford and 24 at South Allington.

The first census, taken in 1801, recorded a population of 562. Population increased to 637 in 1821, but declined much earlier than the typical parish, and then almost continuously to the end of the century when it had decreased to only 40 per cent of the 1821 figure, although the number of houses was to remain much more constant. This could be explained by farmers having accommodated their workers within the farmhouses, only for labour to be shed as arable farming became increasingly uneconomic in the face of competition from abroad, and was replaced by less labour-intensive livestock farming.

The 1831 census provided more detail than the three previous ones. Of the 149 adult males, 15 were farmers employing 91 labourers, while four employed no labour; this does suggest no great change from the 17 villeins and smallholders of 1086. In 1831 there were 26 males employed 'in Retail, Trade, or in Handicraft as Masters or Workmen' with 8 more as labourers, while oddly, since most parishes would have had at least a resident curate, no one came into the category of 'Capitalists, Bankers, Professional and other Educated Men'.

In the 1841 census the total population was of 579 (from Tim Blyth). The 1851 census provides the most detailed picture of the parish thus far. There were by then two very large farms: both Richard Foss at East Prawle and John Huxham at Chivelstone were farming 500 acres (possibly some of it in adjoining parishes). The former employed 18 labourers, while Nicholas Pitts worked his 350 acres at South Allington with 14 labourers. East Prawle continued to be the largest settlement, with 10 fishermen and seven coastguards. It also supported two victuallers, two blacksmiths, two shoemakers and two carpenters, as well as a shopkeeper, a grocer draper and a mole catcher. At South Allington were the curate, four tailors and two masons, a grocer, carpenter and blacksmith. At Ford the only trades were a victualler and a miller, while at Chivelstone itself there were only a 'victualler hawker' and a stone mason.

Tim Blyth also found the census results in the table below:

Parish	1801	1851	1901	1931	1961	1971	1981
Chivelstone	562	571	385	433	349	297	208

From Kelly's Directories we have the following population information for Chivelstone:

1881	1891	1901	1911	1921	1931
426	436	385	439	443	611

The first half of the century had seen a slight increase in population, reaching a maximum of 461 in 1951; but the decline was then steep, to a minimum of 208 in 1981, no doubt the result of the trend to second homes and holiday cottages. There has been a modest recovery since then, to 286 in 2001, but by then over 40 per cent of the houses in the parish were second homes, and the figure for East Prawle village was 60 per cent. Another change was that the farms which in 1851 had employed up to 18 workers now employed only casual labour, and at that date the parish population was almost exactly double what it was in 2001.

According to Wikipedia and 'The Parish Population of 2011', the population of Chivelstone Parish taken at the 2011 census was 280.

Appendix II

White's, Billings and Kelly's Directories 1850 – 1939:

Listings of the post offices at Chivelstone (South Allington) and East Prawle

Date	Post Office	Sub-Postmaster/ mistress	Information
1850	(White's)	W Lidstone	Post to Kingsbridge 1 aftn
1857	(Billings)	W Lidstone	Mr W Lidstone, Sub-Master. Arrival by Foot Post from Kingsbridge 11.30 a.m. Despatch immediately afterwards, - the messenger waiting while the bag is made up, Money Order Office, Kingsbridge.
1878-1879	South Allington/ Chivelstone	Mr Edward Yabsley	Letters are received at 9.25 a.m. and despatched at 3.40 p.m. week days only, via Kingsbridge. Torcross is the nearest Money Order Office. Letters are received at Prawle at 11.30 a.m. from Kingsbridge. There is a WALL LETTER BOX here, cleared at 3 p.m. week days only. Salcombe is the nearest Money Order Office.
1888	Chivelstone	Edward Yabsley	Letters from Kingsbridge by foot post received at 10.50 a.m. and dispatched at 2.25 p.m. The nearest money order office is at Torcross & telegraph office at Salcombe.
1889	Chivelstone	Edward Clayton	Letters from Kingsbridge by foot post received at 9.25 a.m. and dispatched at 3.56 p.m. The nearest money order & telegraph office is at Torcross.
1893	Chivelstone	Edward Clayton	As 1889 but now the nearest money order & telegraph is at Frogmore. Postal orders are issued here, but not paid.
1902	Chivelstone	Edward Clayton	Letters from Kingsbridge by foot post received at 8.35 a.m.; dispatched at 4 p.m. Postal orders are issued here, but not paid. The nearest money order office is at East Prawle.
	East Prawle	William George Samuel Beer	Post & M.O. O., S.B. & Annuity & Insurance Office. Letters from Kingsbridge, via Frogmore, received at 9.35 a.m.; dispatched 3.20 p.m. Chivelstone is the nearest telegraph office, 2 miles distant.
1906	Chivelstone	Edward Clayton	Letters from Kingsbridge by foot post received at 8.20 a.m.; dispatched at 8.30 a.m. & 4 p.m. No Sunday delivery. The nearest money order office is at East Prawle, 2 miles distant.
	East Prawle	William George Samuel Beer	Post & M.O. O., S.B. & Annuity & Insurance Office. Letters from Kingsbridge, via Frogmore, received at 9.15 a.m.; dispatched at 3.30 p.m. No Sunday delivery. Chivelstone telegraph office, 2 miles distant. There is also a telegraph office at Prawle Coastguard station, with a general delivery of telegrams within half a mile only.
1914	Chivelstone	Nicholas Edward Powlesland	Post & T. & Telephone Office. Letters from Kingsbridge by foot post received at 7.50 a.m. & 4.10 p.m.; dispatched at 8 a.m. & 4.20 p.m. No Sunday delivery. The nearest money order office is at East Prawle, 2 miles distant.

Date	Post Office	Sub-Postmaster/ mistress	Information
	East Prawle	William George Samuel Beer	Post & M. O. Office. Letters from Kingsbridge, via Frogmore, received at 8.30 a.m. & 4.50 p.m.; dispatched at 11 a.m. & 3.40 p.m. No Sunday delivery. Chivelstone telegraph office, 2 miles distant.
1919	Chivelstone	Nicholas Edward Powlesland	Post & T. & Telephone Office. Letters from Kingsbridge. The nearest money order office is at East Prawle, 2 miles distant.
	East Prawle	Mrs Emma Helena Putt	Post & M. O. Office. Letters from Kingsbridge. Chivelstone, 2 miles distant, is the nearest telegraph office.
1926	Chivelstone	William Feegan	Post & T. Office (Messages may be telephoned for treatment as express letters). Letters from Kingsbridge. The nearest money order office is at East Prawle, 2 miles distant.
	East Prawle	Mrs Emma Helena Putt	Post, M.O., T. & T. E. E Office. Letters from Salcombe.
1930	Chivelstone	No name	as 11926.
	East Prawle	No name*	Post, M.O., T. & T. & T. E. D. Letters from Salcombe.
1939	Chivelstone	No name	Post & T. Office. Letters from Kingsbridge. East Prawle nearest M.O. office.
	East Prawle	No name*	Post, M.O. & T. Office. Letters from Kingsbridge.

We know that Mrs Putt was running the East Prawle Post Office from 1915, and her daughter, Pat Farleigh, joined her when she left school and continued until the post office closed in 1993.

Appendix III

Old Maps

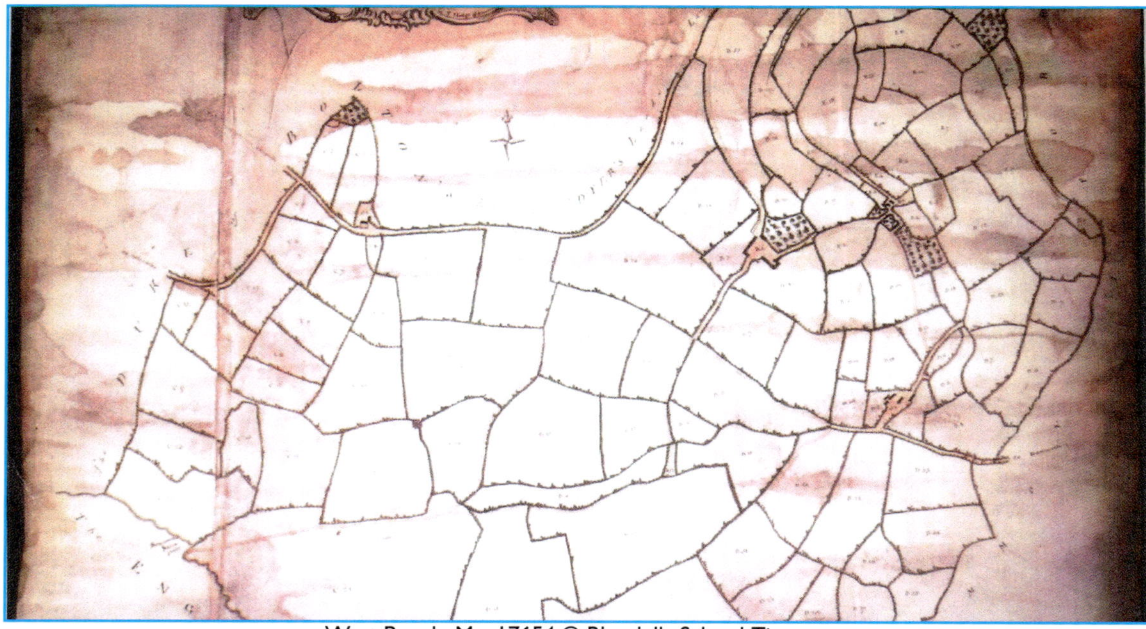

West Prawle Map17654 © Blundells School, Tiverton

Benjamin Donn Map of Devon 1765

(The originals of this map and the Greenwood map on the next page can be found at the Devon Rural Archive)

Historical Map 1809 ©Cassini Publishing Ltd

Greenwood 1827

Appendix IV

South Devon Water Board Maps

Drawings reproduced with kind permission of South West Water
RAF Station-Prawle proposed water supply, drawing no. 18/564/41, dated 4/3/1941,
from Sherford to West and East Prawle (on two pages)

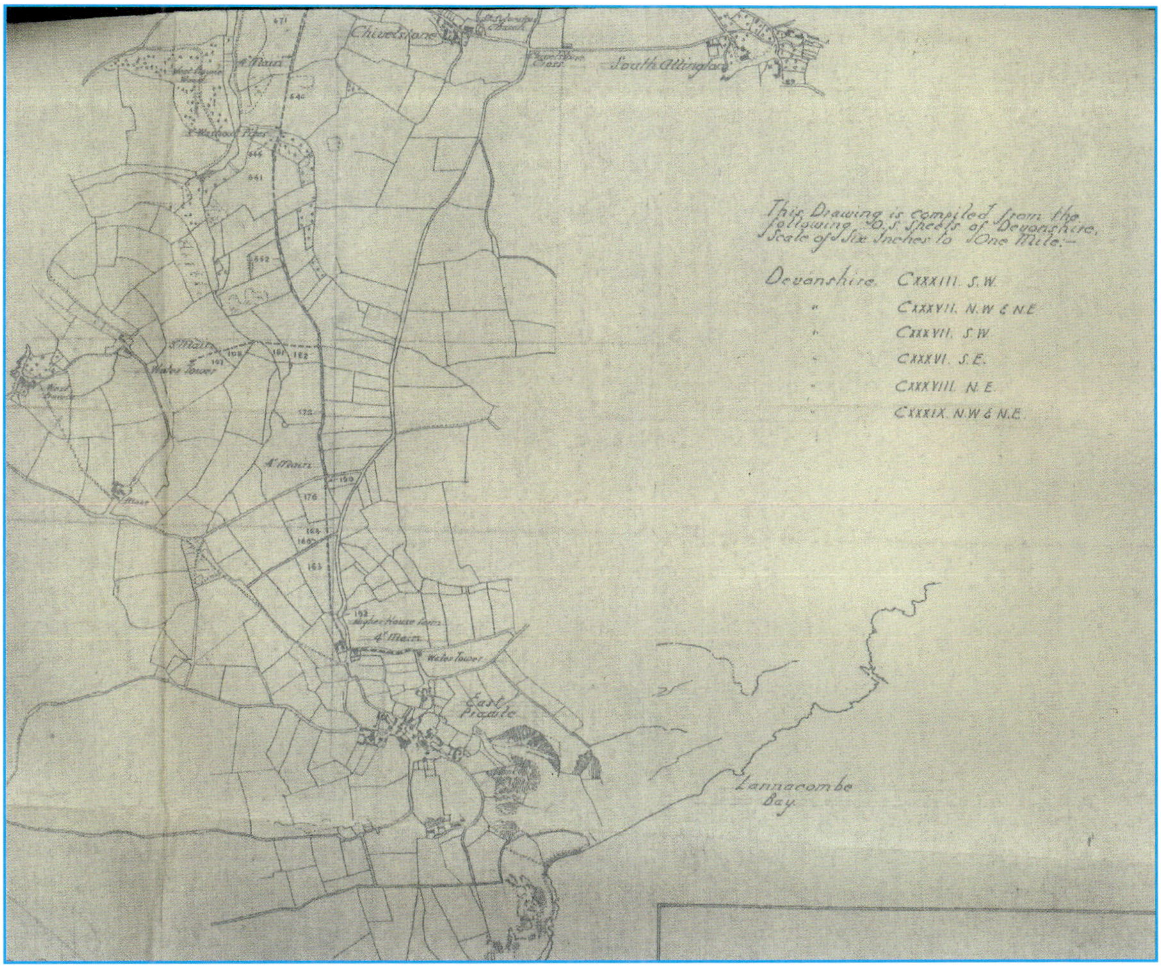
Chivelstone
South Allingdon
This Drawing is compiled from the following O.S. Sheets of Devonshire, Scale of Six Inches to One Mile.—
Devonshire CXXXIII. S.W.
" CXXXVII. N.W & N.E
" CXXXVII. S.W.
" CXXXVI. S.E.
" CXXXVIII. N.E.
" CXXXIX. N.W & N.E.
Water Tower
Higher House Farm
East Prawle
Lannacombe Bay

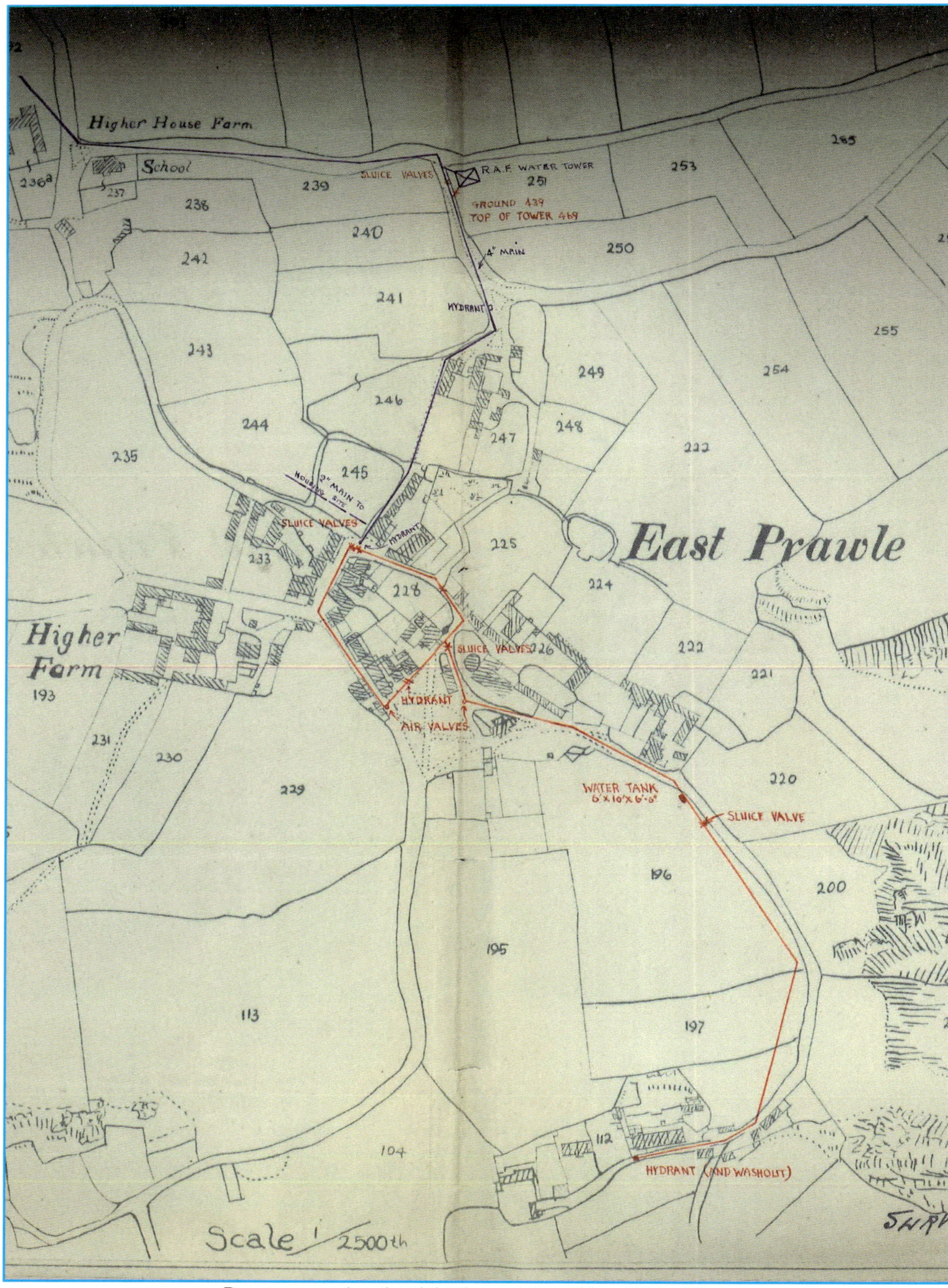

Drawing reproduced with kind permission of South West Water
Drawing no.1042/3, Kingsbridge Rural District Council 1949 of existing and proposed mains

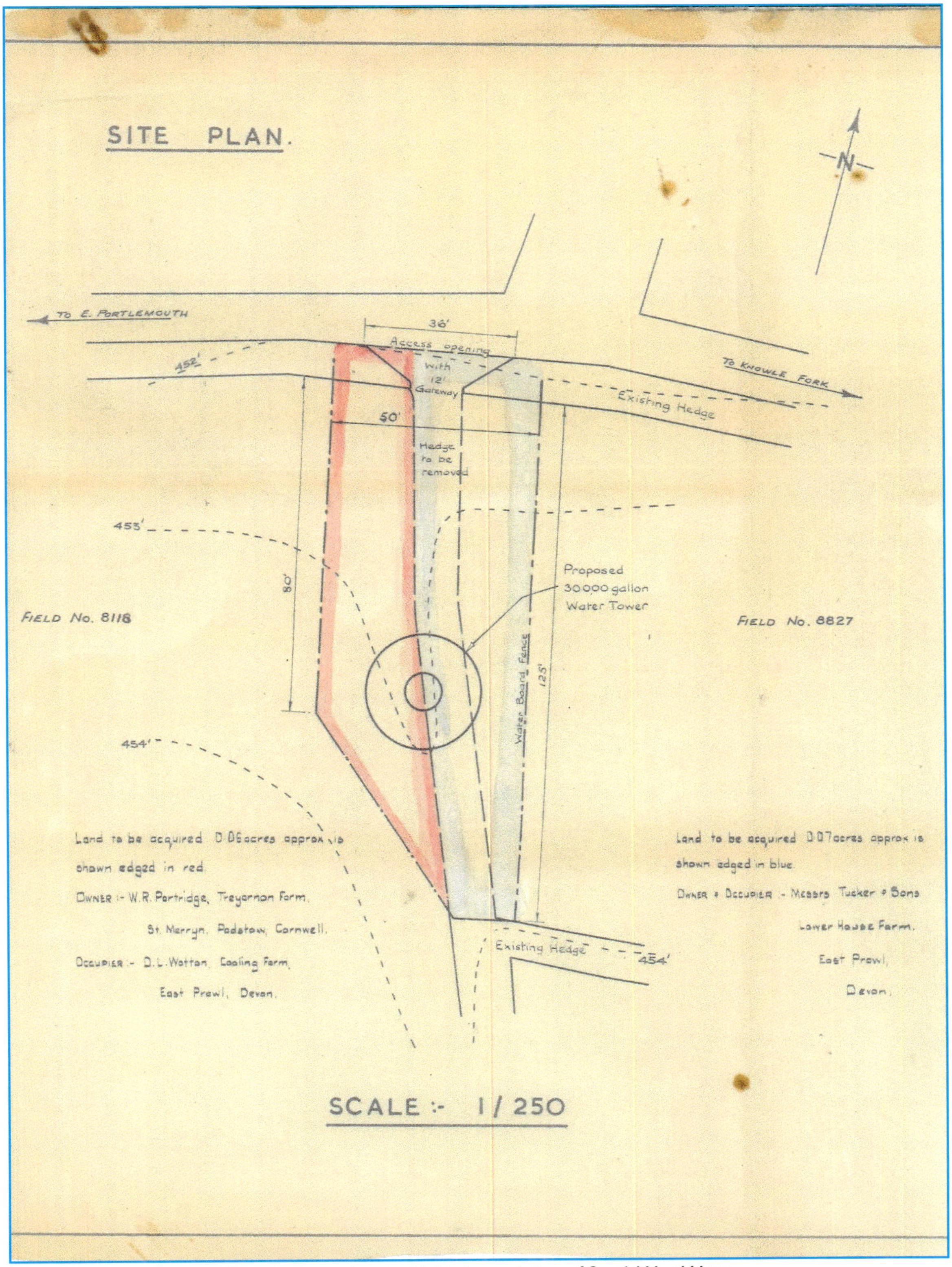

Drawing reproduced with kind permission of South West Water
Drawing of the site for the East Prawle water tower, drawing no.454/11 dated 12/4/1960

Appendix V

Extracts from 1907 and 1925 Ordnance Survey Maps showing local lanes and features

The names of local lanes and other landscape features around East Prawle compiled by Richard and Jane Partridge on the 1925 one inch to one mile Ordnance Survey map. The inset on the next page is from the 1907 six inch to one mile Ordnance Survey map.

Key to Map on page 188
1 Levers
2 Ford Hill
3 Ridge Road
4 Quarry Lane
5 Orchard Lane
6 Sue Hannaford's Lane
7 Pucka Pitts
8 Mellon Hill
9 Abbeygate/Chivelstone Hill
10 Borough Road
11 Broad Road
12 Half Way Tree
13 Whitegate Corner
14 Knole Hill Road
15 Merrymore Lane
16 Through Aerodrome
17 Higher Road
18 Common's Lane
19 Shell Hill
20 Prawle Point Road
21 Lollipop Lane
22 Sharper's Lane
23 Horsley Road
Inset Map below
24 Brake Park Pool Corners

Key to Inset Map below
25 School
26 Town Road
27 Stuggy Lane
28 Woodcombe Road
29 Billator Road
30 Butt's Gate
31 Lower Road or Thurt Lake
32 Moor Well Pond
33 Higher Farm Corner
34 Summergate
35 Torrings Lane
36 Head Town
37 Chapel Lane
38 Providence Hill
39 Fore Street
40 Duck's Lane
41 Town Hill
42 Around Castle
43 Penny Hill
44 The Green
45 Holloway Hill
46 West End
47 New Houses
48 New Houses Hill
49 Shadycombe Bottom

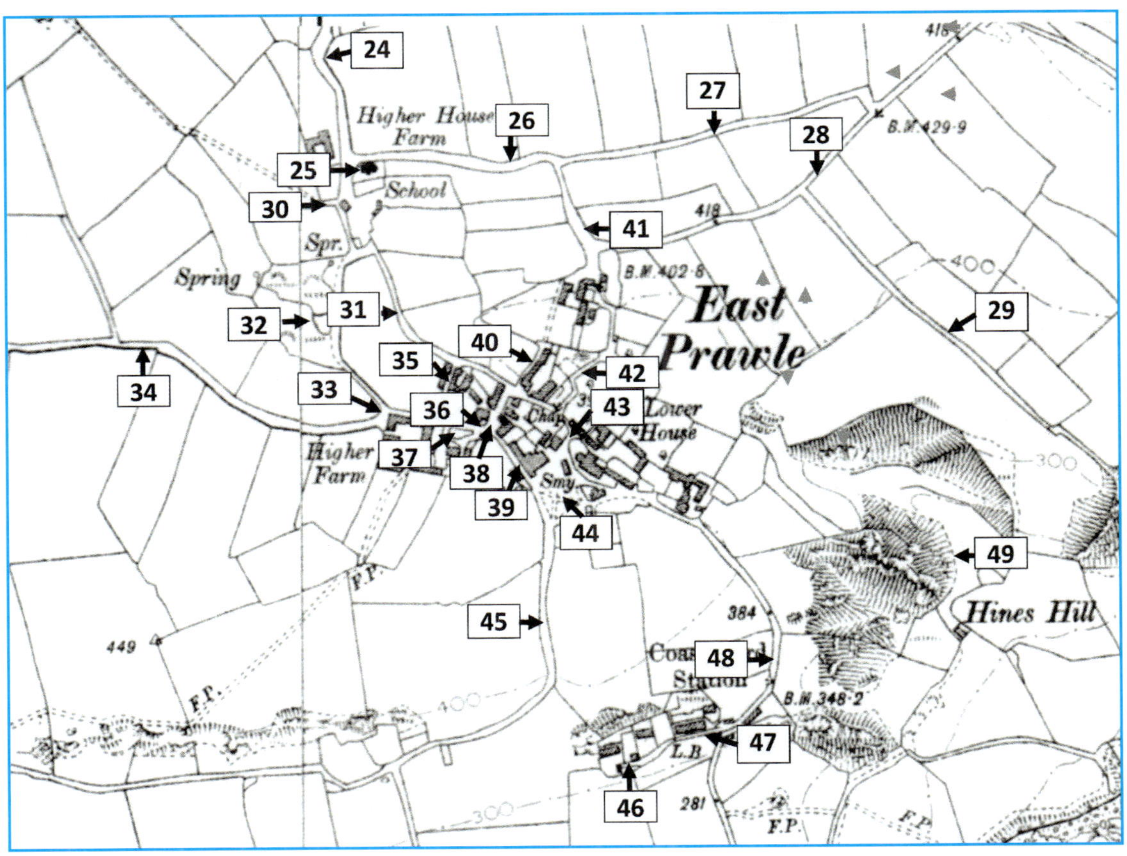

Bibliography

Why This Book?

Roberts, W A. *Elizabethan Court Rolls of Stokenham Manor 1560 – 1602.* W A Roberts, Beeson. 1984.

A Bit of History

Barrett, Roger. *Prawle Point and the Coast between Start Point and Salcombe Bar.* Kingfisher Print and Design Ltd. 2011.

Waterhouse, Robert. *East Portlemouth Heritage Appraisal. An Archaelogical History of the Parish.* The Coast & Countryside Service. 2002.

Born, Anne. *The History of Kingsbridge and Salcombe.* Orchard Publications, Chudleigh, Devon. 2002.

Murray, John. *Handbook for Travellers in Devon and Cornwall.* London. 1850 (and 1865).

Luscombe, Ellen & Young Francis. *Myrtles and Aloes.* G P Friend, Kingsbridge 1861.

Fox, Sarah Prideaux. *Kingsbridge and its Surroundings.* Printed for the compiler by G.P. Friend, Plymouth. 1874.

White, Walter. *Londoner's Walk to the Land's End.* Chapman and Hall. 1865.

www.devon.gov.uk/print/index/environmentplanning/natural_environment/geology/southerndevon.htm#15

Louden, Philippa. 'Physical Aspects of the Prawle Point Area of Devon'. Thesis. 1964-1965.

Hoskins, W G. *Devon,* Collins, London. 1954.

'The National Gazetteer of Great Britain and Ireland'. 1868.

Tucker, Roger. '120 Years Farming in and around East Prawle'. Presentation.

Stanes, Robin. *A History of Devon.* Oxford University Press. 1986.

www.ironbarkresources.com/slaves/whiteslaves07.htm

www.english-heritage.org.uk/content/imported-docs/p-t/salcombe_archaeological_report_final_version_figs.pdf

Reed, S. J. *Archaeological Excavation and recording of a burial at Prawle Point, South Devon.* Exeter Archaeology Report No. 03.27. June 2003.

Coope, Rev Frank Egerton, MA. *Thurlestone church and Parish.* Published by the author. 1900.

Fox, Sarah Prideaux. *Kingsbridge Estuary with Rambles in the Neighbourhood.* Kingsbridge. 1864.

Waterhouse, Robert. *Stokenham Heritage Appraisal, an Archaeological History of the Parish.* The Coast & Countryside Service. 2002.

Roberts, W A. *Stokenham Occasional Papers 1 (Queen Katherine's rental 1547).* W A Roberts, Beeson. 1984.

The Village

Hoskins, W G. *Devon,* Collins, London, 1954.

Exeter Archaeology. *Chivelstone Parish Heritage Appraisal.* In conjunction with the people of Chivelstone parish. 2006/7.

Stanes, Robin. *Old Farming Days Life on the Land in Devon and Cornwall.* Halsgrove. 2005.

Waterhouse, Robert. *East Portlemouth Heritage Appraisal. An Archaelogical History of the Parish.* The Coast & Countryside Service. 2002.
Chivelstone Parish Millennium Book. 2000-2001.
Kelly's Directories. 1888 – 1930.
Milton, Ruth and Frank. *Sisters Against the Sea.* Halsgrove. 2005.
Barrett, Roger. *A History of Prawle Point and the Coast between Start Point and Salcombe Bar.* Kingfisher Print and Design Ltd. 2011.
Adams, Rev B N. *Devon's Most Southerly Parish,* a description. J R Gill & Don. Kingsbridge.

About the House

www.roadtickle.com/things-you-didnt-know-about-may/
Pedrick, Stephen. *A Century of Memories.* Nick Walker Printing, Kingsbridge, 2009.
Toyn, Shân. *Devon Privies, a nostalgic trip down the garden path.* Countryside Books. 1998.
Shepherd, Doreen. *South Pool Portrait of a South Devon Village in the mid-twentieth century.* Rosemary Publications, South Pool. 1997.
Milton, Ruth and Frank. *Sisters Against the Sea.* Halsgrove. 2005.
Kelly's Directory. 1939.
www.goosefat.co.uk/page/history

In the Kitchen

Seymour, John. *The National Trust Bo`ok of Forgotten Household Crafts.* Dorling Kindersley Ltd. 1987.
Lidstone, Hugh R G. *Lidstone of the South Hams of Devon.*The Western Litho Company of Plymouth. 1989.
Shepherd, Doreen. *South Pool Portrait of a South Devon Village in the mid-twentieth century.* Kingfisher Print and Design Ltd. 1997.
Milton, Ruth and Frank. *Sisters Against the Sea.* Halsgrove. 2005.
Hartley, Dorothy. *Food in England.* Macdonald & Co. (Publishers) Ltd. 1954.
Pedrick, Stephen. *A Century of Memories.* Nick Walker Printing, Kingsbridge. 2009.
Cream Separator Advert from '*The Lister Standard*'. June 1929.
Roberts, W A. *Elizabethan Court Rolls of Stokenham Manor 1560 – 1602.* W A Roberts, Beeson, 1984.
Stanes, Robin. *A History of Devon.* Oxford University Press. 1986.
Stanes, Robin. *Old Farming Days Life on the Land in Devon and Cornwall.* Halsgrove. 2005.
Exeter Archaeology. *Chivelstone Parish Heritage Appraisal.* In conjunction with the people of Chivelstone parish. 2006/7.
www.tea.co.uk/catherine-of-braganza

Water

Documents regarding East Prawle's water supply provided by South West Water.
Pedrick, Stephen. *A Century of Memories.* Nick Walker Printing, Kingsbridge. 2009.

Schools

www.en.wikipedia.org/wiki/Dame_school
Kelly's Directory. 1888, 1889, 1893 and 1902.
Welch, David. 'East Prawle Board School'. Compiled in the 1970s.
discovery.nationalarchives.gov.uk/details/rd/d363f644-8141-4ce1-98b6-6e2509fc40a0

Shops

History, Gazeteer & Directory of Devon. 1850, 1878-79.
Kelly's Directory in 1888, 1889, 1893 and 1902.

Pedrick, Stephen. *A Century of Memories.* Nick Walker Printing, Kingsbridge. 2009.

Communication

www.postalheritage.org.uk/page/rowlandhill
A survey of the Post Offices by an independent researcher named Ken Smith for the British Postal Museum & Archive.
Kelly's Directory. 1902.
Pedrick, Stephen. *A Century of Memories.* Nick Walker Printing, Kingsbridge. 2009.
Fox, Sarah Prideaux. *Kingsbridge and its Surroundings.* Printed for the compiler by G.P. Friend, Plymouth. 1874.
White's Devon Gazeteer. David & Charles Publishers Ltd. 1850.
Billing's Directory and Gazeteeer of Devonshire. 1857.
Pedrick, Stephen. *Daishels and Figgy Duff Further recorded memories of life in the South Hams and elsewhere.* Nick Walker Printing, Kingsbridge. 2012.
Frogmore Village Community Association. *Frogmore, Devon. The Village's History by its residents.* 2009.
Williams, Ken and Reynolds, Dermot. *The Kingsbridge Branch.* Oxford Publishing Co. 1977.
Kelly's Directory. 1935.
'This is Exeter'. 30 January 2009.
www.devonlive.com/bt-answers-box-return/story-11828044-detail/story.html.

Transport

Fairweather-Tall, John. 'Travel by Water'. Published by the Kingsbridge History Society.
Williams, Ken and Reynolds, Dermot. *The Kingsbridge Branch.* Oxford Publishing Co. 1977.
Waterhouse, Robert. *Stokenham Heritage Appraisal: An Archaeological History of the Parish.* The Coat & Countryside Service, South Hams. 2002.
Tanner, Kathy, BA AMA. 'Coaching Days' Cookworthy Papers 3. Published by the William Cookworthy Museum Society. 1978.
Luscombe, Ellen & Young Francis. *Myrtles and Aloes.* G P Friend, Kingsbridge. 1861.
'Surveyors Account of Money Expended on the Highways of the Parish of Chivelstone'. Devon Record Office.
Grimley, Roger. 'Carriers from Chivelstone Parish (Between the two world wars)'. Old Post, Bigbury, Kingsbridge TQ7 4AP
Pedrick, Stephen. *A Century of Memories.* Nick Walker Printing, Kingsbridge. 2009.
Kathy Tanner BA AMA. 'Bringing the railway to Kingsbridge'. Cookworthy Papers. Published by the William Cookworthy Museum Society.
Fox, Sarah Prideaux. *Kingsbridge and its Surroundings.* Printed for the compiler by G.P. Friend, Plymouth. 1874.
Mitchell, Vic and Smith Keith. *Branch Line to Kingsbridge. The Primrose Line.* Middleton Press. 2002.
Hawkins, Abraham. *Kingsbridge and Salcombe with the Intermediate Estuary.* R. Southwood. 1819.
Fairweather, James. *Salcombe and Neighbourhood.* Published by the author. Third edition 1912.
Kelly's Directory. 1888, 1906.
Grimley, Roger, 'Transport to adn from East Prawle'. Old Post, Bigbury, Kingsbridge TQ7 4AP

Religion

http://en.wikipedia.org/wiki/ Melodeon_(organ
Fox, Sarah Prideaux. *Kingsbrige and its Surroundings.* Printed for the compiler by G.P. Friend, Plymouth.

1874.
Watkin, H R. 'History of the Priory of Totnes'. Compiled from original records and published by the author. 1914.
Stabb, John. *Some Old Devon Churches.* Published by Simpkin, Marshall, Hamilton, Kent & Co. 1908.
Kelly's Directory. 1939.
Stubbs C W, M A (Vicar of Stokenham, Chivelstone and Sherford). 'The Church in the Villages'. Cranford's Library, Dartmouth. 1887.
British Listed Buildings. 'Living Waters'. Listing NGR: SX7872842813.
Wilkins J G. Compiler and editor. *The Parish of Stokenham its People and its Ancient Churches.* A limited edition. 1977.
Exeter Archaeology. *Chivelstone Parish Heritage Appraisal.* In conjunction with the people of Chivelstone parish. 2006/7.
Roberts W A. *Stokenham Occasional Papers: Queen Katherine's Rental 1547.* W A Roberts. Beeson, 1980.
Waterhouse, Robert. *East Portlemouth Heritage Appraisal, an Archaeological History of the Parish.* The Coast & Countryside Service. 2004.
'New Venture' the newspaper for the Exeter Diocese. June 1979.
Chivelstone Parish Millennium Book. 2000-2001.
Born, Anne. *The History of Kingsbridge and Salcombe.* Orchard Publications, Chudleigh, Devon. 2002.
Hoskins, W G. *Devon.* Collins, London. 1954.
Waterhouse, Robert. *East Portlemouth Heritage Appraisal. An Archaelogical History of the Parish.* The Coast & Countryside Service. 2002.
James, Jeanne, 'The Medieval Chapel at Prawle, formerly in the Manor and Parish of Stokenham', *Devon & Cornwall Notes & Queries*, Vol. XL, Part V (2009), 136-147.
James, Jeanne, A Note and a Query: 'New light on the site of the medieval chapel at Prawle' and 'Was the entrance to Salcombe Harbour marked by a medieval chapel or even two?', *Devon & Cornwall Notes & Queries*, Vol. XLI, Part VI (2014), 190-196.

Festivities

Kelly's Directory. 1878 and 1888.
Pedrick, Stephen. *A Century of Memories.* Nick Walker Printing, Kingsbridge. 2009.
Raising the Glove www.kingsbridgefairweek.co.uk/information/history/

Farming

Kelly's Directory. 1919, 1926, 1930 and 1935.
Stanes, Robin. *A History of Devon.* Oxford University Press. 1986.
www.goldendays.org.uk/out-and-about/find-out-about-green-lanes/
Born, Anne. *The History of Kingsbridge and Salcombe.* Orchard Publications, Chudleigh, Devon. 2002.
Exeter Archaeology. *Chivelstone Parish Heritage Appraisal.* In conjunction with the people of Chivelstone parish. 2006/7.
Waterhouse, Robert. *Stokenham Heritage Appraisal, an Archaeological History of the Parish.* The Coast & Countryside Service. 2002.
www.legendarydartmoor.co.uk/cattle_moor.htm.
Brunskill, R W. *Traditional Farm Buildings of Britain.* Victor Gollancz Ltd. 1982.]
Dartington Rural Archive. *Horse Power Darlington Rural Archive*, Dotesios Printers Ltd. 1985.
Stanes, Robin. *Old Farming Days Life on the Land in Devon and Cornwall.* Halsgrove. 2005.

Donaldson Frances. *Four Years Harvest.* Faber and Faber Limited. 1945.
Williams Ken and Reynolds Dermot. The Kingsbridge Branch. Oxford Publishing Co. 1977.
Waterhouse, Robert. *Stokenham Heritage Appraisal, an Archaeological History of the Parish.* The Coast & Countryside Service. 2002.
Waterhouse, Robert. *East Portlemouth Heritage Appraisal, an Archaeological History of the Parish.* The Coast & Countryside Service. 2002.
myweb.tiscali.co.uk/andyspatch/gintraps.htm
Fox, Harold. *The Evolution of the Fishing Village: Landscape and Society along the South Devon Coast, 1086-1550*, Leopard's Head Press, Oxford. 2001.
Luscombe, Ellen & Young Francis. *Myrtles and Aloes.* G P Friend, Kingsbridge. 1861.
Fraser, Robert. *General View of the County of Devon with Observations on the Means of its Improvement.* London: Printed by C. Macrae M DCC XCIV (1714), Reprinted by Porcupines, Pilton Street, Barnstaple. 1970.
Pedrick, Stephen. *A Century of Memories.* Nick Walker Printing, Kingsbridge. 2009.

Fishing

Milton, Ruth and Frank. *Sisters Against the Sea.* Halsgrove. 2005.
Pedrick, Stephen. *A Century of Memories.* Nick Walker Printing, Kingsbridge. 2009.
Dickinson, M G. *A Living from the Sea, Devon's Fishing Industry and its Fishermen.* Devon Books, Tiverton. 1987.
Fox, Harold. *The Evolution of the Fishing Village: Landscape and Society along the South Devon Coast, 1086-1550.* Leopard's Head Press, Oxford. 2001.
Hoskins, W G. *Devon.* Collins, London. 1954.
Roberts, W A. *Elizabethan Court Rolls of Stokenham Manor 1560 – 1602.* W A Roberts, Beeson. 1984.
Wilkins J G, compiler and editor. *The Parish of Stokenham its People and its Ancient Churches.* A limited edition. 1977.
Exeter Archaeology. *Chivelstone Parish Heritage Appraisal.* In conjunction with the people of Chivelstone parish.2006/7.
en.wikipedia.org/wiki/Newfoundland_(dog) and lewisandclarktrail.com/newfoundland.htm.
Fox, Sarah Prideaux. *Kingsbridge and its Surroundings.* Printed for the compiler by G.P. Friend, Plymouth. 1874.
Melia, Steve. *Hallsands a Village Betrayed.* Forest Publishing. 2004.

Eyes along the Coast

Exeter Archaeology. *Chivelstone Parish Heritage Appraisal.* In conjunction with the people of Chivelstone parish. 2006/7.
Luscombe, Ellen & Young Francis. *Myrtles and Aloes.* G P Friend, Kingsbridge. 1861.
National Coastwatch Prawle Point: www.nci-prawlepoint.org.uk/hist.htm

Smuggling

Waugh, Mary. *Smuggling in Devon and Cornwall 1700-1850.* Countryside Books. 1991.
Wigley, Brian. *Smuggling and other transgressions in the South Hams, Devon.* Orchard Publications. 2003.
Born, Anne. *The History of Kingsbridge and Salcombe.* Orchard Publications, Chudleigh, Devon. 2002.
Pedrick, Stephen. *A Century of Memories.* Nick Walker Printing, Kingsbridge. 2009.
Roberts, W A. *Stokenham Occasional Papers 1 (Queen Katherine's rental 1547): Wreck of the Sea: 1588.* W A Roberts, Beeson. 1980.

Wrecks and the Rocket Apparatus

McDonald, Kendall. *Shipwrecks of the South Hams.* Wreckwalker Books. 2002.
Barrett, Roger. *Prawle Point and the Coast between Start Point and Salcombe Bar.* Kingfisher Print and Design Ltd. 2011.
South West Maritime Archaeological Group: www.swmag.org/index.php/moroccan-gold-coins.
National Coastwatch Prawle Point: www.nci-prawlepoint.org.uk/hist.htm.
Fox, Sarah Prideaux. *Kingsbridge and its Surroundings.* Printed for the compiler by G.P. Friend, Plymouth. 1874.
Fairweather J A S. *Eye-witness accounts of the Great Blizzard of March 9th and 10th 1891 in the South Hams of Devon.* Reset edition published by the Kingsbridge History Society. 2002.

Times of War

Exeter Archaeology. *Chivelstone Parish Heritage Appraisal.* In conjunction with the people of Chivelstone parish. 2006/7.
en.wikipedia.org/wiki/Spanish_Armada
Barrett, Roger. *Prawle Point and the Coast between Start Point and Salcombe Bar.* Kingfisher Print and Design Ltd. 2011.
Born, Anne. *The History of Kingsbridge and Salcombe.* Orchard Publications, Chudleigh, Devon. 2002.
Waterhouse, Robert. *East Portlemouth Heritage Appraisal. An Archaelogical History of the Parish.* The Coast & Countryside Service. 2002.
Luscombe, Ellen & Young Francis. *Myrtles and Aloes.* G P Friend, Kingsbridge. 1861.
Giles, Frank. *Napoleon Bonaparte England's Prisoner.* Constable & Robinson Ltd. 2001.
Cordingly, David. *Billy Ruffian.* Bloomsbury. 2003.
Williams Ken and Reynolds Dermot. *The Kingsbridge Branch.* Oxford Publishing Co. 1977.
Pedrick, Stephen. *A Century of Memories.* Nick Walker Printing, Kingsbridge. 2009.
Pedrick, Stephen. *Daishels and Figgy Duff Further recorded memories of life in the South Hams and elsewhere.* Nick Walker Printing, Kingsbridge. 2012.
Passmore Mike and Andrew. *Royal Air Force Air-Defence Radar Stations in Devon, the Second World War and Beyond.* Imprintdigital.net, 2008.
www.nationalarchives.gov.uk/cabinetpapers/themes/agriculture-second-world-war.htm
www.nature.com/nature/journal/v144/n3645/abs/144473a0.html
www.carrotmuseum.co.uk/history4.html.

Royal Events

Golden Jubilee of Queen Victoria South Hams Celebrations. Reset editon published by Kingsbridge History Society. June 1987.

Appendices

Exeter Archaeology. *Chivelstone Parish Heritage Appraisal.* In conjunction with the people of Chivelstone parish. 2006/7.
Kelly's Directory in 1881, 1891, 1901, 1911, 1921, 1931.
. White's Devon Gazeteer. David & Charles Publishers Ltd. 1850.
Billing's Directory and Gazeteeer of Devonshire. 1857.

Index

For the purposes of clarity, in the case of Partridges and Tuckers, I have indicated the relationship to Richard and Roger respectively. It is interesting to note that they share a grandfather.

22046610R00119

Printed in Great Britain
by Amazon